IMAGES
of Sports

Wildcat Hockey

Ice Hockey at the University of New Hampshire

IMAGES
of Sports

WILDCAT HOCKEY
ICE HOCKEY AT THE UNIVERSITY OF NEW HAMPSHIRE

Elizabeth Slomba and William E. Ross

ARCADIA
PUBLISHING

ISBN 978-0-7385-1102-3

Published by Arcadia Publishing
Charleston, South Carolina

Printed in the United States of America

Library of Congress Catalog Card Number: 2002108570

For all general information contact Arcadia Publishing at:
Telephone 843-853-2070
Fax 843-853-0044
E-mail sales@arcadiapublishing.com
For customer service and orders:
Toll-Free 1-888-313-2665

Visit us on the Internet at www.arcadiapublishing.com

Contents

ACKNOWLEDGMENTS

The authors wish to thank the people who contributed assistance and insight to the development of this book. These include Doug Prince, Lisa Nugent, Ron Bergeron, and Beverly Conway of UNH Photographic Services. Their helpfulness and expertise in locating and duplicating images from both Photographic Services and Special Collections added greatly to this book. Many thanks go to our colleagues Mylinda Woodward and Dale Valena, who helped with the research and in locating images and artifacts. We thank Nancy Holt, Brad Holt, and Brenda Holt Mullaney for their invaluable assistance in identifying photographs from the 1960s, 1970s, and 1980s. We also extend thanks to Prof. Steve Hardy for his support and encyclopedic knowledge of hockey history.

William Ross wishes to acknowledge his own "hat trick" of Katie, Stuart, and Stephen. Elizabeth Slomba appreciates her brother Mike, who loves sports, and Laura, who loves him.

INTRODUCTION

A Longstanding Tradition

Shortly after the turn of the last century, the *New Hampshire College Monthly* reported that "ice polo" was being played on the Durham campus. It is not a stretch to picture pickup games and interclass contests on the frozen ponds and flooded, low-lying fields near campus. By 1911, land had been flooded behind New Hampshire Hall and fraternities played a series of hockey games in pursuit of a silver cup. In 1914, a group of students took it on themselves to form an ice hockey team with a student as manager. The team members purchased uniforms and played a four-game schedule, primarily against nearby club teams. They went 2-2 and captured the imagination of many of their classmates, but there would be no 1915 season.

In the spring of 1924, more than 100 students volunteered to spend Campus Day clearing brush and stones for the proposed site of a new skating rink, the future home of ice hockey at the University of New Hampshire. Later that year, more than 30 young men answered football coach Hank Swasey's call for students to play ice hockey. The team, then nicknamed the "Bulls," went 2-2 and played in the first intercollegiate hockey game in the Boston Arena. The UNH ice hockey team was in the history books and, unlike the 1914 team, it was here to stay.

The following year, assistant football coach and UNH graduate Ernest Christensen took over head coaching duties. In 1927, his newly christened Wildcats finished 6-0, the only undefeated season in men's ice hockey history. For over a decade, Christensen and his teams had to deal with skilled opponents and the uncertainties of New England weather. Playing on an outdoor rink, the team often had to curtail practice time or cancel scheduled games due to warm or snowy weather. In 1939, the university moved the rink near College Woods. There, it was closer to the men's locker room in the new field house, and the proximity to College Woods sheltered the ice from the afternoon sun.

The Wildcats, first under one-year head coach George Thurston and then under Anthony Dougal, struggled with the weather and the team's relative mediocrity. As the nation became involved in World War II, scheduling games became harder. Fuel shortages made it more difficult to travel and, by 1943, many players left college life and ice hockey behind to fight in the war. After an abbreviated, two-game season in 1943, ice hockey at UNH took a four-year sabbatical.

Hockey returned in 1947, as did a number of veterans of both the war and previous teams. The team experienced only limited success. In 1949, weather forced UNH to cancel 11 varsity games; the freshman team never played a game. To the rescue came Harry C. Batchelder, Class of 1913, who earned his fortune in the ice-making industry. He provided his alma mater with the machinery with which to make artificial ice and, in 1955, Batchelder Rink was built at a site near the original rink, behind New Hampshire Hall.

With a consistent ice surface and more regular practice sessions, the fortunes of UNH hockey changed for the better. Head coach Horace "Pepper" Martin also stepped up recruiting, luring such stars as Albert "Albie" Brodeur and Rod Blackburn from Berlin, New Hampshire, and Ray March from Milton, Massachusetts. The late 1950s brought another revolution to UNH ice hockey as Ken McKinnon, a native of the Toronto area, became the first Canadian hockey player to play for the Wildcats. He would not be the last.

There would be more significant changes, as well. In 1964, the university administration decided to enclose the rink in an indoor arena, which would be named for longtime coach A. Barr "Whoop" Snively, who had taken over as head coach for ice hockey two years before. The university hired Rube Bjorkman, former head coach at Rensselaer Polytechnic Institute, later in 1964. Bjorkman's mission was to build the program and to take the Wildcats into Division I ice hockey. As a result, better competition brought bigger crowds, and "Lively Snively" was born. Playing in Snively paid dividends, as the Wildcats enjoyed a 21-4 advantage on home ice between 1966 and 1968. In 1968, Bjorkman was named New England Coach of the Year, but soon thereafter he resigned to return to the Midwest and later, to the head coaching post at the University of North Dakota.

Charlie Holt, who had led Colby College to an Eastern Collegiate Athletic Conference (ECAC) II championship, took over the ice hockey program for the 1968–1969 season. He picked up the rich talent left by Bjorkman and made it his own; UNH made it to the first round of the ECAC playoffs in Holt's first year. By the mid-1970s, Holt and his staff had added new talent to his "Offense of the Seventies." The 1976–1977 team had five 20-goal scorers and still holds team records for points in a season. The team capped the season with a trip to the four-team National Collegiate Athletic Association (NCAA) Tournament; eight players from that squad made their way to the National Hockey League.

In 1979, the Wildcats went into the playoffs with a 19-3 regular season record for their last 22 games. They remained hot in the playoffs, with victories over Yale and Cornell, en route to a Boston Garden showdown with home-state rival Dartmouth. In the end, UNH won 4-3. Thus, the Wildcats closed the decade with their first and only ECAC championship banner.

In the late 1970s, a new team brought additional excitement to Snively. Under the direction of head coach Russ McCurdy, the UNH women's ice hockey team began play in 1977. In its inaugural season, the women's team "ran the table," going 15-0-0. In its second season, McCurdy's team ended one game in a tie, but the women did not lose a game until the 1981–1982 season. McCurdy's teams won the Eastern Association for Intercollegiate Athletics for Women (EAIAW) and ECAC championships four times each. They failed to win a national championship only because none existed at the time.

The UNH men's ice hockey team made it to the ECAC tournament again in 1984, but it would be their last ECAC tournament. The 1985 season opened with UNH as a charter member of a new league, Hockey East. The new scheduling structure permitted regular-season games against some of the western powerhouses, such as Wisconsin and Minnesota. Nevertheless, in 1985, Charlie Holt announced his intention to retire at the end of the season. Bob Kullen, Holt's assistant, took over coaching duties in 1986 but had to sit out the 1987–1988 season due to heart problems. The Wildcats made the Hockey East playoffs for the first time in three years during the 1988–1989 season, but Kullen's health forced him to resign as head coach in 1990.

Former UNH star and associate head coach Dick Umile was selected to take the Wildcats into the 1990s. He continued the tradition of aggressive recruiting, and his teams have added a few more All-Americans and the University's first Hobey Baker Award winner to the list. Moreover, Umile's teams have advanced to post-season play with increasing regularity as they consistently make it to the Hockey East playoffs. Under Umile, they have advanced to the

NCAA regionals and/or tournament eight times and to the NCAA "Frozen Four" three times. In the end, however, any men's ice hockey campaign will have to face a tough Hockey East schedule and the realization that the Maine Black Bears will always be lying in wait.

Russ McCurdy stepped aside as head coach of the women's team in 1992. His successor, Karen Kay, helped maintain the tradition of success in an era of increasing competitiveness in women's ice hockey. The UNH women's ice hockey team was ECAC champion in 1995–1996 and, in 1998, it defeated Brown 4-1 for the national title. UNH lost to Harvard in the title game the following year. In addition, the women's ice hockey team has produced two All-Americans, four members on the 1998 U.S. Olympic women's ice hockey team, and three members of the 2002 U.S. Olympic team. Coach Brian McCloskey, the former assistant coach of the men's team, took over coaching duties for the women following the 2001–2002 season.

In recent years, the UNH ice hockey teams have enjoyed the move from the cozy confines of Snively Arena to the new Whittemore Center. The new arena feature the larger playing surface of Towse Rink and has a capacity of 6,000 for ice hockey games. As before, "home ice" really means something to both Wildcat teams; however, fears that the larger space would absorb crowd noise were wholly unfounded. The "Whitt" has already been home to new traditions and even greater successes for UNH hockey. Home ice in the Whittemore Center launched the UNH women to the national championship in 1998, saw the men go to the NCAA national championship tournament three times and, in 2002, played host to the Women's "Frozen Four." The men's team has a long history of play in Hockey East, but the 2002–2003 season marks the beginning of the Hockey East Women's League. As with all new beginnings, it is not hard to imagine that the Whitt will see a few more championship teams in the not-so-distant future.

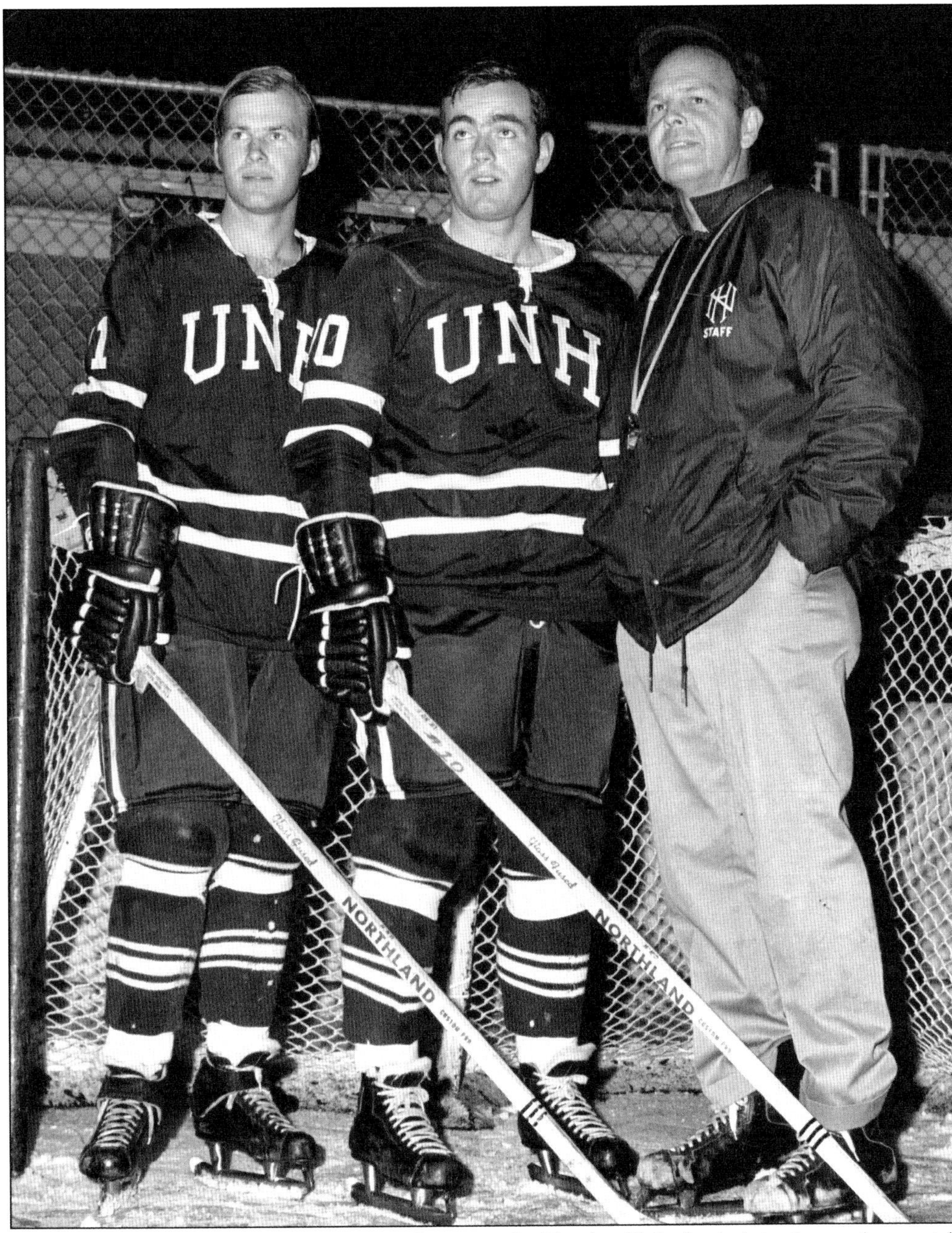

Second-year University of New Hampshire coach Charlie Holt (right) is shown here with the co-captains from the 1969–1970 ice hockey team, Ryan Brandt (left), and Alan Clark. (UNH Archives.)

One

Hockey Takes Root

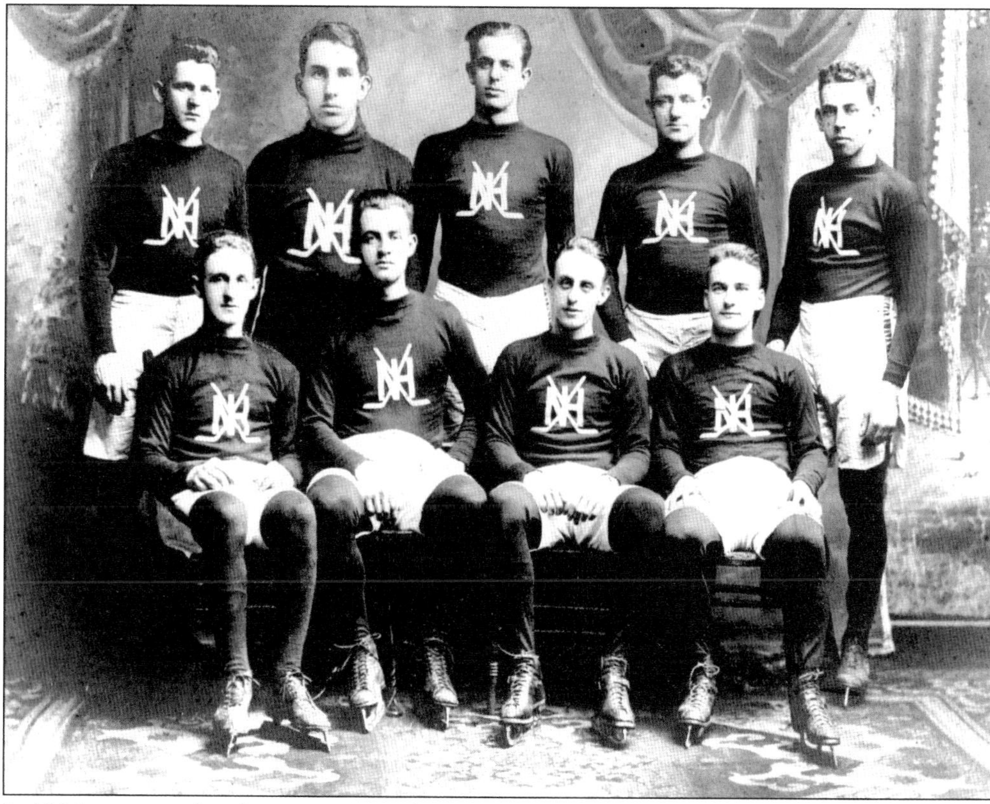

In 1914, a group of students came together to form the first ice hockey team of New Hampshire College (later the University of New Hampshire). A student, R.E. Haines (front row, second from left), managed the team against opponents that included the Exeter Athletic Association, Phillips Exeter, and Lowell Textile. The team finished with a 2-2 record but disbanded after one season. (UNH Archives.)

NEW HAMPSHIRE COLLEGE 173

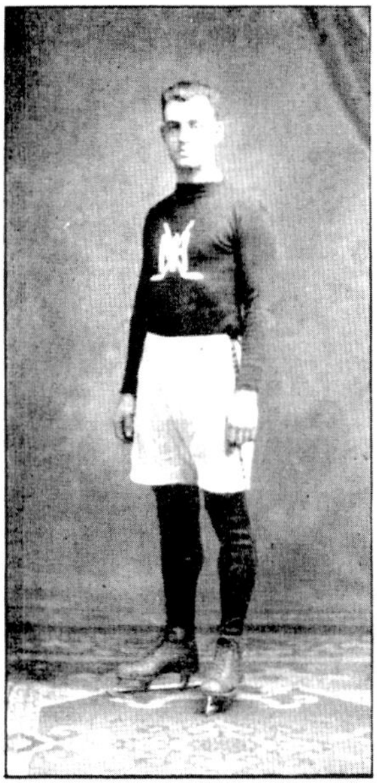

Manager Haines

Hockey

Season of 1914

R. E. HAINES, '15	*Manager*

THE TEAM

W. H. L. BRACKETT, '14	*Rover*
C. R. DANIELS, 2-year, '14	*Center*
T. F. CRAM, 2 year, '15	*Center*
J. F. HOBBS, '15	*Right Wing*
G. W. HAZEN, 2 year, '15	*Left Wing*
R. E. HAINES, '15	*Cover Point*
H. G. WOODMAN, 2 year, '14	*Point*
M. F. McMAHON, 2 year, '15	*Point*
W. T. TAPLEY, '16	*Guard*

Results of Season

New Hampshire 1	Exeter Athletic Association 5
New Hampshire 1	Phillips Exeter 7
New Hampshire 3	Lowell Textile 0
New Hampshire 2	Exeter Athletic Association 1

This page from the 1916 yearbook *Granite* includes the team roster and results for the 1914 season. (UNH Archives.)

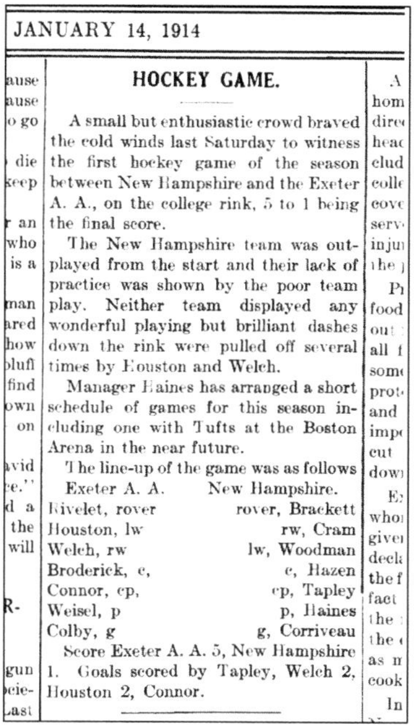

JANUARY 14, 1914

HOCKEY GAME.

A small but enthusiastic crowd braved the cold winds last Saturday to witness the first hockey game of the season between New Hampshire and the Exeter A. A., on the college rink, 5 to 1 being the final score.

The New Hampshire team was outplayed from the start and their lack of practice was shown by the poor team play. Neither team displayed any wonderful playing but brilliant dashes down the rink were pulled off several times by Houston and Welch.

Manager Haines has arranged a short schedule of games for this season including one with Tufts at the Boston Arena in the near future.

The line-up of the game was as follows

Exeter A. A.	New Hampshire.
Rivelet, rover	rover, Brackett
Houston, lw	rw, Cram
Welch, rw	lw, Woodman
Broderick, c,	c, Hazen
Connor, cp,	cp, Tapley
Weisel, p	p, Haines
Colby, g	g, Corriveau

Score Exeter A. A. 5, New Hampshire 1. Goals scored by Tapley, Welch 2, Houston 2, Connor.

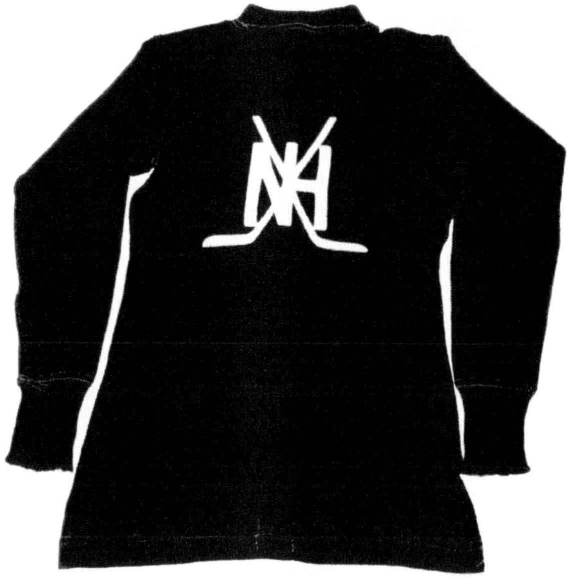

These relics represent the early days of ice hockey at the University of New Hampshire. The account of the first extramural ice hockey game played in Durham is from the *New Hampshire* of January 14, 1914. It is accompanied by the ice hockey jersey worn by Ted Cram, Class of 1916, one of the members of the 1914 team. (Left photograph UNH Archives, right photograph UNH Museum.)

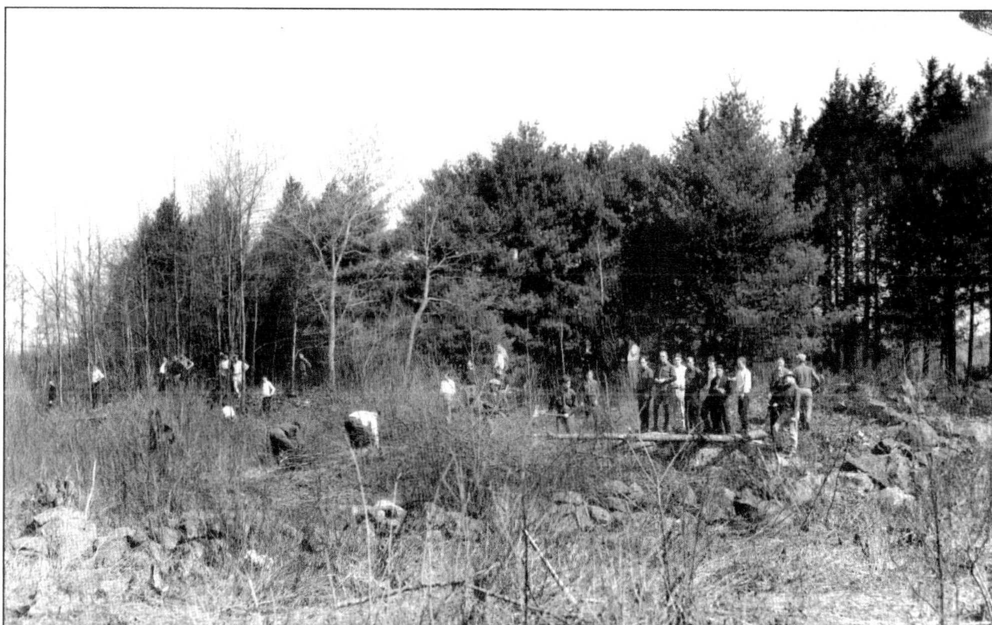

On May 7, 1924, UNH students gathered on Campus Day to engage in projects to improve the campus. More than 100 students volunteered to help remove brush and rocks in preparation for the construction of a new ice hockey and ice-skating rink behind New Hampshire Hall. (Clement Moran photograph. UNH Archives.)

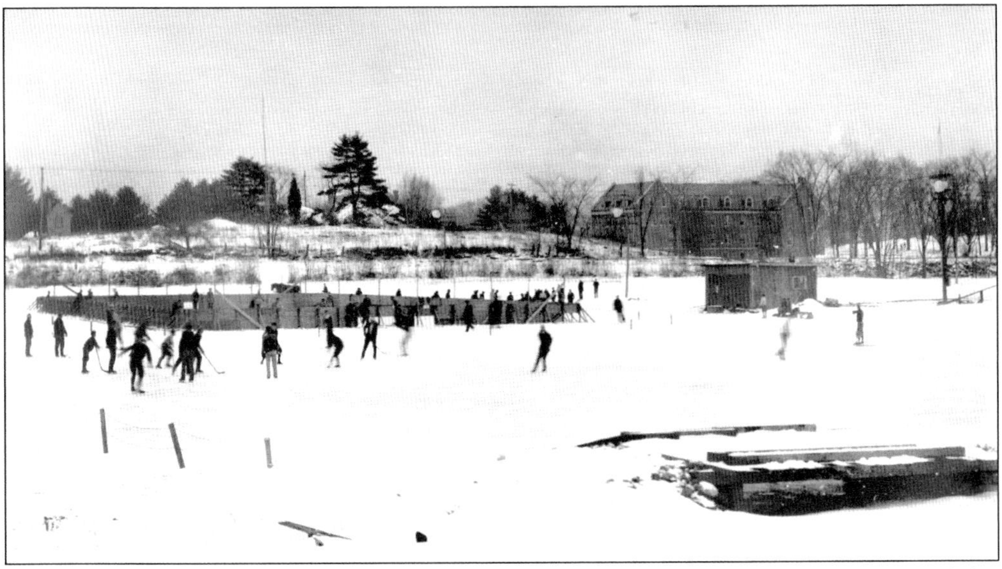

Ice hockey is being played on the new skating rink in 1924. Because of the early date of this photograph, the game is probably an intramural or pickup game. (Clement Moran photograph. UNH Archives.)

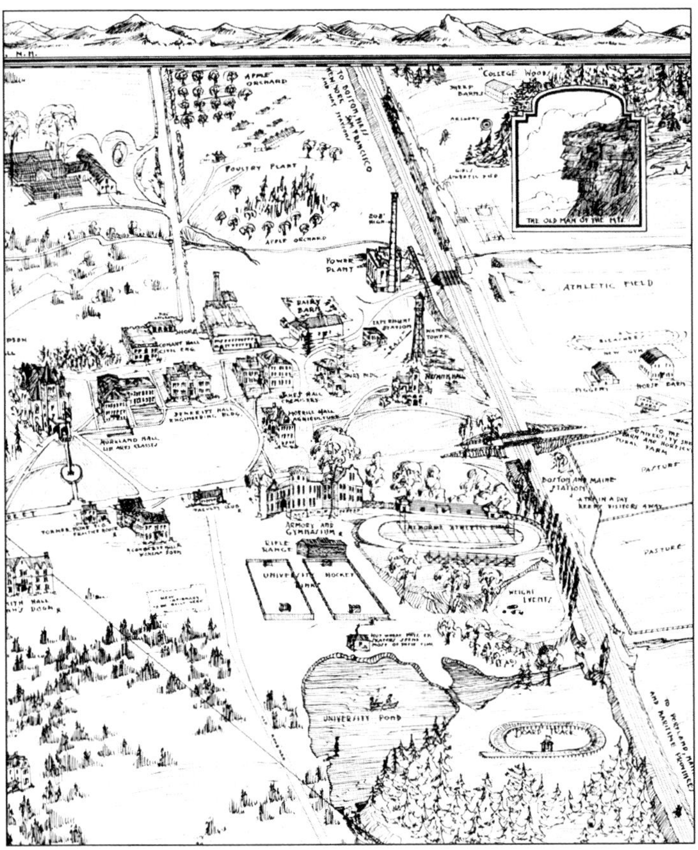

This 1930 map shows the location of the first ice hockey rink at the University of New Hampshire. (UNH Museum.)

In 1924, coach Hank Swasey formed the first intercollegiate ice hockey team, the Bulls, at the University of New Hampshire. In its only year under Swasey, the team played all four games away, with victories against Bates and Colby. (Clement Moran photograph. UNH Archives.)

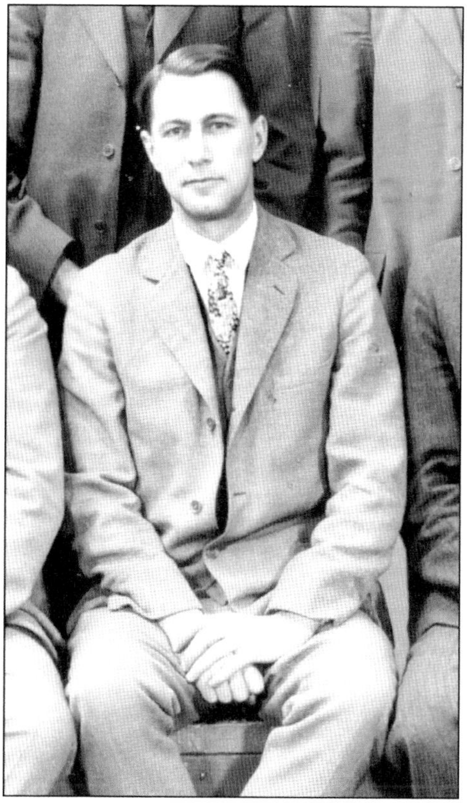

NEW HAMPSHIRE HOCKEY PLAYERS DEFEAT BATES AND COLBY ON TRIP

First Maine Invasion By Granite State Skaters Proves Blue And White Sextet Of High Grade

DEFEATED BY FAST LEWISTON AMATEUR CLUB

First Game Played In Blinding Snowstorm Against Bates On Home Rink—Colby No Match For Locals—Return Game Looked For With St. Dominique Club, Only Outfit To Defeat Swasey's Men

Playing the first game of varsity hockey by a New Hampshire team, the varsity sextet, coached by Henry Swasey, defeated the Bates outfit on their own rink at Lewiston by a two to one score, traveled up to Waterville and defeated Colby 5 to 0 on the second night and returned to Lewiston to meet defeat at the hands of the St. Dominique Club, one of the fastest of amateurs playing together outside the big cities.

New laurels were added to the fame of Captain Bill Sayward, for three years a varsity football player and his team-mates in the first contests of the new sport. In addition to Sayward himself, a rare find has been unearthed in the person of Bill Proudman, '27, from West Roxbury, Mass., whom the Lewiston papers proclaimed the best college player yet seen on Colby's ice. John Morton, '25, and Elliot Wyman, another sophomore, also showed that Coach Swasey has developed a team that will give a good account of itself for the remainder of its schedule.

With the temperature hovering around the zero mark, in addition to a raging blizzard, the New Hampshire "Bulls" played its first game of hockey, emerging a winner over Bates with a score of 2 to 1. On account of the weather, four 10-minute periods were played and the rink was swept off after each period. This made it possible to play good hockey for about two minutes of each period. For the most part each team shot from anywhere on the ice, as small snowdrifts made it impossible to carry the puck.

Corey for Bates was the first to send the rubber into the net on a long shot from the side of the rink. In the third period Proudman, by clever dribbling, took the puck through the whole Bates team, drew the goal-tender out, and slipped the pill in, tying the score. About the middle of the extra period both teams started, with a bang, to break the tie. On a face-off in front of the Bates goal, after about three quarters of the period had elapsed, Morton, on a rebound from his own shot, hooked in the winning score. For Bates, Corey and Dimlick played a fine brand of hockey, while the New Hampshire offense of Proudman, Morton and Wyman and the defense of Sayward, Blewett and Fudge was a noteworthy feature.

The summary:

New Hampshire (2)	Bates (1)
Wyman, lw	rw, Corey
Morton, c	c, O'Connor
Proudman, rw	lw, Lane
Fudge, rd	ld, Stanley
Sayward, ld	rd, Dimlick
Blewett, g	g, Wyllie

Goals scored by Corey, Proudman, and Morton. Penalties, Fudge and Corey. Referee, Haines, New Hampshire.

(Continued on Page Four)

This account in the *New Hampshire* of January 29, 1925, discusses the UNH ice hockey team's first games. In their first intercollegiate game, the Bulls defeated Bates College 2-1. (UNH Archives.)

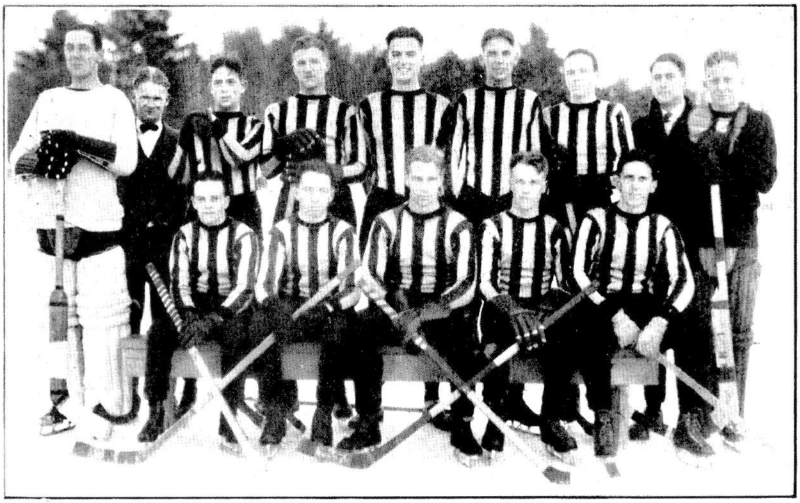

VARSITY HOCKEY TEAM 1925

Hockey

With the construction of a skating rink came the addition of hockey to the list of major sports at New Hampshire.

Coach Swasey took charge of the new sport and issued a call for candidates. Approximately 30 men answered his call and with these men he proceeded to mold the first hockey team to represent the University of New Hampshire in intercollegiate competition.

The squad was soon hard at work every day on the ice, Swasey soon got a line on the men and he picked a team and began to whip them into shape for the first game.

"Bill" Sayward was elected captain of the team and the team journeyed to Lewiston, Maine, to make their debut against Bates on January 20th.

The first game that was ever played by the New Hampshire hockey team was a victory for them. The game was played in a snowstorm so team-work was out of the question. New Hampshire won, the score being 2-1.

Coverage of UNH's first intercollegiate ice hockey team appears in the 1926 *Granite*. (UNH Archives.)

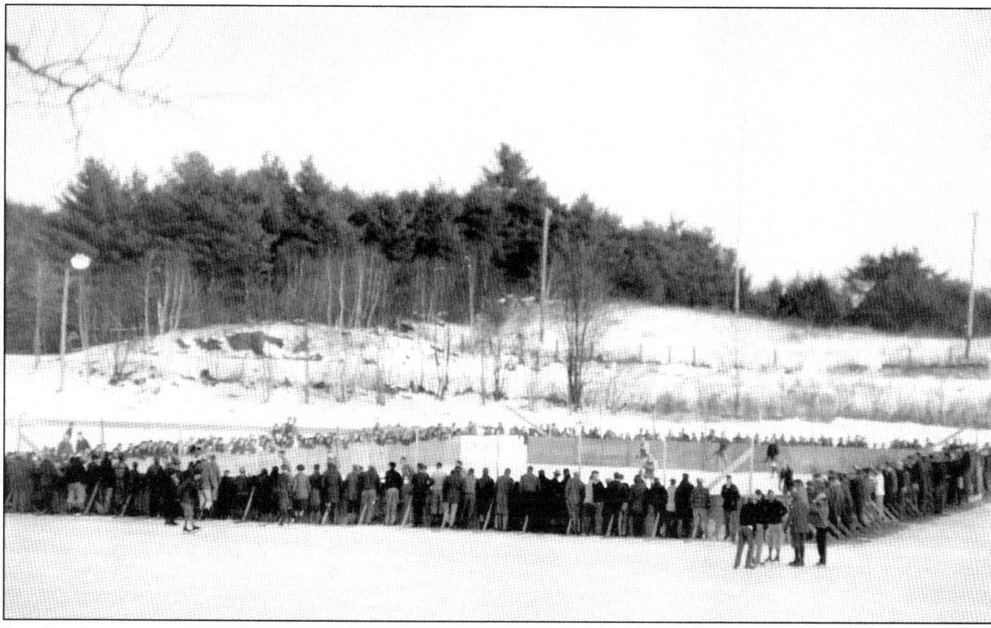

Ice hockey action at the rink behind New Hampshire Hall is shown here c. 1925. (Clement Moran photograph. UNH Archives.)

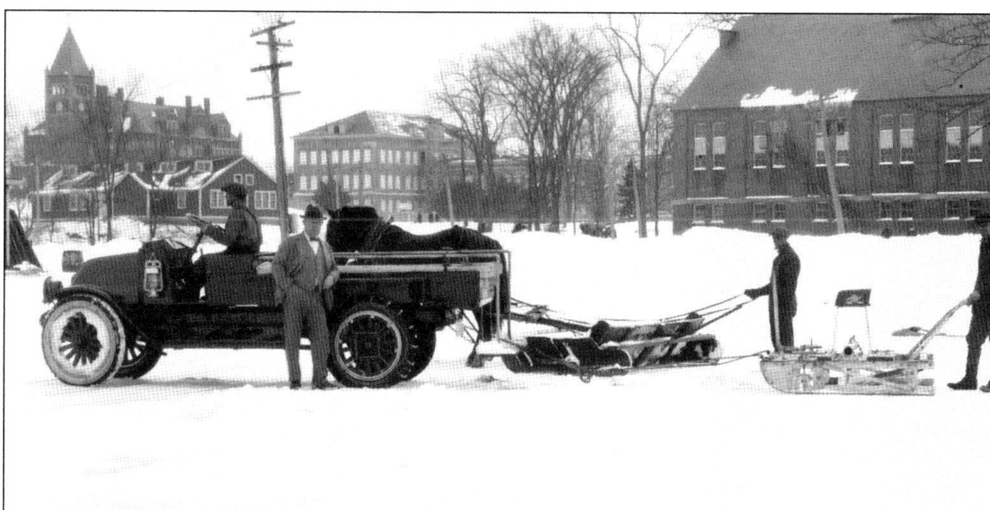

The Athletic Department employed truck-drawn ice scrapers to groom the ice on the outdoor rink, as seen in this 1926 photograph. (Clement Moran photograph. UNH Archives.)

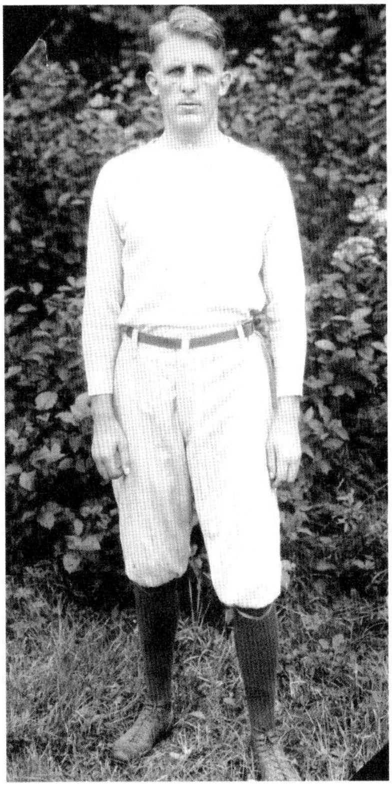

Ernest Christensen took over coaching duties for the UNH ice hockey team during the 1926 campaign. His team skated to a 1-3 record. Christensen coached for 12 of the next 13 years, with a career record of 55 wins, 54 losses, and 8 ties. Christensen also served as lacrosse coach and as assistant football coach, as pictured here. (Clement Moran photograph. UNH Archives.)

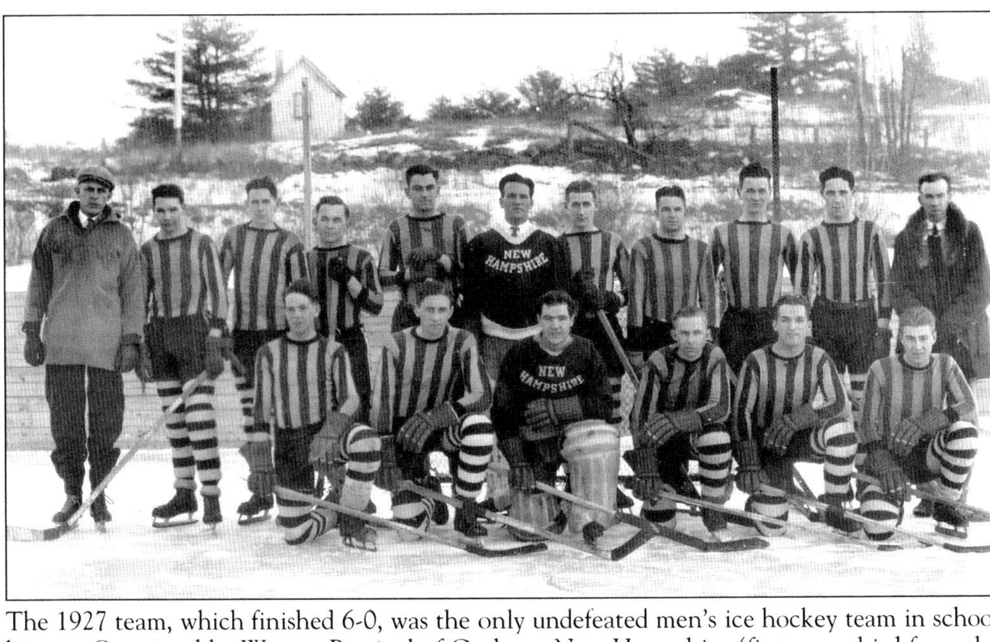

The 1927 team, which finished 6-0, was the only undefeated men's ice hockey team in school history. Captained by Warren Percival of Gorham, New Hampshire (first row, third from the right), the UNH team defeated Bates College, Bowdoin College, Springfield College (twice), Brown University, and Providence College. (Clement Moran photograph. UNH Archives.)

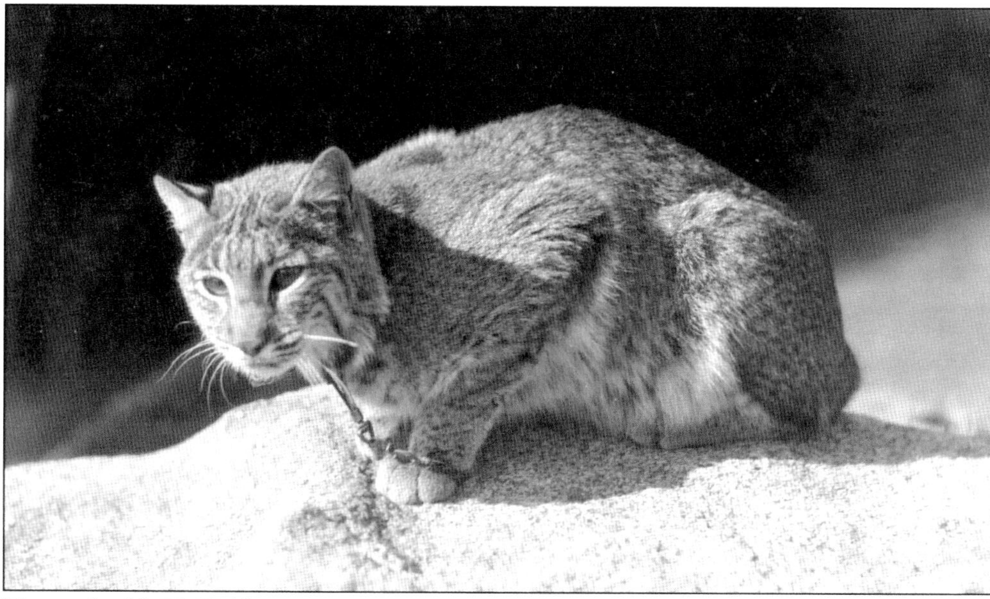

This is the UNH Wildcat in 1934. Prior to the 1927 season, the UNH ice hockey team was called the Bulls. In 1926, the New Hampshire Club voted to adopt the wildcat as the official school mascot. According to the *New Hampshire*, the wildcat, like the state, was "small and aggressive." The bull was considered sluggish and more appropriate for a larger school. On a practical note, the club also determined that a live wildcat was more portable than a bull. (Clement Moran photograph. UNH Archives.)

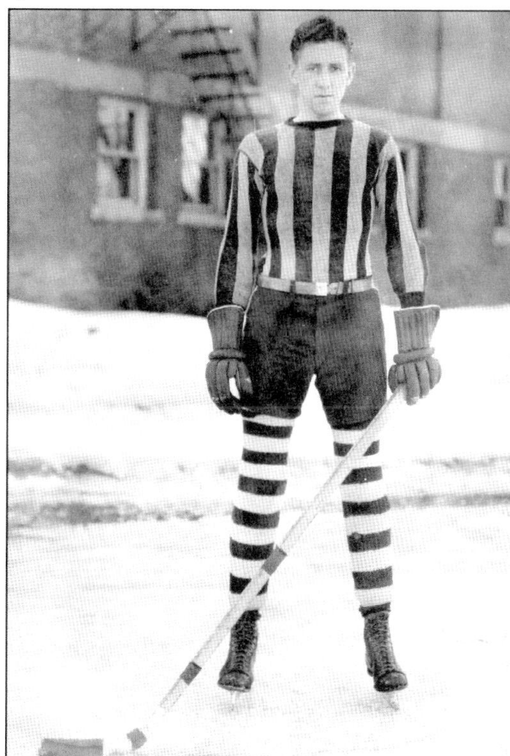

Roland Chandler of Waltham, Massachusetts, captained the 1928 UNH Wildcats to a 7-1-1 record, despite the fact that the team only played three games at home. (Clement Moran photograph. UNH Archives.)

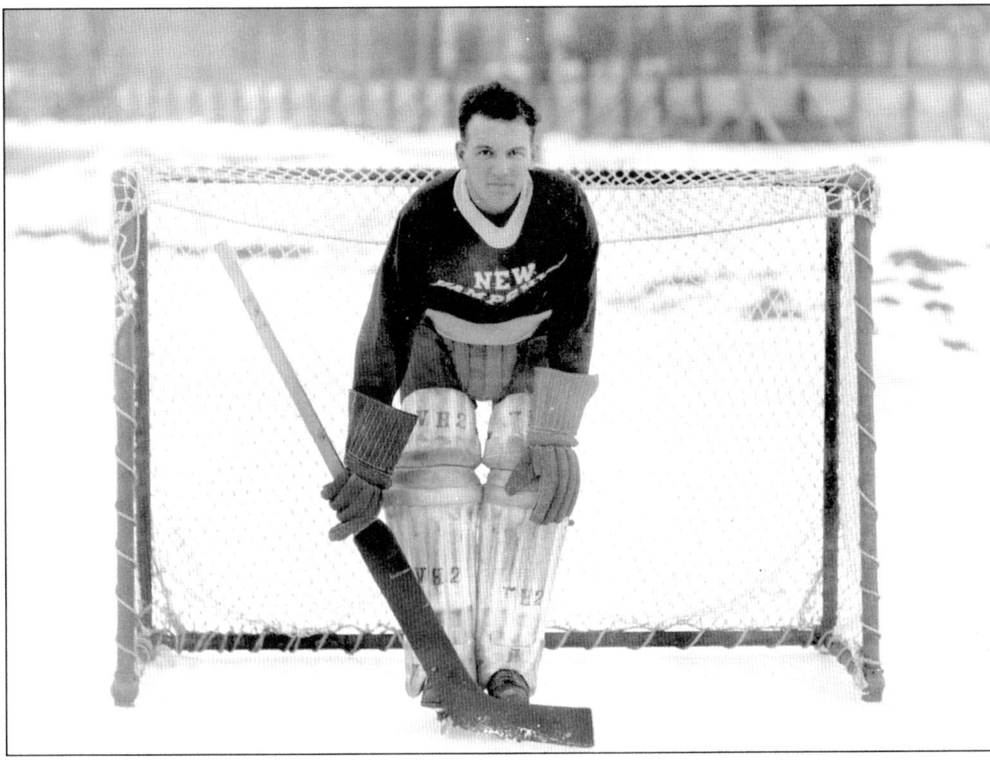

Goalie Ed Hunt of Exeter, New Hampshire, was a mainstay in goal in 1928 and 1929. In 1929, Hunt recorded four shutouts in only eleven games. His record was tied four times but was not broken until the 2000–2001 season when Ty Conklin had five shutouts. (Clement Moran photograph. UNH Archives.)

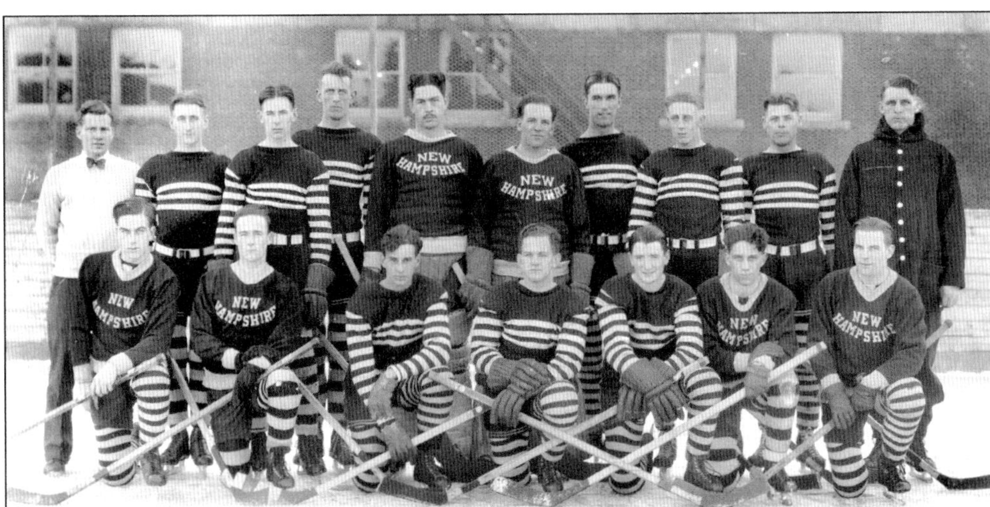

The 1929 UNH Wildcats, captained by Alvin Reinhart of Medford, Massachusetts, finished with a 6-4-1 record. With Hunt in goal, the team featured a 1.82 goals against average. (Clement Moran photograph. UNH Archives.)

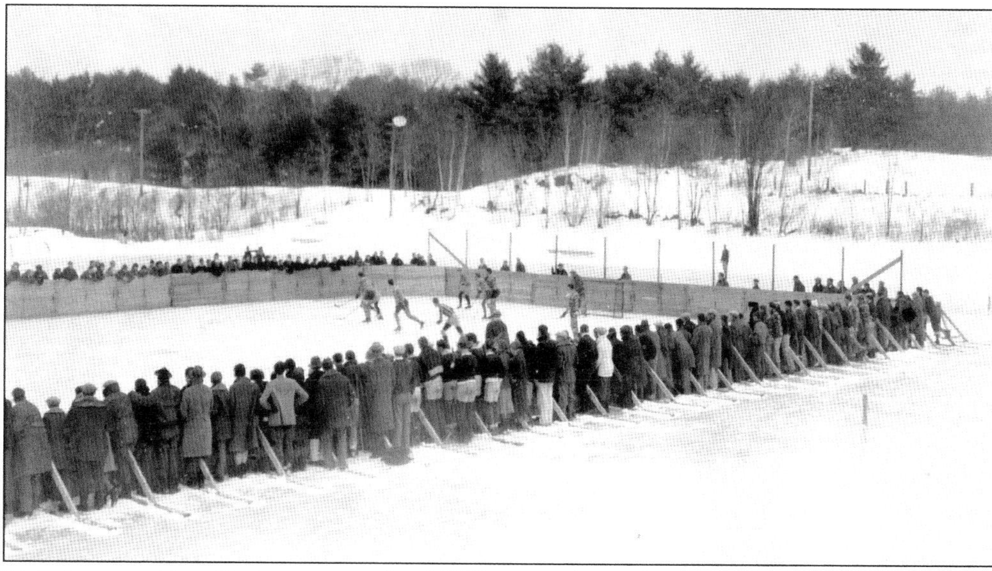

This is an unidentified game on the UNH ice rink in the late 1920s. (Clement Moran photograph. UNH Archives.)

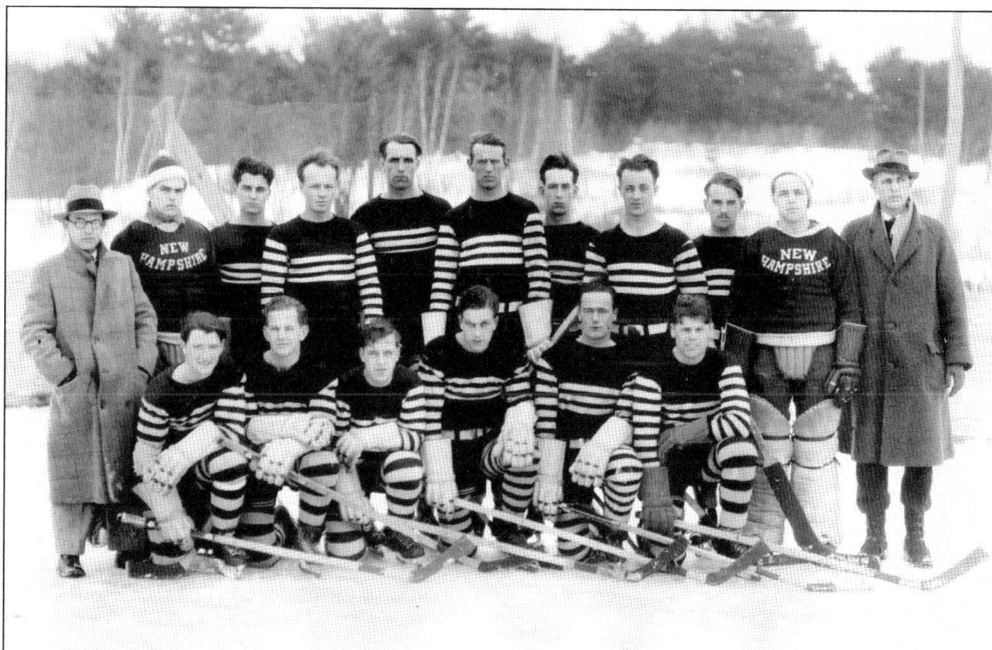

The 1930 team, coached by Ernest Christensen and captained by Donald McFarland of Concord, New Hampshire, fell to a 3-8-2 record. Wins came against Pennsylvania, Amherst, and Army. (Clement Moran photograph. UNH Archives.)

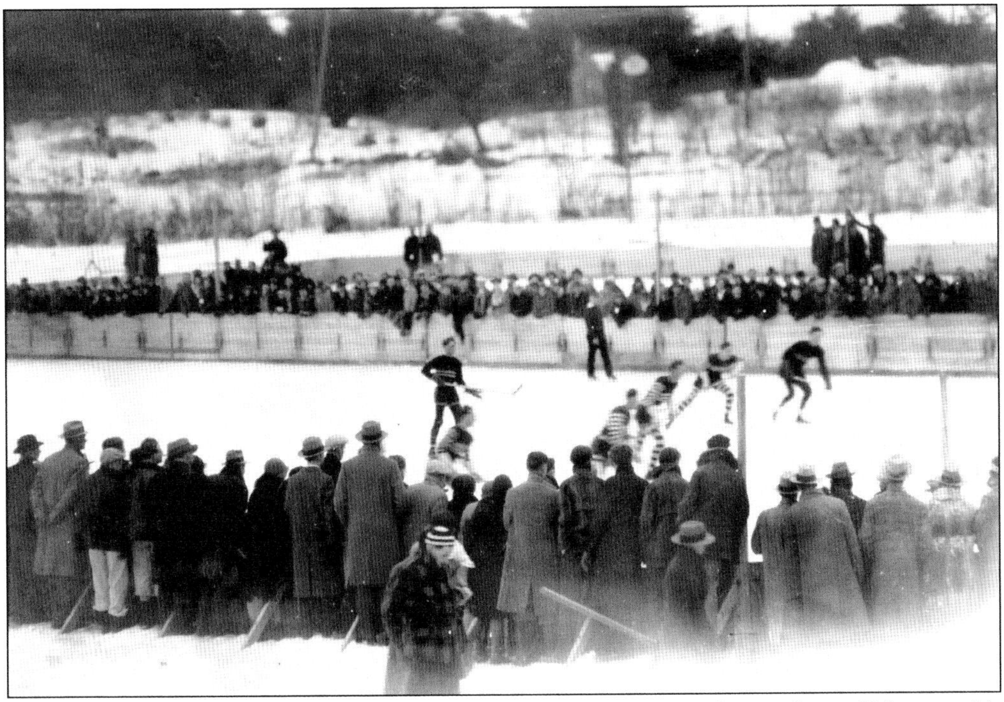

An ice hockey game is being played at the 1931 Winter Carnival on February 14. (UNH Museum.)

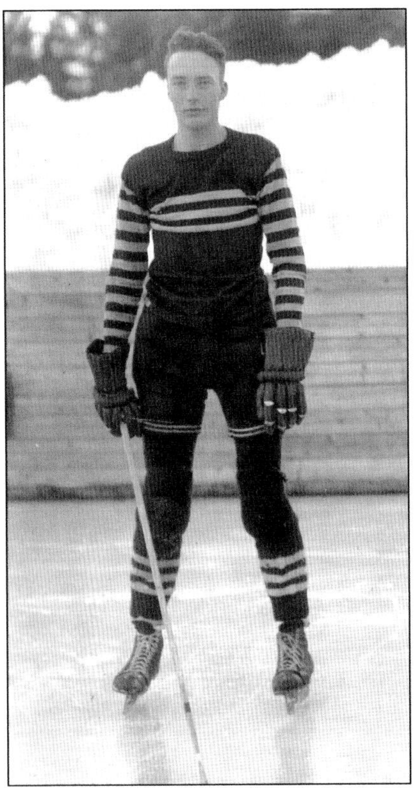

Captain Karl "Bob" Manchester led the 1935 freshman team, known as the Kittens, to a 7-2-3 record. A native of Providence, Rhode Island, Manchester also played varsity hockey, football, and ran track while at UNH. (Clement Moran photograph. UNH Archives.)

Hockey

Coach, ERNEST CHRISTENSEN
Co-Captain, CHARLES GROCOTT
Co-Captain, JAMES E. STEFFY
Manager, BERTRAM B. TOWER

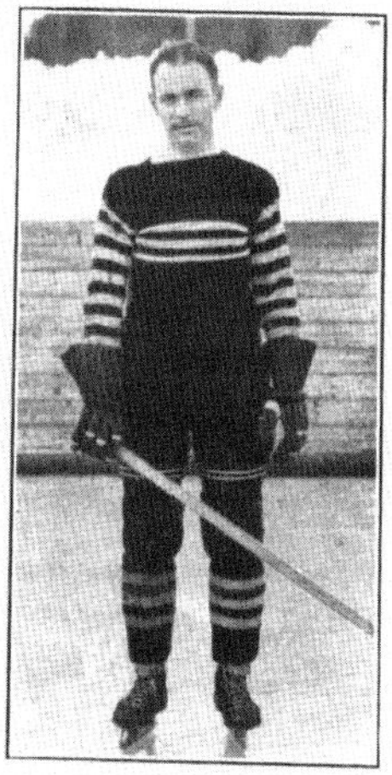

Co-Captain Grocott

Rising from its slump of previous years, the fast varsity hockey team led by Co-Captains Grocott and Steffy went places as it scored seven wins, suffered three losses and tied two games. It was the most successful season in recent years.

The season got off to an excellent start when the team played three games before a reversal was registered against

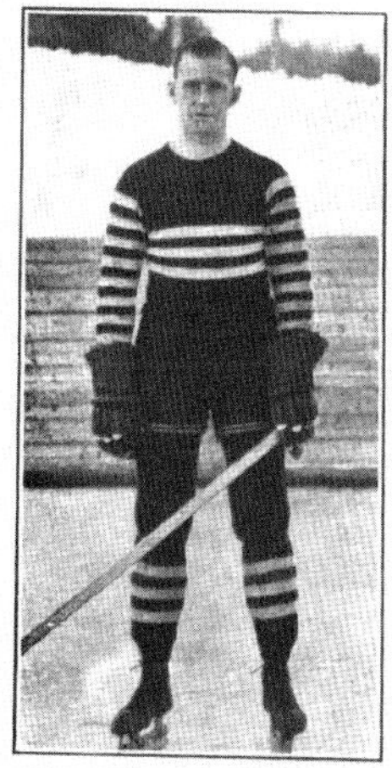

Co-Captain Steffy

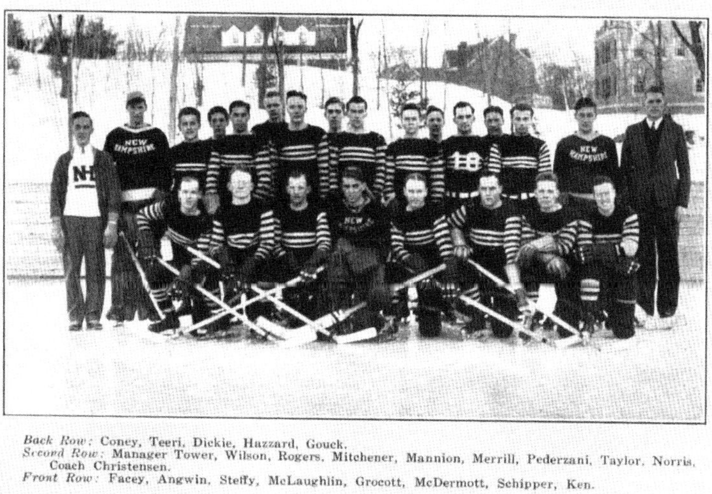

Back Row: Coney, Teeri, Dickie, Hazzard, Gouck.
Second Row: Manager Tower, Wilson, Rogers, Mitchener, Mannion, Merrill, Pederzani, Taylor, Norris, Coach Christensen.
Front Row: Facey, Angwin, Steffy, McLaughlin, Grocott, McDermott, Schipper, Ken.

[200]

This coverage of the 1935 season comes from the 1936 *Granite*. After several losing seasons, including a disastrous 0-8 campaign in 1932, the Wildcats got back on track with a 7-6 record in 1935. (UNH Archives.)

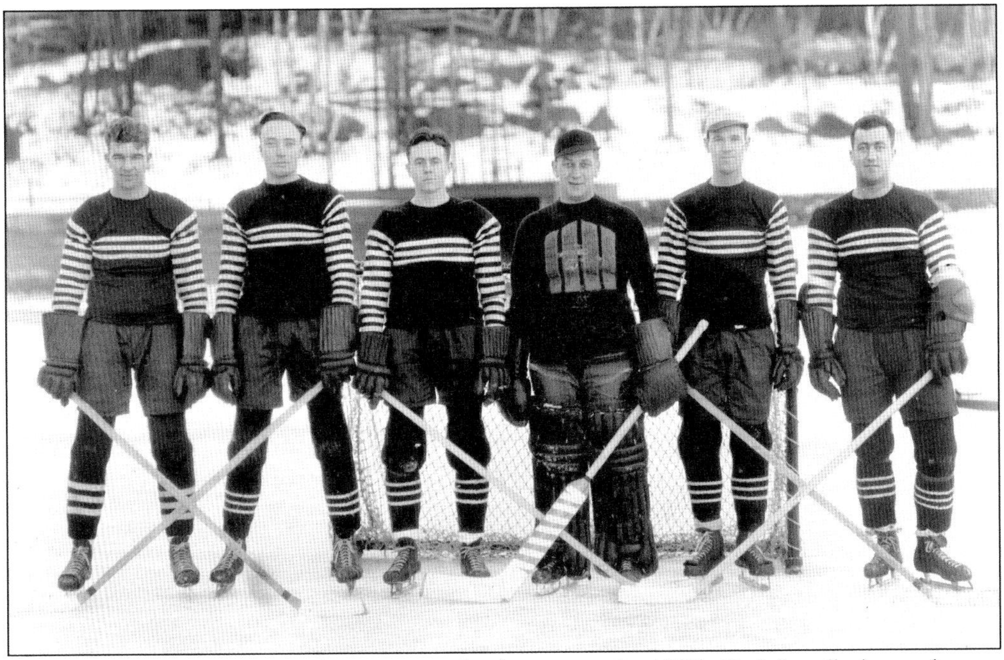

These are the starters from the 1937 ice hockey team. In 1937, Carl Lundholm took over coaching duties from the ailing coach Ernest Christensen. The transition, coupled with poor ice conditions for practice, contributed to a 3-5 record. The starters, from left to right, are Wendell "Bull" Martin, Bob Manchester, co-captain Herbert Merrill, Kenneth Norris, co-captain William Facey, and Russell "Russ" Martin. (Clement Moran photograph. UNH Archives.)

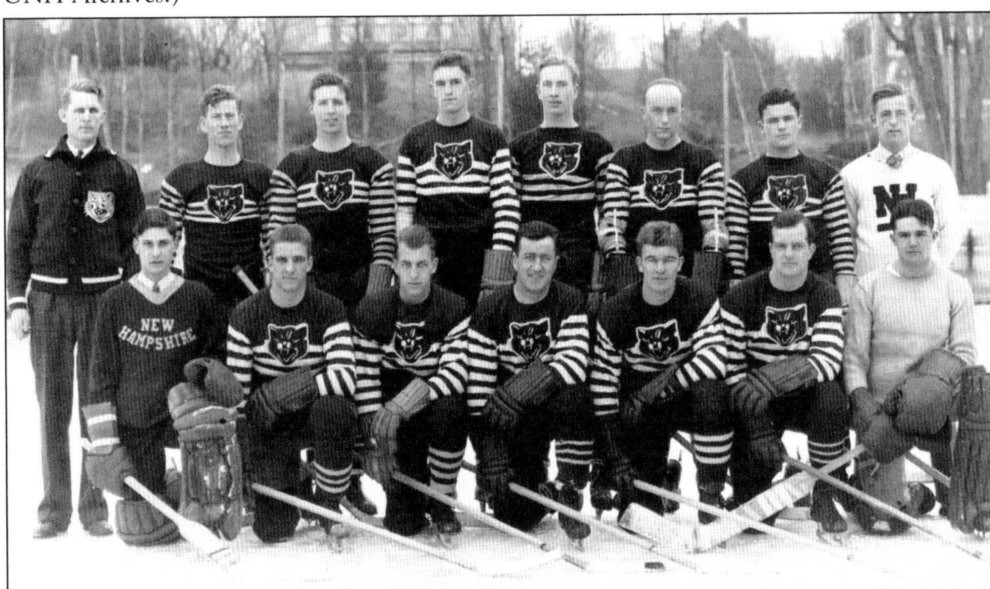

The 1938 Wildcats were captained by Russ Martin. That season saw the return of coach Ernest Christensen, a much-improved record (6-1-3), and new uniforms featuring the wildcat mascot. Martin, while playing in only 31 games over three seasons, finished with 75 career points. (Clement Moran photograph. UNH Archives.)

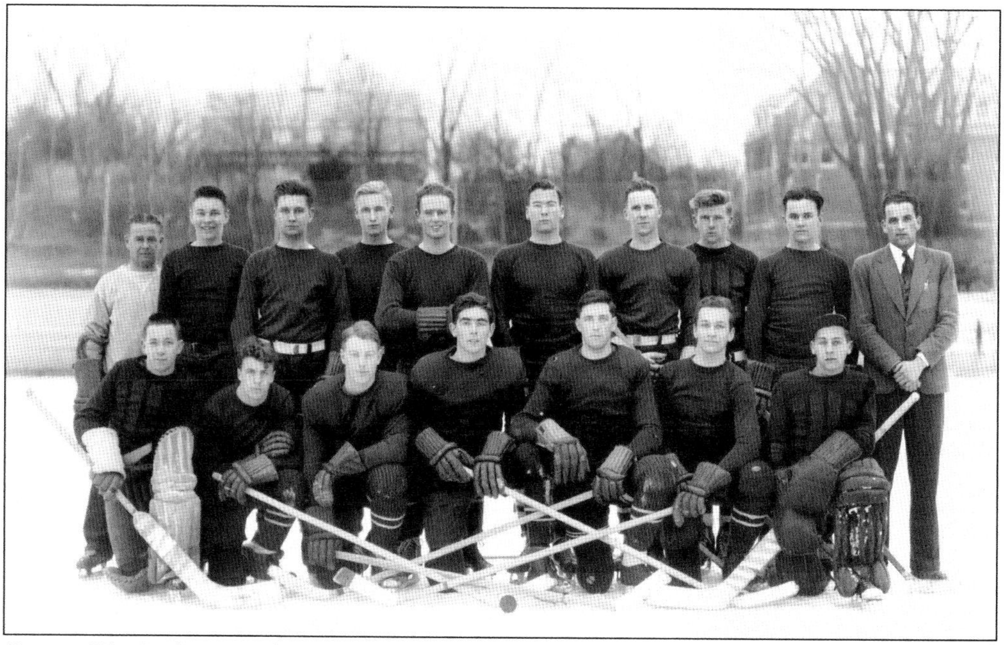

George "Fuzz" Thurston (rear left) is pictured here with the 1937–1938 freshman ice hockey team. Thurston, an amateur ice hockey player of some renown, coached the varsity team the following season. (Clement Moran photograph. UNH Archives.)

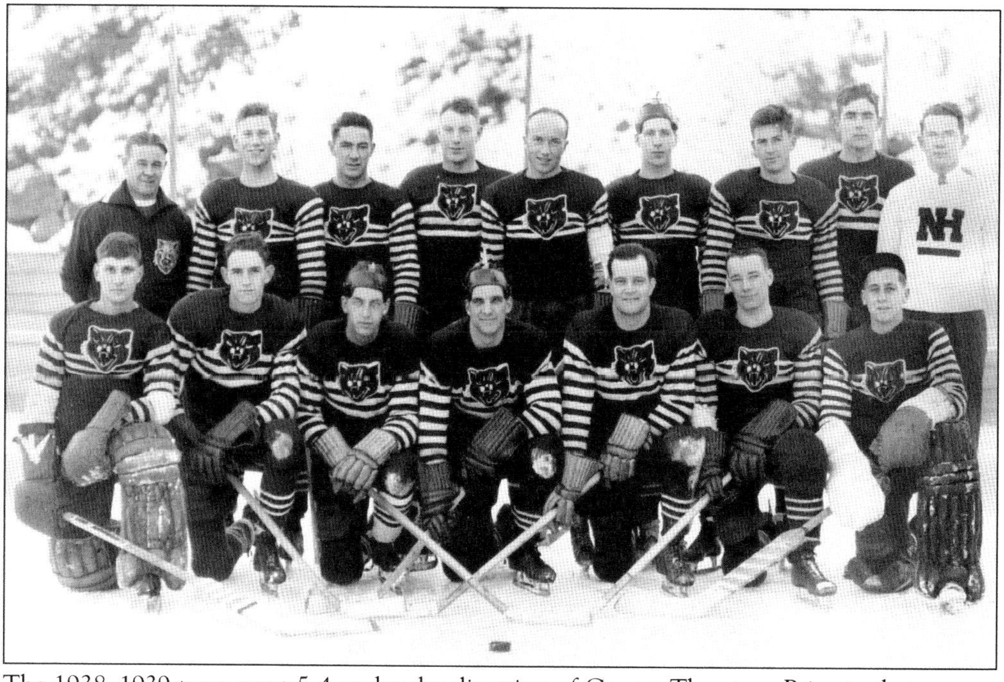

The 1938–1939 team went 5-4 under the direction of George Thurston. Prior to that season, the rink was moved behind the new field house near College Woods. The new location provided better access to the new men's locker rooms. In addition, the afternoon shade helped protect the natural ice from the elements. This is the first team photograph in which players wore protective headgear. (Clement Moran photograph. UNH Archives.)

University of New Hampshire Athletic Association

ATHLETIC REPORT

N. H. (Varsity) vs. Middlebury Event Hockey

Date of Contest January 13, 1939 Where Played Durham

Official Score: N. H. 11; Middlebury 0

Time of Game or Length of Meet 3 - 20's Attendance 150

Contract $100.00 Home Gate Receipts

Officials:

PAID Fee	Expenses	NAME	ADDRESS
$15		1. Kelleher	
$10		2. N. Raymond	
		3.	
		4.	

Injuries: only N. H. players.

None

(REMARKS:—Suggestions for same trip, Weather, Sportsmanship, Hospitality, Playing Facilities.)

The ice was good, and the weather cold. A fight started in the second period, and turned into a riot.

Shown are the athletic report (left) and manager's game report (below) from the January 13, 1939 home game against Middlebury College. Although manager Edward Reed recorded an inordinate number of penalties, the *Granite* contained a more vivid account of the rough-and-tumble contest: "The game was featured in the second period by a fight between the players which saw spectators and substitutes entering the fisticuffs." (UNH Archives.)

MANAGER'S GAME REPORT

Summary:

	New Hampshire		Middlebury
lw.	Quinn, Carlson, Couser, Huff, Richardson	lw.	Reichert, Hawes
c.	Davison, Wood, Brunel	c.	Jarrell, Berry
rw.	Patten, Roper, Richardson, Carlson, Spearman	rw.	Cobb, Hutton
ld.	Fournier, Martin, McCrum	ld.	Mayo, Stabile, Hutton
rd.	Otis, Gilgun	rd.	Kinsey, Mayo, Hutton
g.	Wentzell, Haseltine	g.	Martin

Goals:

First Period:	Davison (Patten)	12' 31"
	Carlson (Unassisted)	18' 15"
Second Period:	Patten (Fournier)	25"
	Quinn (Davison)	31"
	Otis (Patten)	2' 24"
	Fournier (Unassisted)	12' 40"
	Roper (Unassisted)	19' 39"
Third Period:	Couser (Unassisted)	1' 21"
	Huff (Fournier)	8' 5"
	Quinn (Unassisted)	13' 6"
	Brunel (Unassisted)	18' 45"

Penalties:

First Period:	Jarrell (Hooking)
	Otis (Tripping)
	Hawes (Anti-defense)
	Davison (Leg check)
	Mayo (Interference)
Second Period:	Otis (Holding)
	Fournier (Charging)
	Wood (Charging into the boards)
	Mayo (Board check)
	Patten (Fighting) (Disqualified for remainder of game)
	Kinsey (") (" ")
Third Period:	Fournier (Tripping)
	Jarrell (Roughing)
	Gilgun (Roughing)
	Mayo (Flank check)

Official Score: New Hampshire 11
Middlebury 0

Time of game: Jan. 13, 1939 4:00 P.M. 3 - 20's

Anthony Dougal took over coaching duties for the 1939–1940 season. In his first season, the Wildcats dropped to 1-9, but among the bright spots for Dougal was a young defenseman named Horace "Pepper" Martin. Martin later coached the UNH ice hockey team for 11 seasons, from 1951 until 1962. (UNH Archives.)

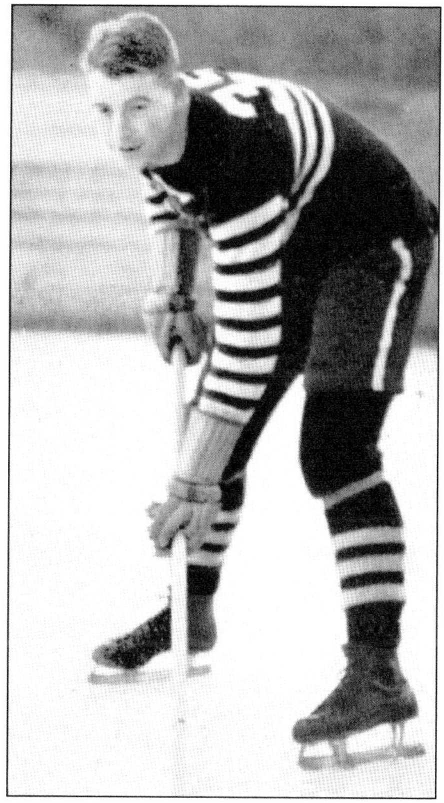

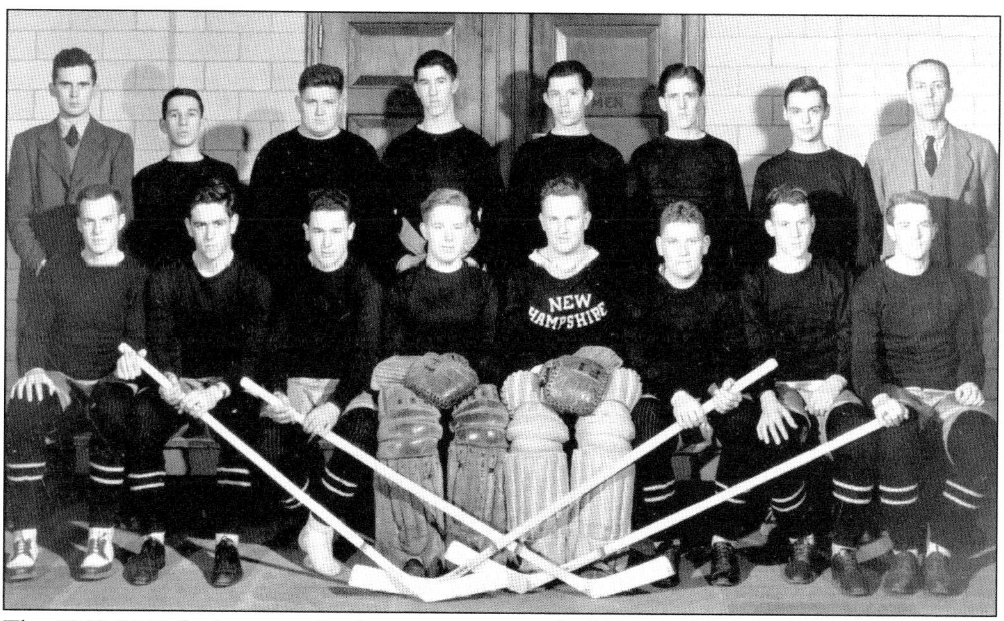

The 1940–1941 freshmen ice hockey team was coached by Harold Rood. The team had a 1-5 season and featured a young center from Concord, New Hampshire, named Karl "Red" Adams. (UNH Archives.)

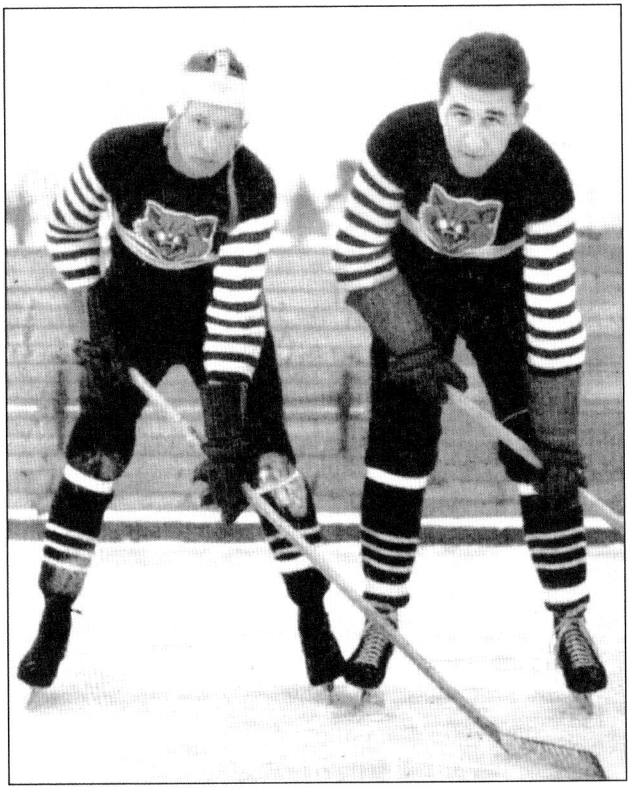

In Anthony Dougal's second season (1940–1941), the varsity improved to a 5-7 record. Captained by veteran goalie Jack Wentzell, the "Dougalmen" featured defensemen Don Perkins (left) and Al Sakoian (right). Perkins returned to UNH after the war to captain the 1946–1947 team. (UNH Archives.)

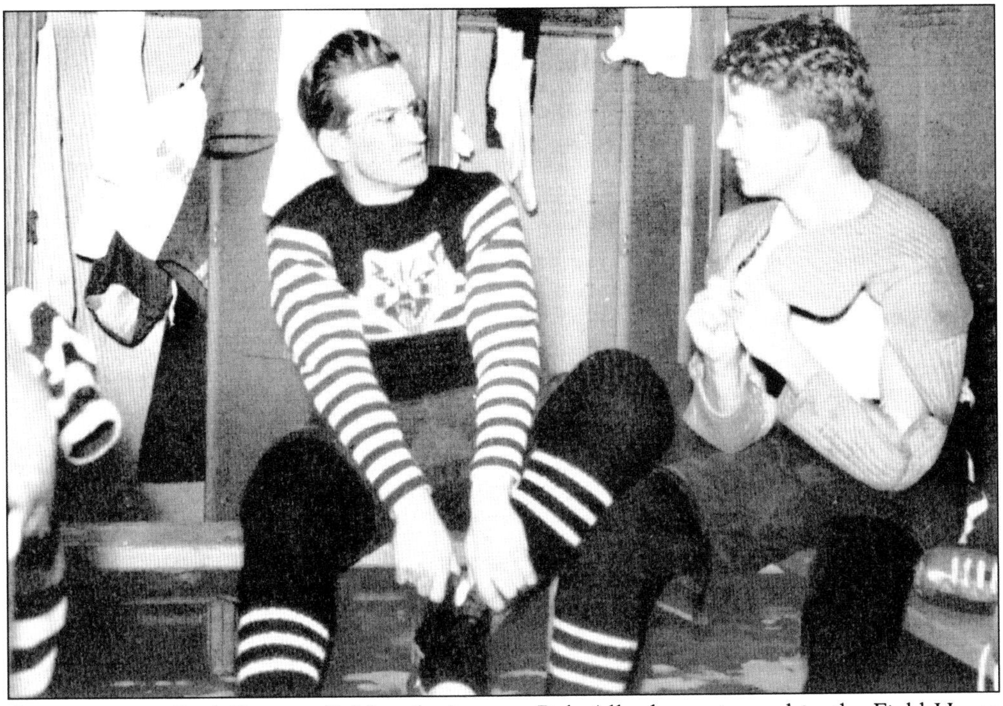

Starting center Paul Conway (left) and wingman Bob Allard are pictured in the Field House locker room in 1941. (UNH Archives.)

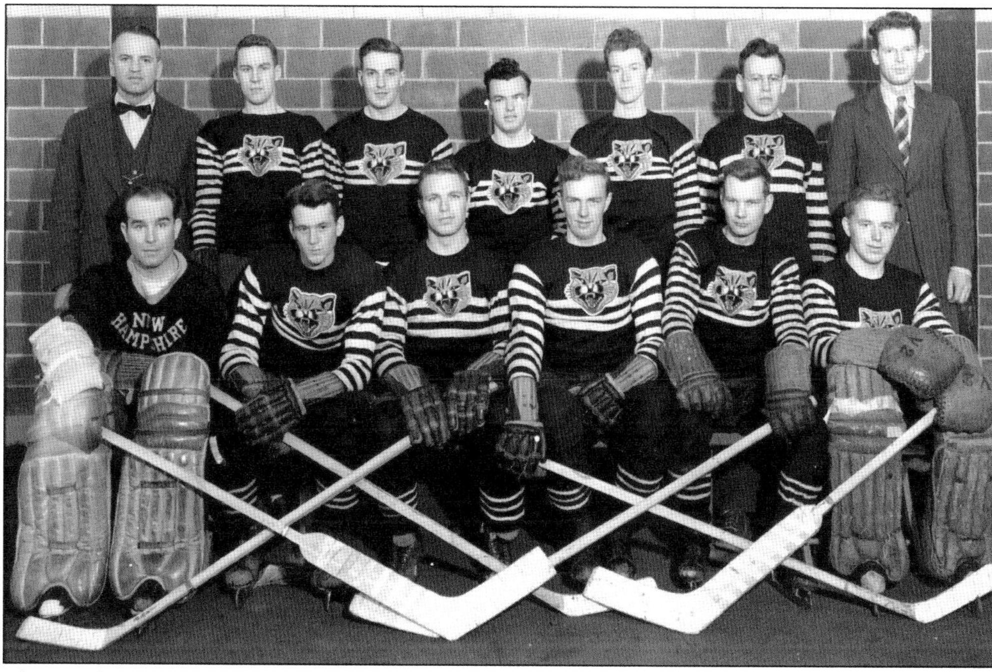

This is the 1941–1942 varsity team with coach Anthony Dougal (top, left). The Wildcats struggled through a 4-10 season, but World War II made this the last UNH team to play a full season until 1947. (UNH Archives.)

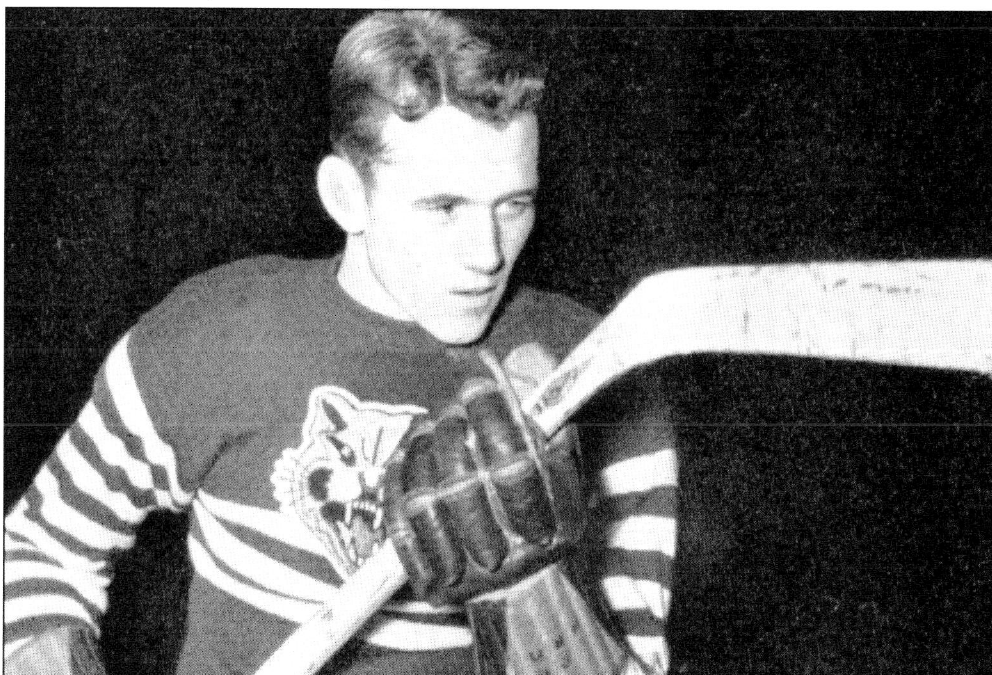

The 1941–1942 season was brightened by the play of sophomore sensation Red Adams. As starting center he proved himself the best stickhandler and fastest skater on the team. At the end of the season, Adams was a unanimous All–New England Team pick. (UNH Archives.)

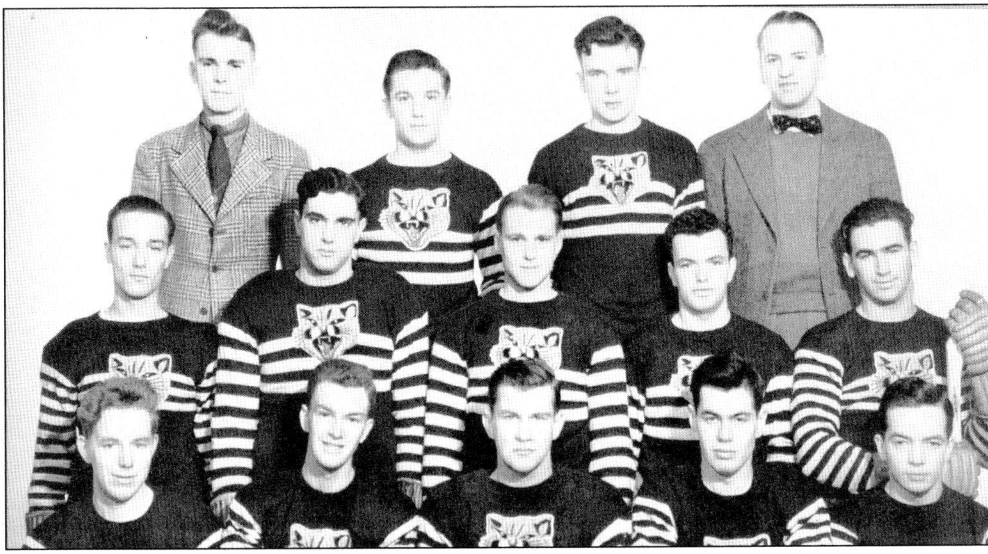

These are the members of the ill-fated 1942–1943 ice hockey team. The Department of Athletics decided to cancel ice hockey for the season, but captain Albert Sakoian and the team protested. The administration relented after team members agreed to assume maintenance of the rink. (UNH Archives.)

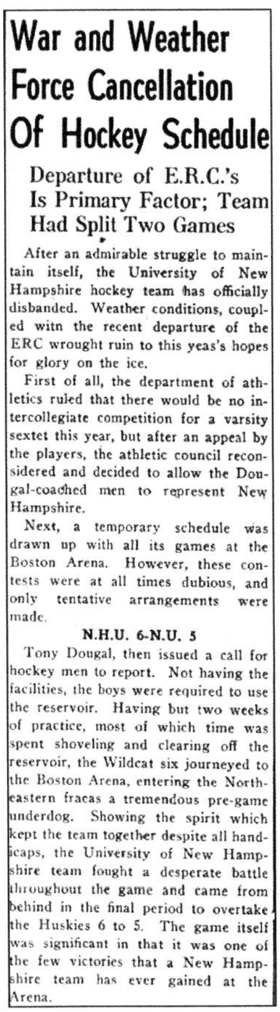

War and Weather Force Cancellation Of Hockey Schedule

Departure of E.R.C.'s Is Primary Factor; Team Had Split Two Games

After an admirable struggle to maintain itself, the University of New Hampshire hockey team has officially disbanded. Weather conditions, coupled witn the recent departure of the ERC wrought ruin to this yeas's hopes for glory on the ice.

First of all, the department of athletics ruled that there would be no intercollegiate competition for a varsity sextet this year, but after an appeal by the players, the athletic council reconsidered and decided to allow the Dougal-coached men to represent New Hampshire.

Next, a temporary schedule was drawn up with all its games at the Boston Arena. However, these contests were at all times dubious, and only tentative arrangements were made.

N.H.U. 6-N.U. 5

Tony Dougal, then issued a call for hockey men to report. Not having the facilities, the boys were required to use the reservoir. Having but two weeks of practice, most of which time was spent shoveling and clearing off the reservoir, the Wildcat six journeyed to the Boston Arena, entering the Northeastern fracas a tremendous pre-game underdog. Showing the spirit which kept the team together despite all handicaps, the University of New Hampshire team fought a desperate battle throughout the game and came from behind in the final period to overtake the Huskies 6 to 5. The game itself was significant in that it was one of the few victories that a New Hampshire team has ever gained at the Arena.

A clipping from the February 10, 1943 *New Hampshire* reports the termination of the 1943 season. With limited practice, scheduling problems, fuel rationing, and enlistments in the military, the season ended after a 13-2 defeat against Harvard University. The team's other contest was a surprising 6-5 victory over Tufts University, not Northeastern University as this article erroneously reported. (UNH Archives.)

Two

THE RISE TO DIVISION I

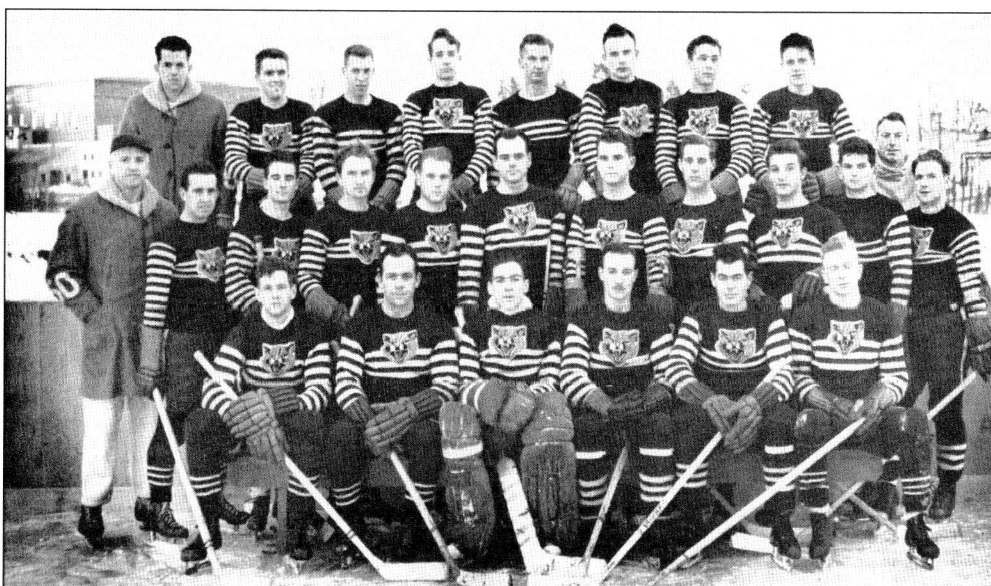

Anthony Dougal is shown here with the 1946–1947 Wildcats. After a lapse of four years, a number of former UNH ice hockey players returned from the war to anchor Dougal's most successful team. Dougal put together a high scoring "Punch Line" of veterans Don Perkins, Bill Forbes, and Ronnie Sleeth. The team scored nearly six goals a game and finished the season 4-1. (UNH Archives.)

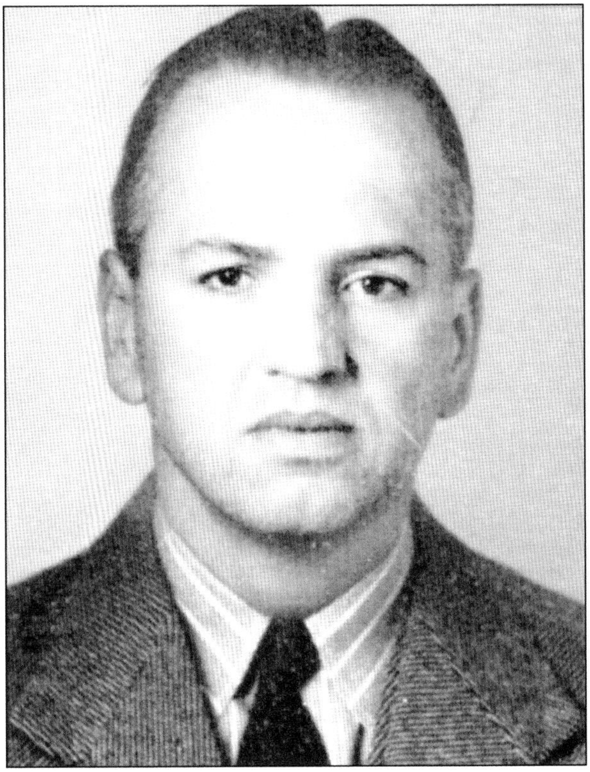

Anthony Dougal, UNH ice hockey coach (1939–1943, 1946–1947), also coached lacrosse and was an assistant football coach. (UNH Archives.)

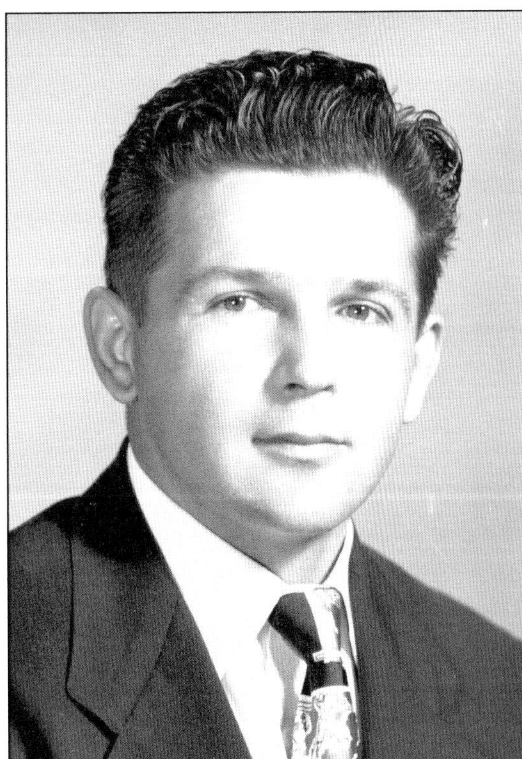

Joseph "Pat" Petroski coached UNH ice hockey from 1947 to 1951. Petroski's teams suffered from poor practice facilities and from a couple of warmer-than-usual winters. These combined to wreak havoc on both practice and playing schedules. (UNH Archives.)

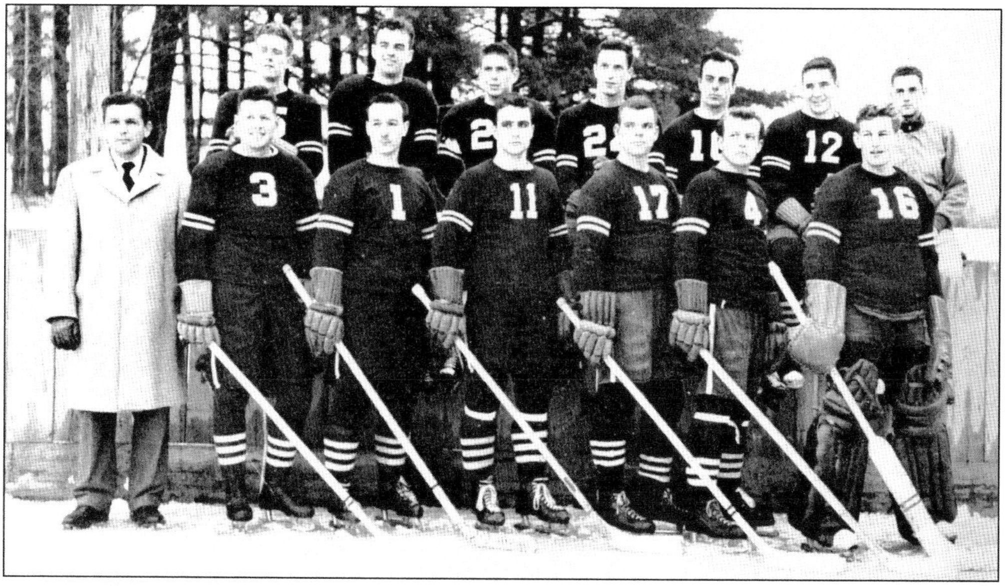

Pat Petroski is shown here with the 1949–1950 UNH Wildcats. The 1950 team suffered from the lack of experienced goaltending and unseasonably warm weather. The team is pictured on the rink adjacent to College Woods. (UNH Archives.)

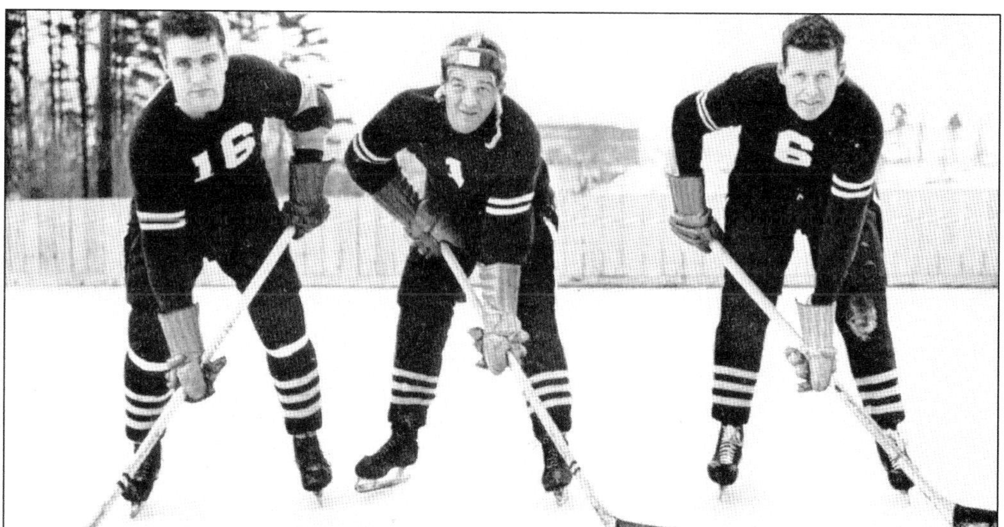

In the 1950–1951 season, Petroski's team rebounded from two abbreviated and winless seasons to post a 5-4 record. Success came in spite of the fact that weather conditions limited them to fewer than 10 practice sessions. They were led by, from left to right, George Healey, captain Walter Fournier, and John Simpson. (UNH Archives.)

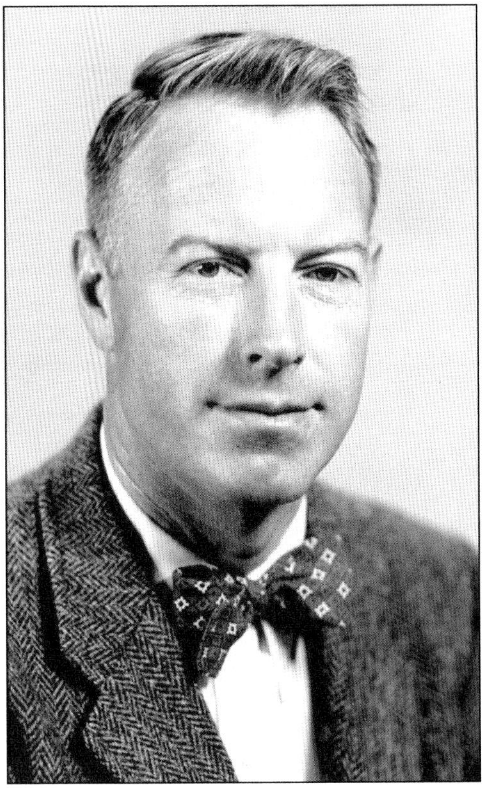

In 1951, Horace "Pepper" Martin became the varsity ice hockey coach. Martin skated with the Wildcats prior to his graduation from UNH in 1941. He also served as coach of the freshman team in 1944. (UNH Archives.)

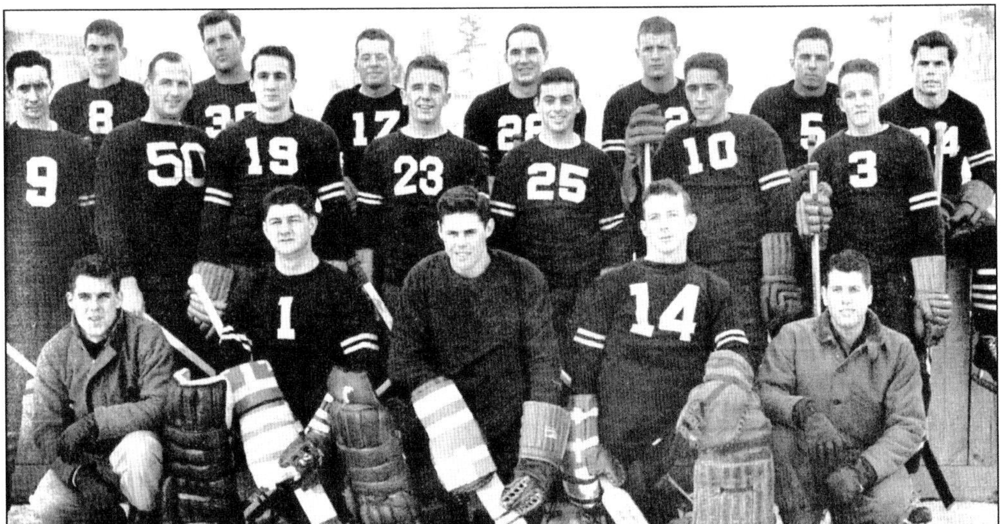

The 1951–1952 Wildcats, coached by Pepper Martin, skated to a 5-5 record. Co-captained by George Healey and John Simpson, the team benefited from the best ice conditions in five years. (UNH Archives.)

Pete Swanson anchored the second line for the Wildcats. His hat trick led the way in a 10-2 thrashing of the Massachusetts Institute of Technology (MIT) on January 13, 1952. (UNH Archives.)

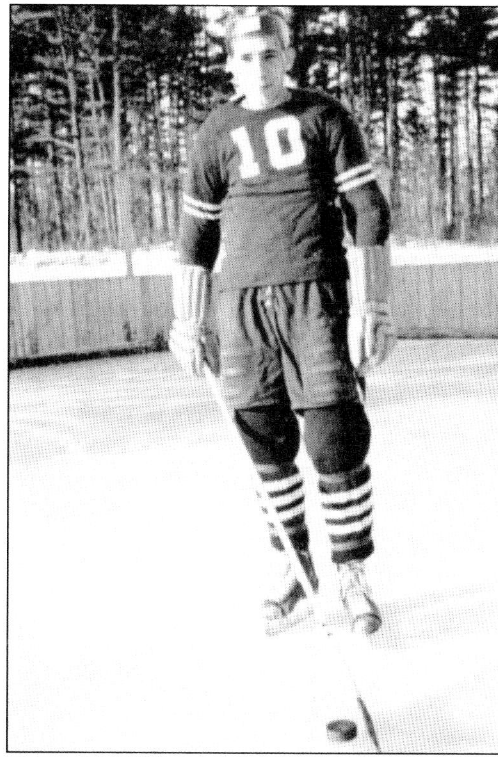

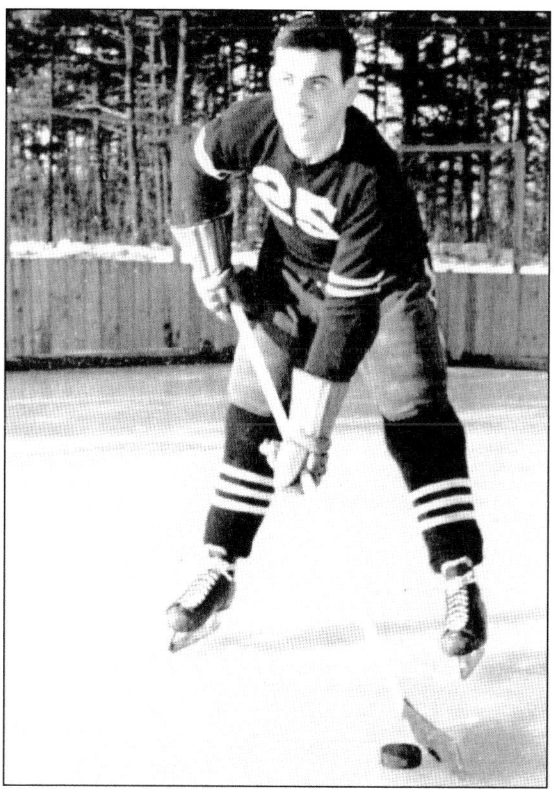

Lawrence "Bambi" King played on Martin's high-powered first line with Tom Dolan and co-captain John Simpson. The team suffered late in the season after King was declared ineligible to play and Dolan and Simpson graduated midyear. (UNH Archives.)

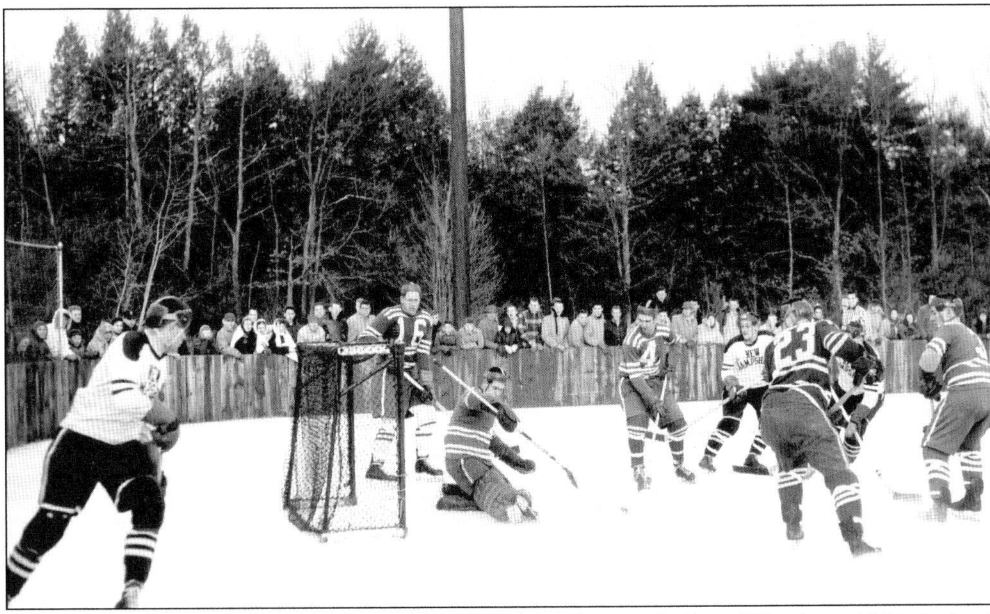

This unidentified game is being played on the old rink near College Woods in 1954. In both 1953 and 1954, weather seemed to be the Wildcats most persistent adversary. In 1954, the team went winless until posting back-to-back wins in mid-February. Alas, just as the team began playing its best hockey, unseasonably warm weather forced the cancellation of the four remaining games on the schedule. (UNH Archives.)

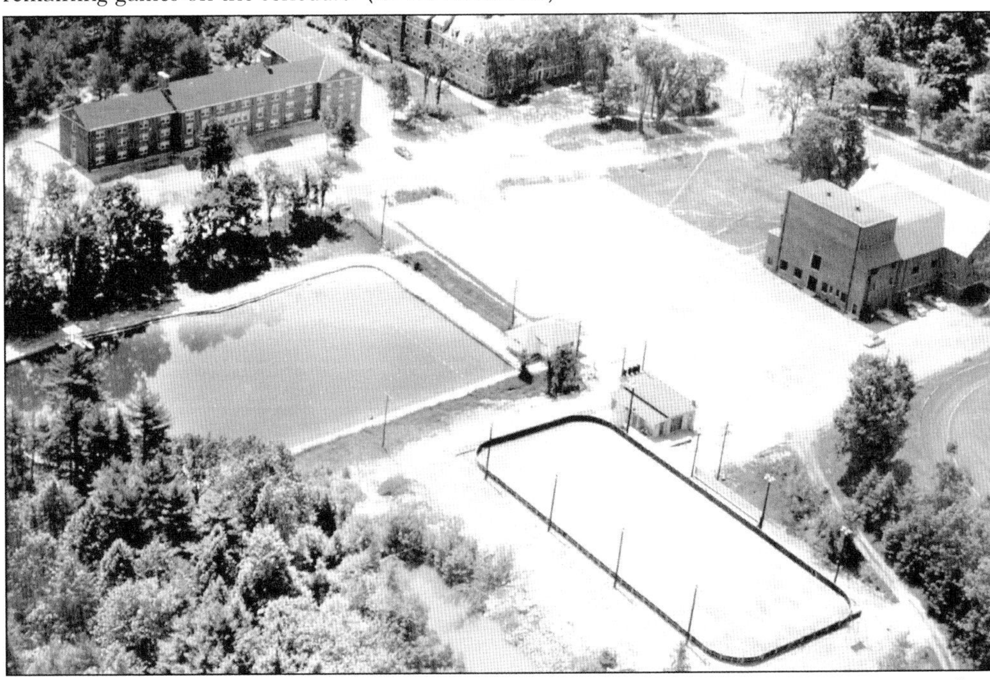

In 1955, Harry C. Batchelder, Class of 1913, donated the equipment necessary to produce artificial ice. In February 1955, the Harry C. Batchelder Rink opened behind New Hampshire Hall, adjacent to where the original UNH ice rink had been located. This is an aerial view of Batchelder Rink in June 1955. (UNH Archives.)

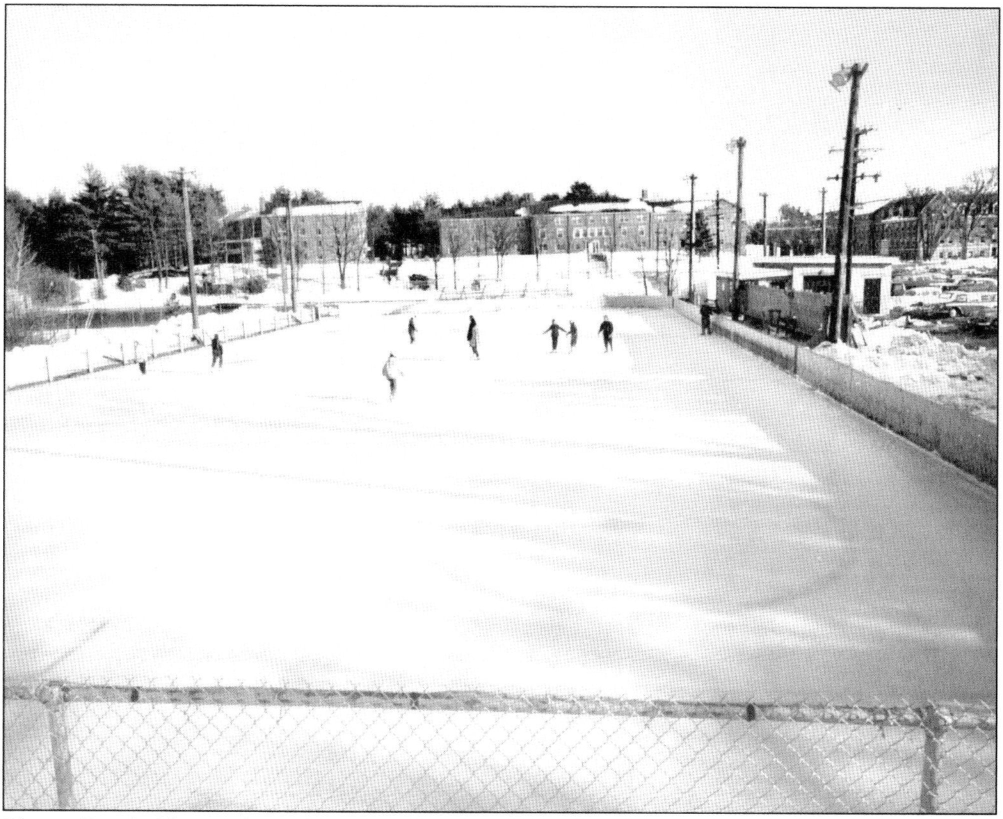

This is Batchelder Rink in the early 1960s, with a chain link fence that was installed for ice hockey games. (UNH Archives.)

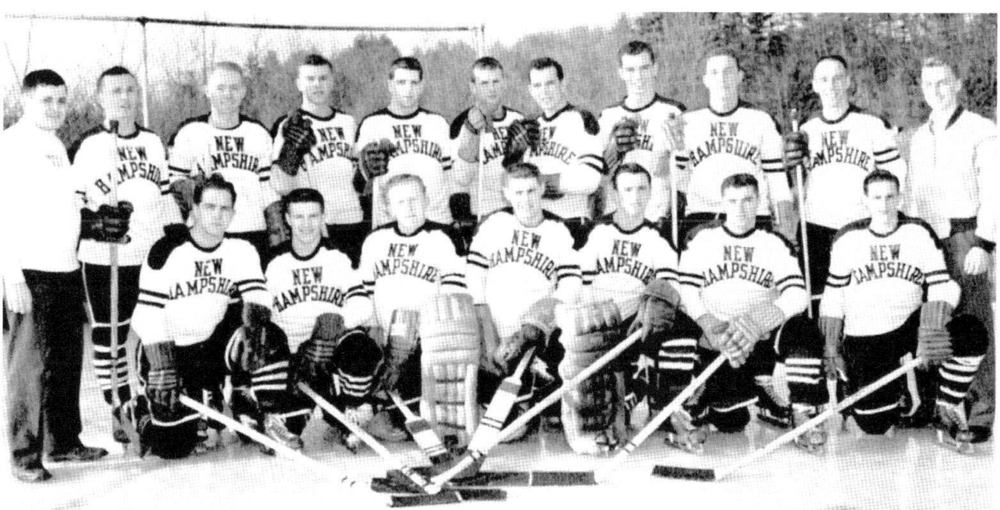

The 1954–1955 team was coached by Pepper Martin and captained by Bill Johnston and Monty Childs. This is the first team photograph taken on Batchelder Rink. (UNH Archives.)

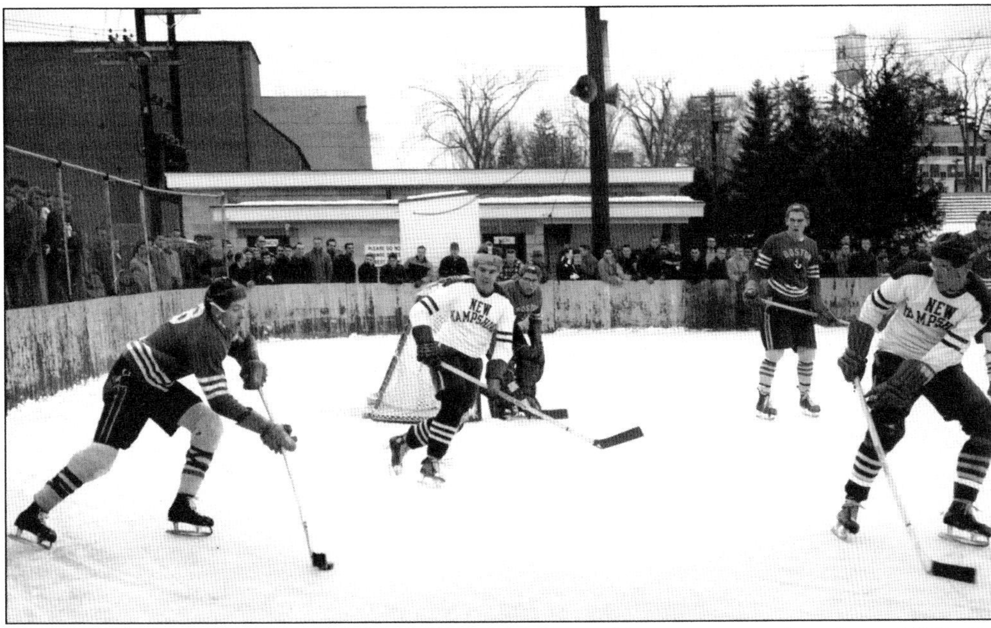

This Wildcat scrimmage against the Boston University Terriers occurred early in 1955. On February 5, 1955, UNH defeated Colby 8-0 in the first official game on Batchelder Rink. The Wildcats finished the season with a 5-8 record. (UNH Archives.)

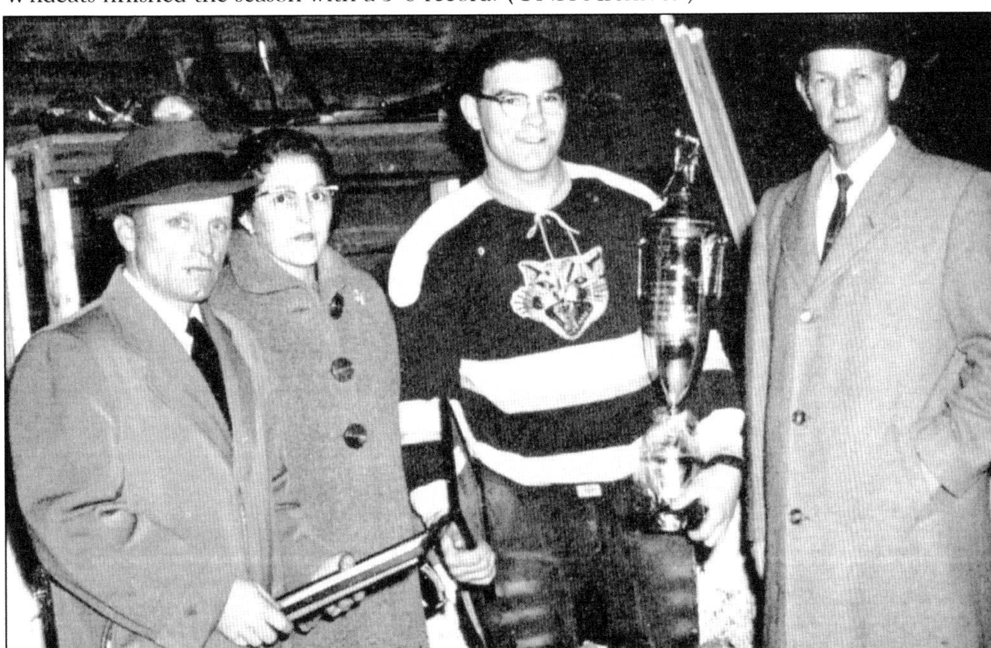

After four losing seasons, the Wildcats posted a 7-7-1 record during the 1956–1957 season. The following year, Martin's team went 13-3. However, the death of player Roger Leclerc in an automobile accident clouded the season. The aggressive, hard-hitting Leclerc was an inspiration to his teammates, and the Roger Leclerc Memorial Trophy, awarded to the team's most valuable player, was inaugurated that year. The first recipient was goalie John "Bozo" Kennedy (third from left). (UNH Archives.)

Albert "Albie" Brodeur, of Berlin, New Hampshire, provided leadership and firepower to Wildcat teams in the late 1950s. Brodeur's 78 career points over three varsity seasons broke the scoring record set by Russ Martin in 1938. (UNH Archives.)

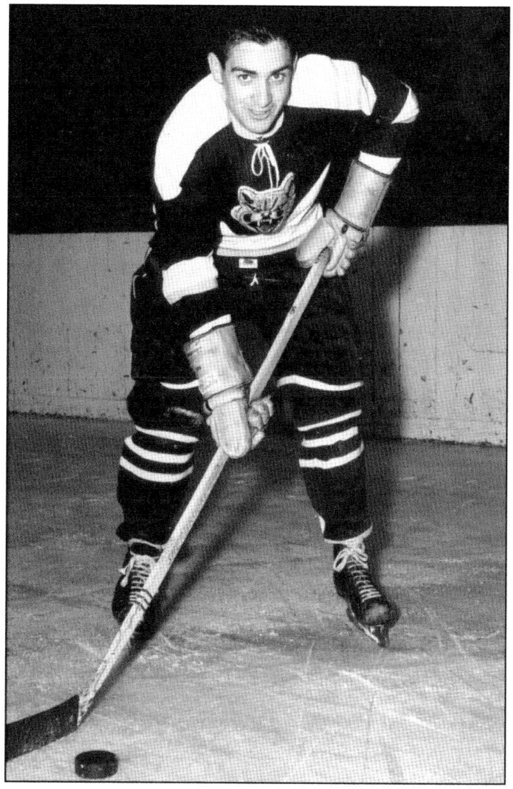

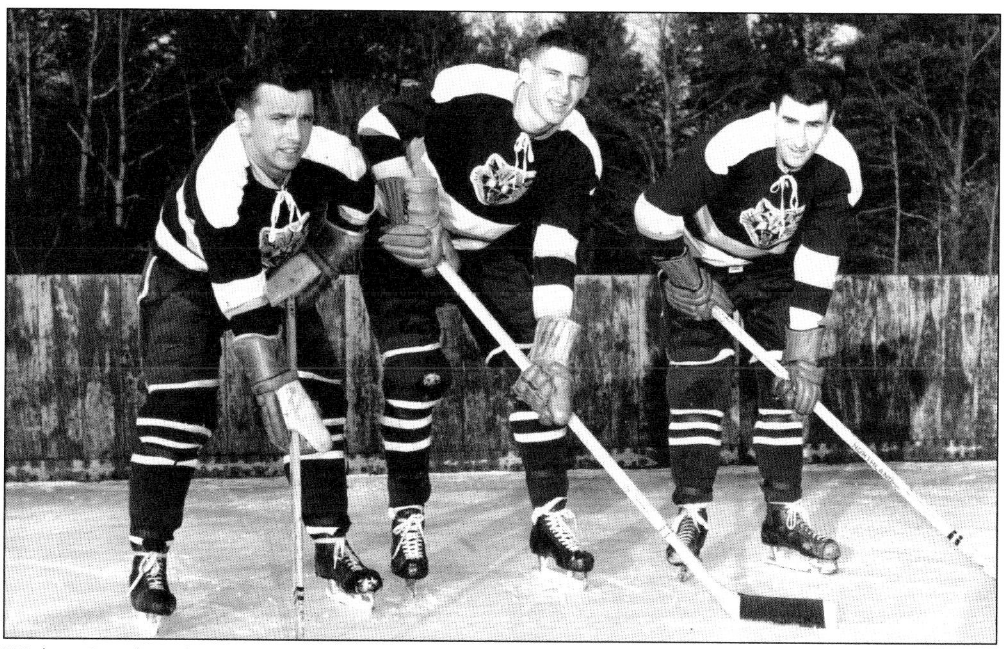

Walter Read, Sylvester "Buster" Clegg, and Albie Brodeur of the 1958–1959 Wildcats are pictured here from left to right. Clegg and Brodeur co-captained the team to a 14-5 record. Between 1957 and 1960, UNH had a combined record of 38-16. (UNH Archives.)

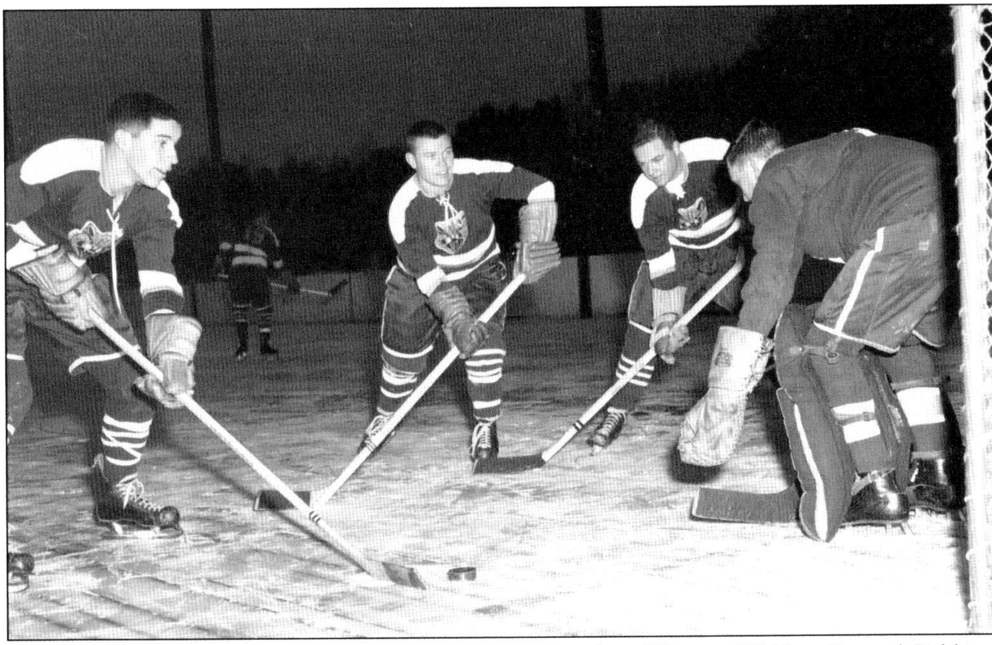

This posed photograph includes 1959–1960 team members Warren Wilder, Samuel Dibbins, and Roger Mageneau, pictured from left to right. The goalie is probably Joe Bellavance. The high-scoring club was led by co-captain Raymond March who, in February 1960, became the first Wildcat hockey player to score 100 career points. He finished with 105. (UNH Archives.)

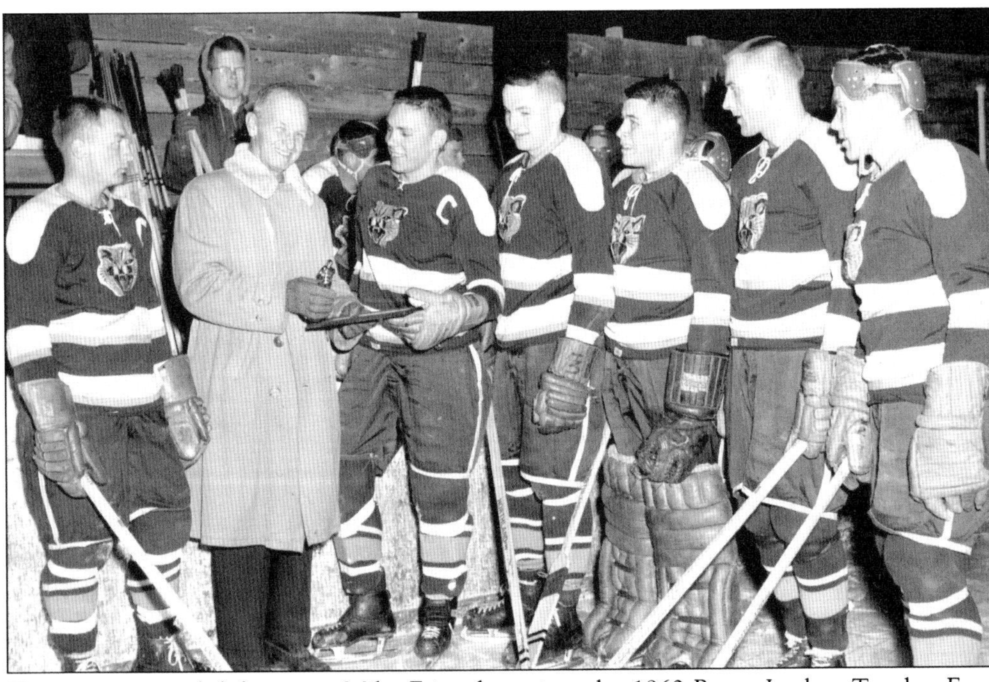

Team captain and defenseman Mike Frigard receives the 1960 Roger Leclerc Trophy. From left to right are Ray March, athletic director Carl Lundholm, Mike Frigard, Ken McKinnon, Joe Bellavance, Bob Patch, and Samuel Dibbins. (UNH Archives.)

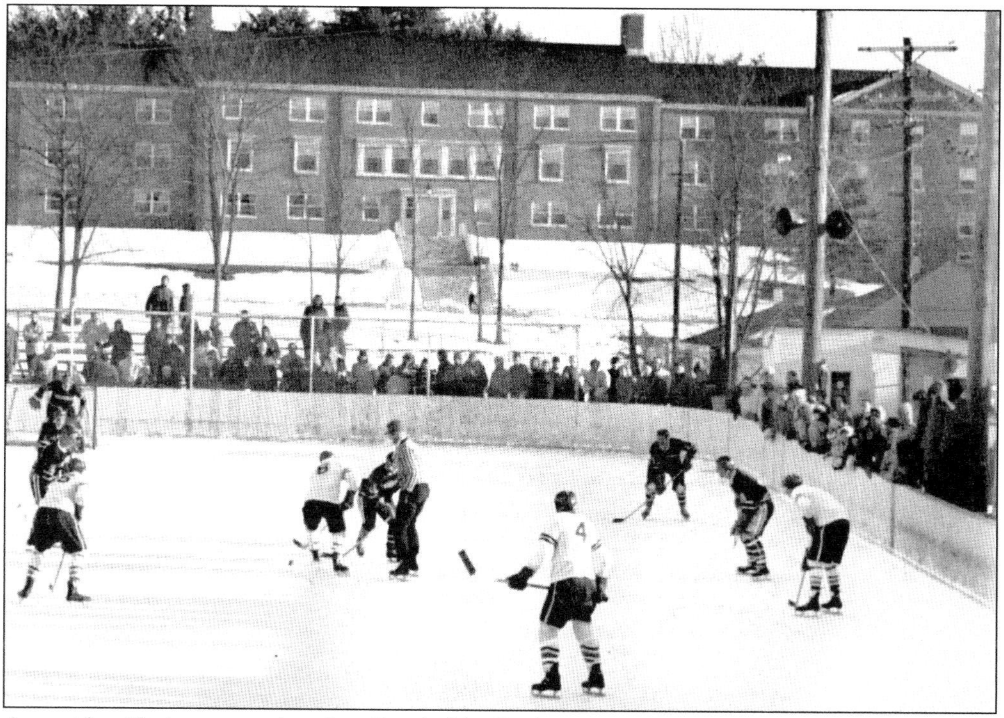

An unidentified game is played on Batchelder Rink in 1960. (UNH Archives.)

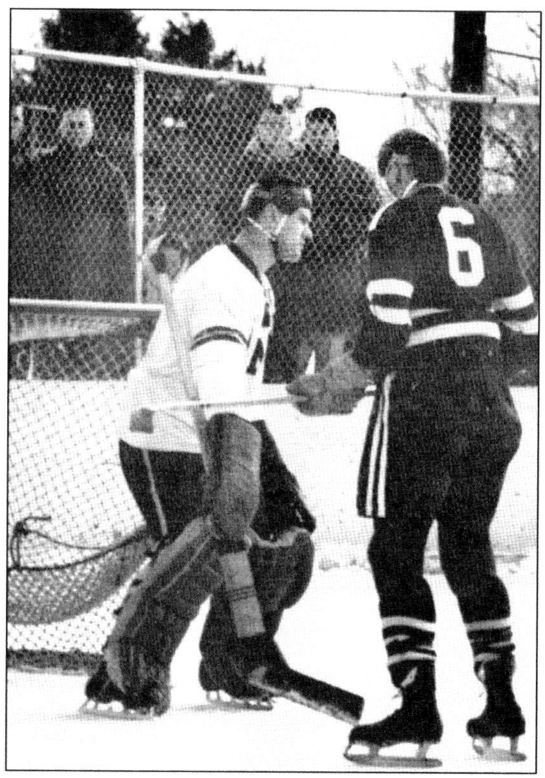

With the graduation of many stars the previous spring, the 1960–1961 season was a rebuilding year. In spite of a 3-11 record, captain and starting goalie Rod Blackburn turned back shot after shot. He finished the year with 589 saves, for an average of 41.4 per game. On March 23, 1961, Blackburn became the first UNH hockey player to be named to the All-American team. (UNH Archives.)

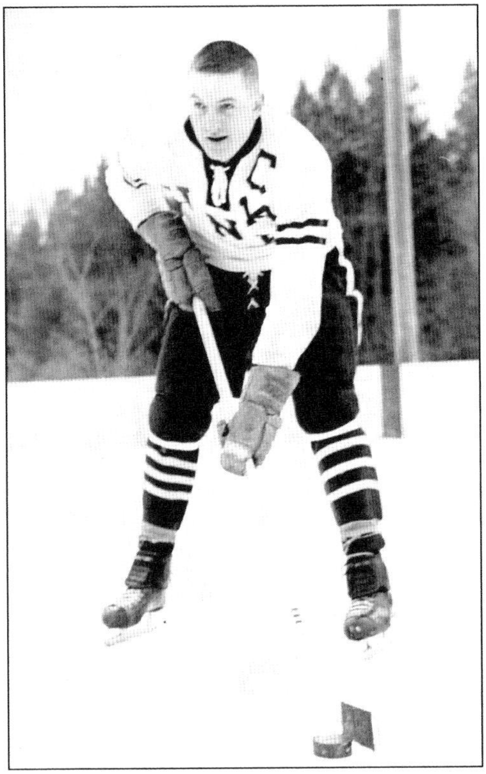

Ken McKinnon was co-captain of the 1961–1962 Wildcats. He was the first Canadian hockey player to attend UNH. He tied a UNH record (held by Ray Patten and Red Adams) by scoring six goals against Connecticut on February 11, 1961. In addition, he opened the door for UNH to recruit a succession of talented Toronto-area players. (UNH Archives.)

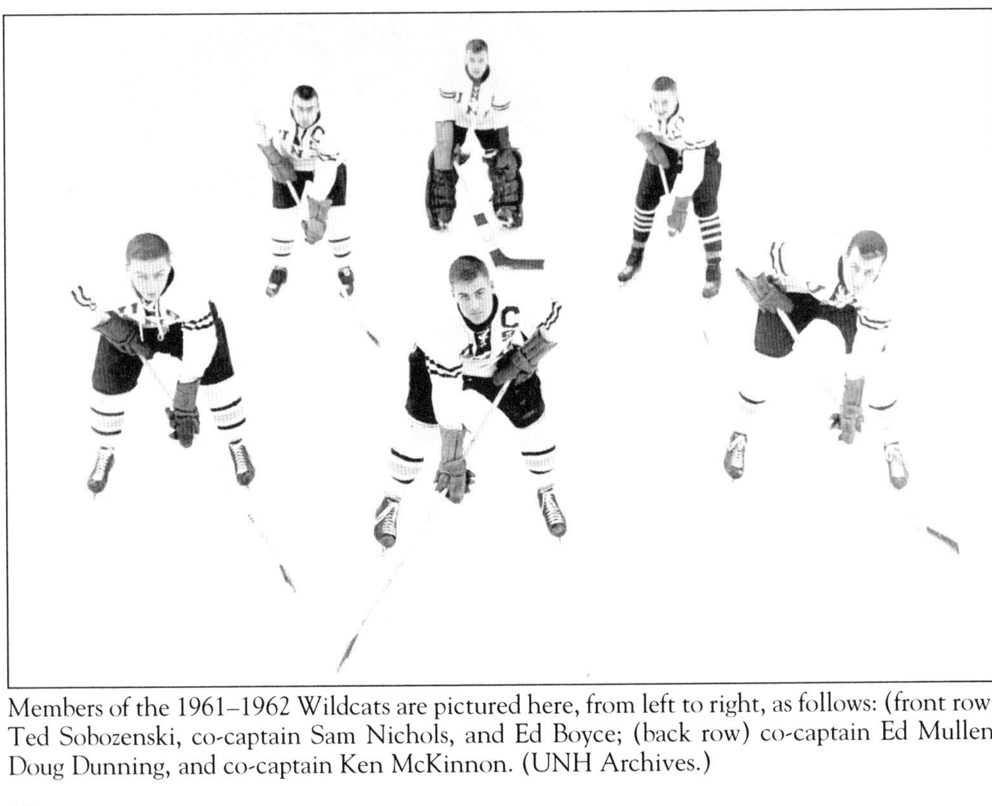

Members of the 1961–1962 Wildcats are pictured here, from left to right, as follows: (front row) Ted Sobozenski, co-captain Sam Nichols, and Ed Boyce; (back row) co-captain Ed Mullen, Doug Dunning, and co-captain Ken McKinnon. (UNH Archives.)

Center Tom Canavan of Willowdale, Ontario, anchored the second line for the 1961–1962 Wildcats. Canavan was the leading scorer for the Wildcats during the 1962–1963 campaign. (UNH Archives.)

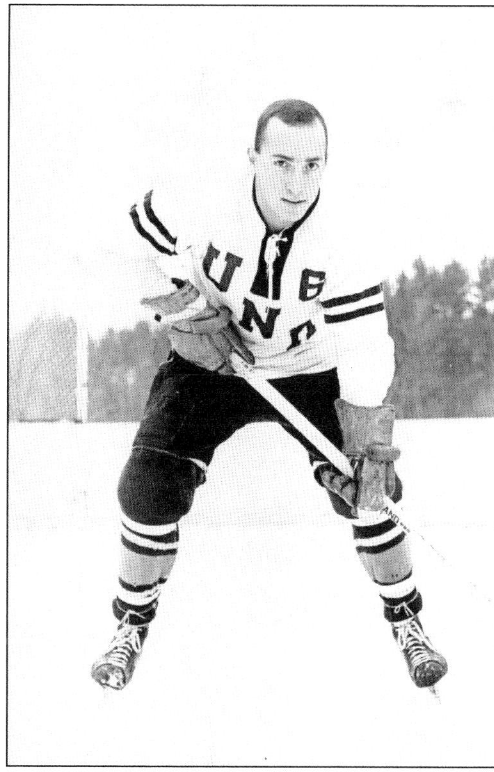

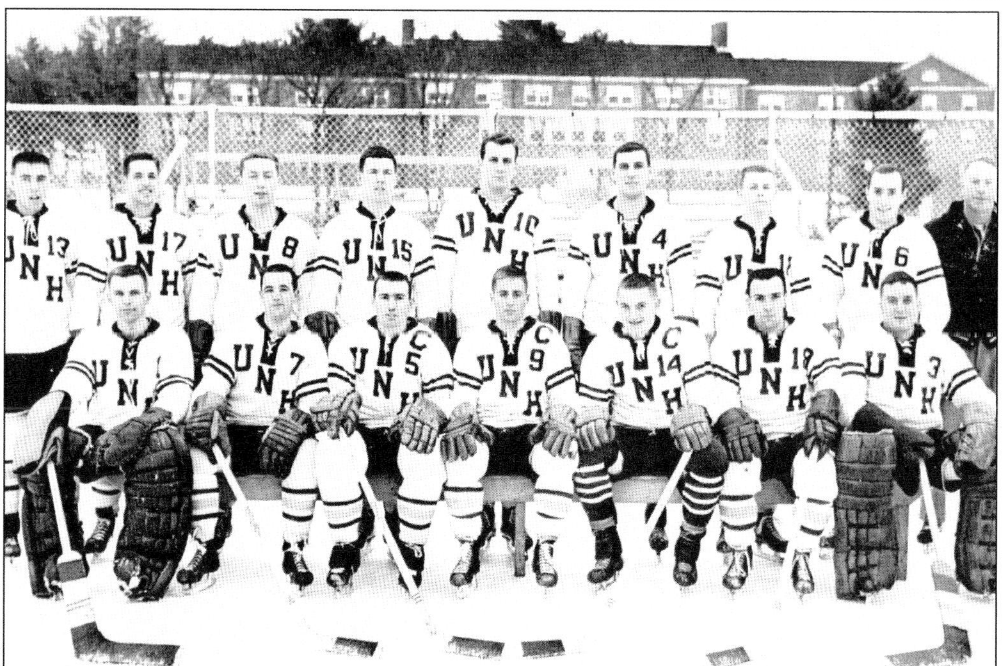

The 1961–1962 UNH Wildcats are pictured here. In Pepper Martin's last year as hockey coach, the Wildcats finished with a record of 10-7-1. The team set a new university record by scoring 103 goals in a season. (UNH Archives.)

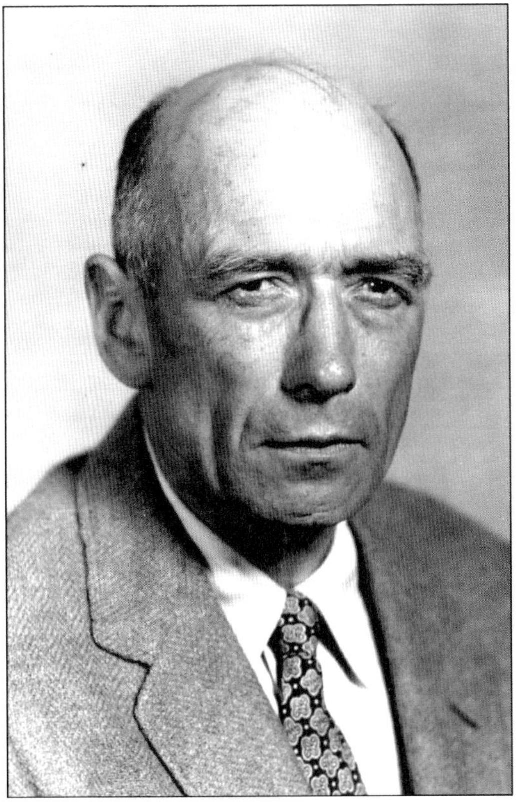

In 1962, A. Barr "Whoop" Snively replaced Pepper Martin as hockey coach. In addition, Snively also served as lacrosse coach and assistant football coach. (UNH Archives.)

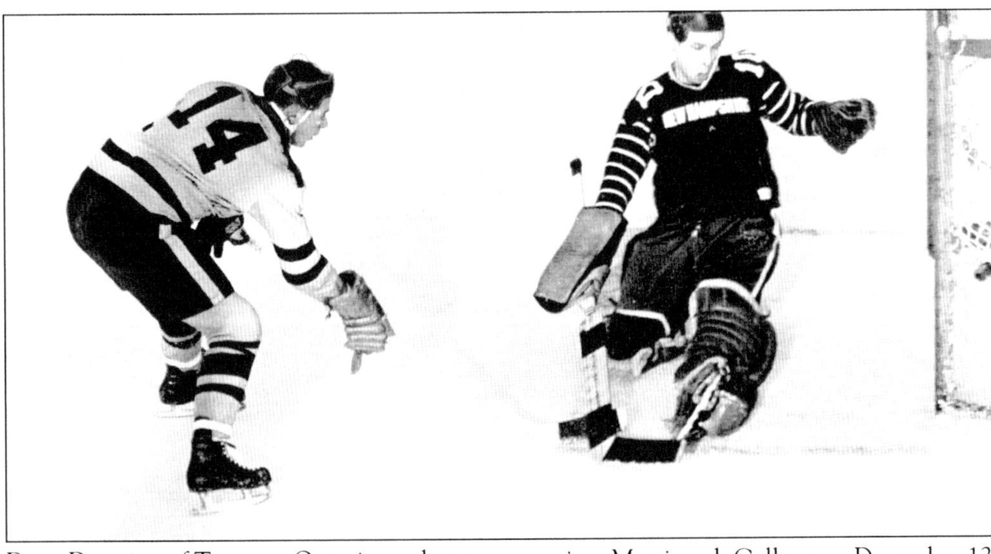

Doug Dunning of Toronto, Ontario, makes a save against Merrimack College on December 12, 1962, at Batchelder Rink. UNH went on to defeat Merrimack 3-2. (UNH Archives.)

Dick Lamontagne was captain of the 1962–1963 hockey team. With an attack that featured Lamontagne, Tom Canavan, and Clarence "Buzz" Littell, and a defense built around goalie Doug Dunning, the Wildcats finished 10-10 in Whoop Snively's first year as coach. (UNH Archives.)

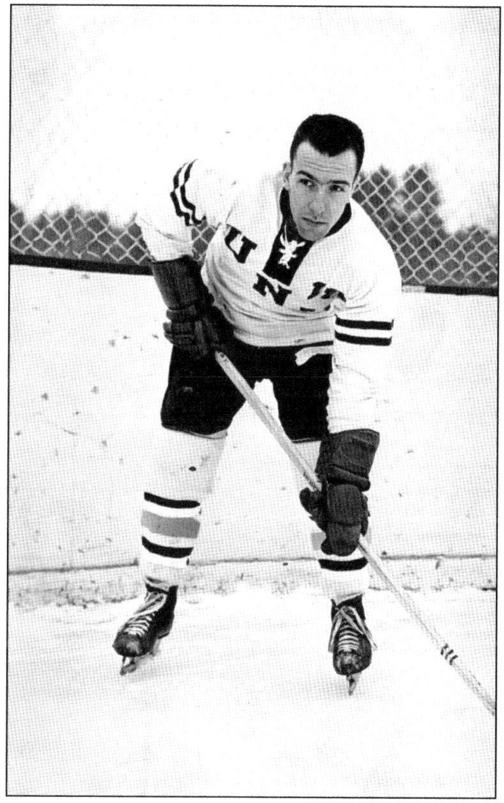

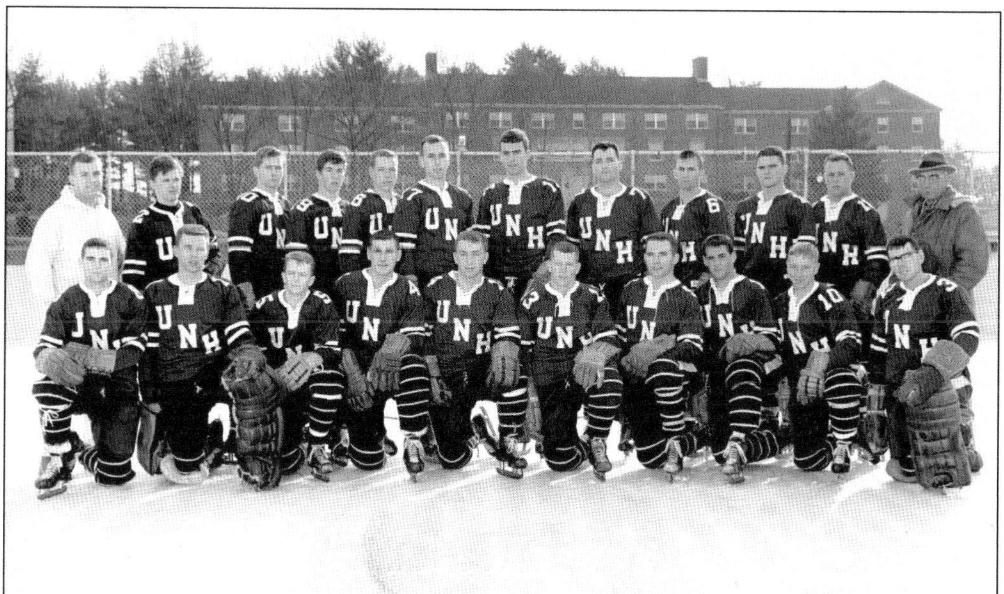

The 1963–1964 UNH Wildcat hockey team, captained by Buzz Littell, finished the year with a 13-12 record. (UNH Archives.)

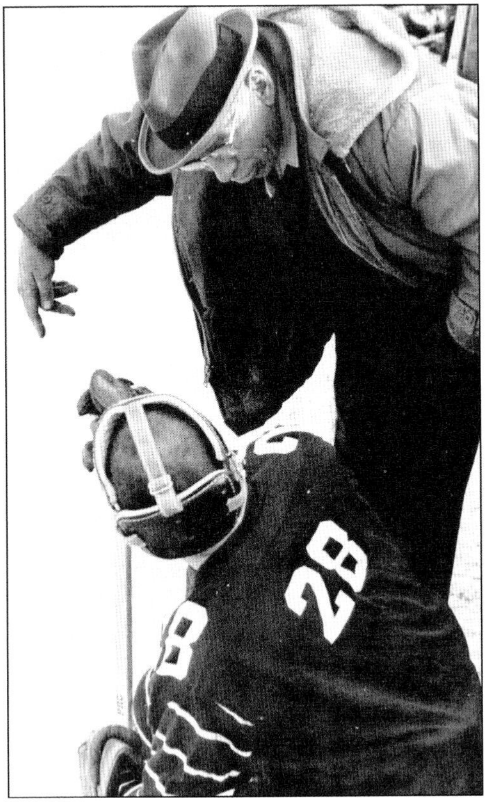

Whoop Snively gives pointers to Tom Canavan, the leading scorer for the 1962–1963 Wildcats. (UNH Archives.)

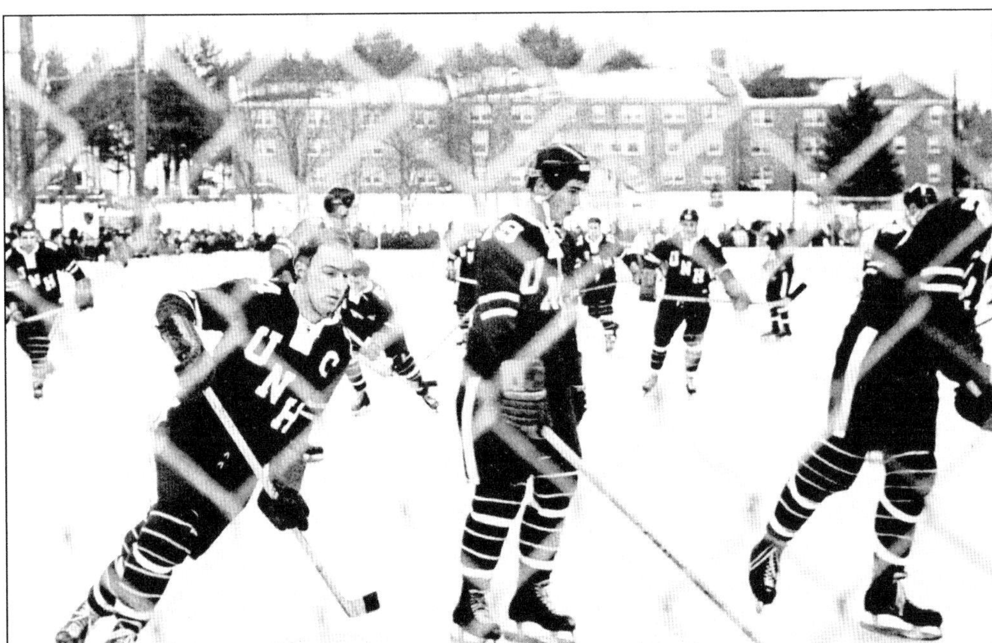

Players warm up on Batchelder Rink during the 1963–1964 season. From left to right are captain Buzz Littell, Al Myer, and Harold "Dude" Thorn. (UNH Archives.)

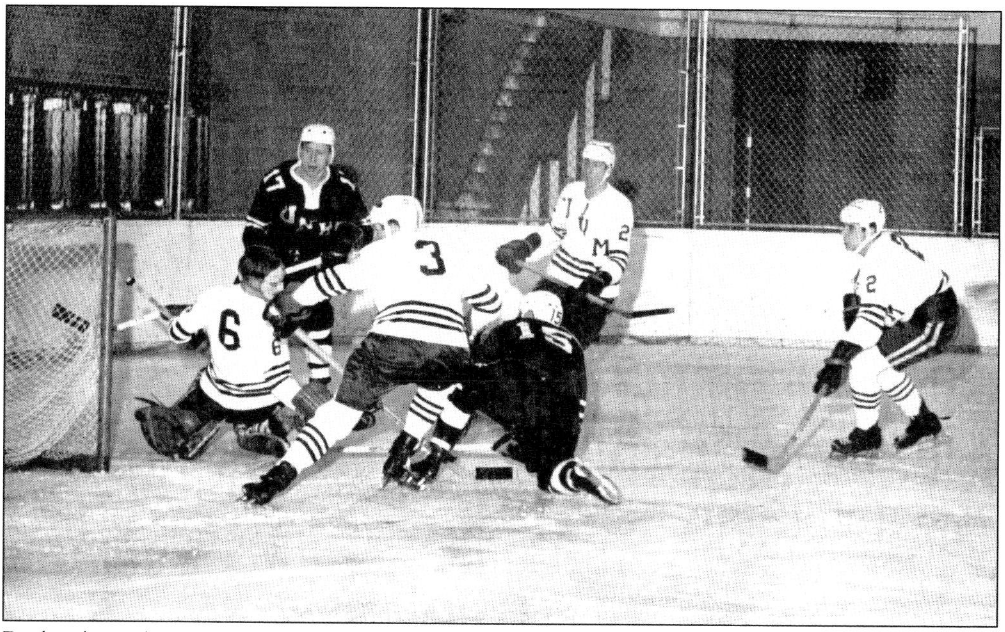

Dude Thorn (No. 15), another import from the Toronto area, was the Wildcats' leading scorer in both 1964 and 1966. He ended his career with 100 points. Here, he caught the University of Vermont goalie going in the wrong direction. (UNH Archives.)

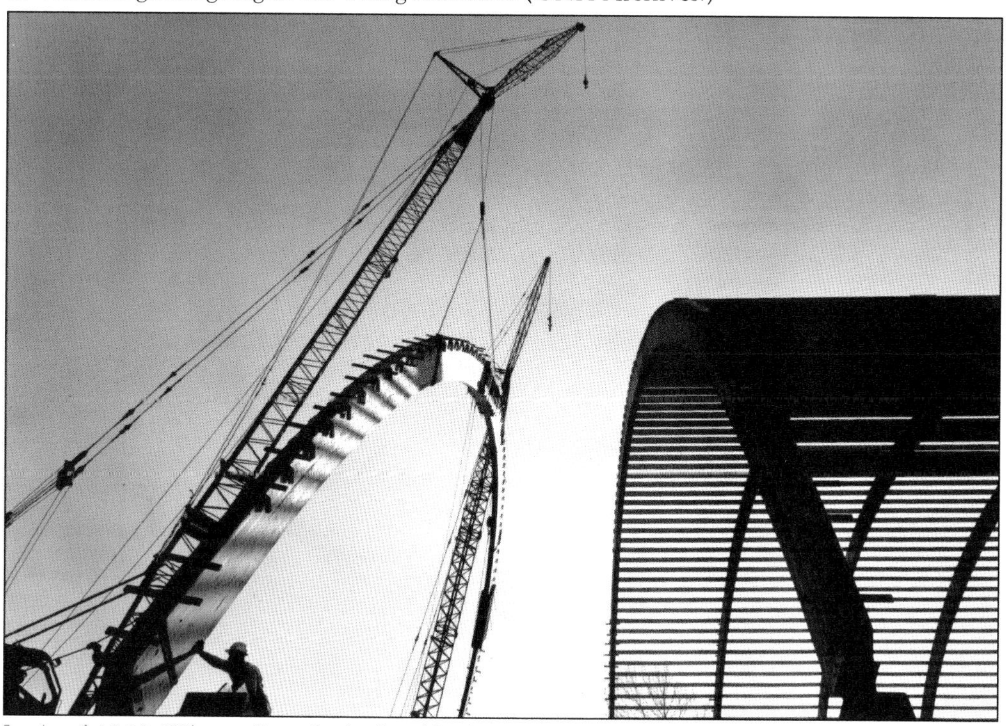

In April 1964, Whoop Snively died suddenly of a heart attack. That same day, the university announced plans to begin enclosing Batchelder Rink with a structure that would be named in Snively's honor. This photograph shows the end beams being installed on October 15, 1964. (Jack Adams photograph. UNH Archives.)

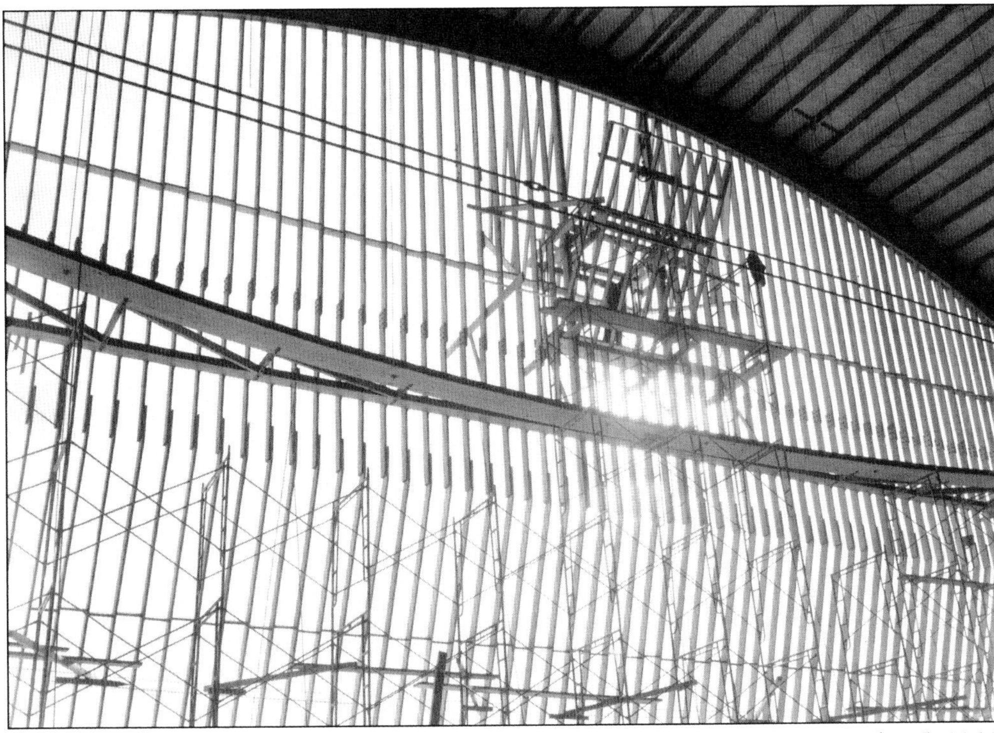

This photograph shows the enclosing of the south end of Snively Arena on December 5, 1964. (Jack Adams photograph. UNH Archives.)

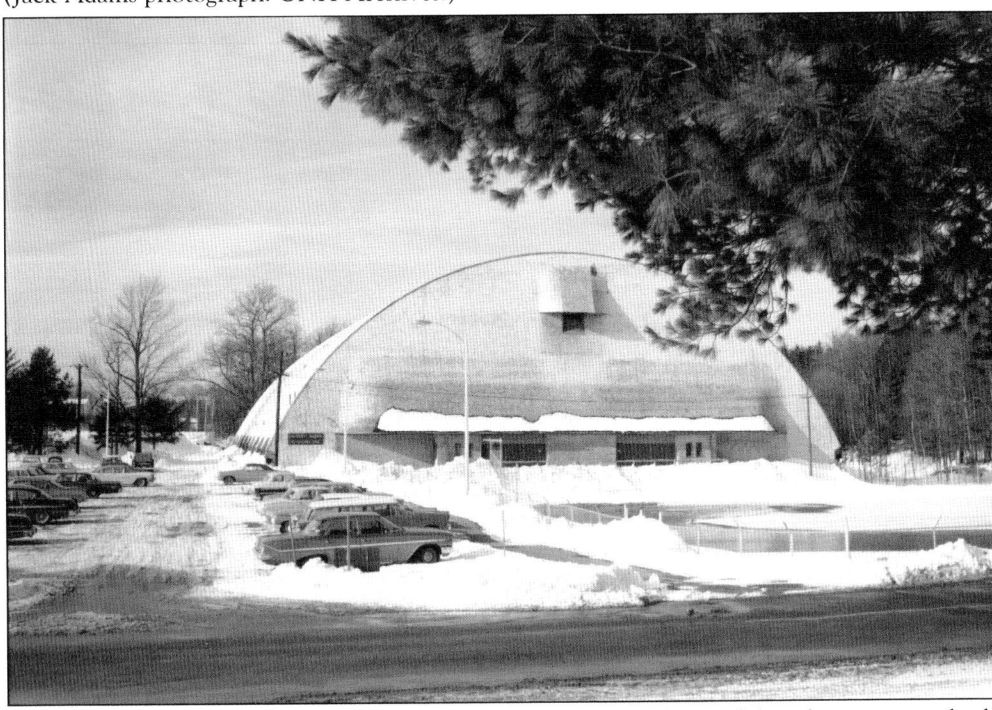

This is the completed Snively Arena in January 1966. The facility took less than a year to build and seated 3,200 for ice hockey. (UNH Archives.)

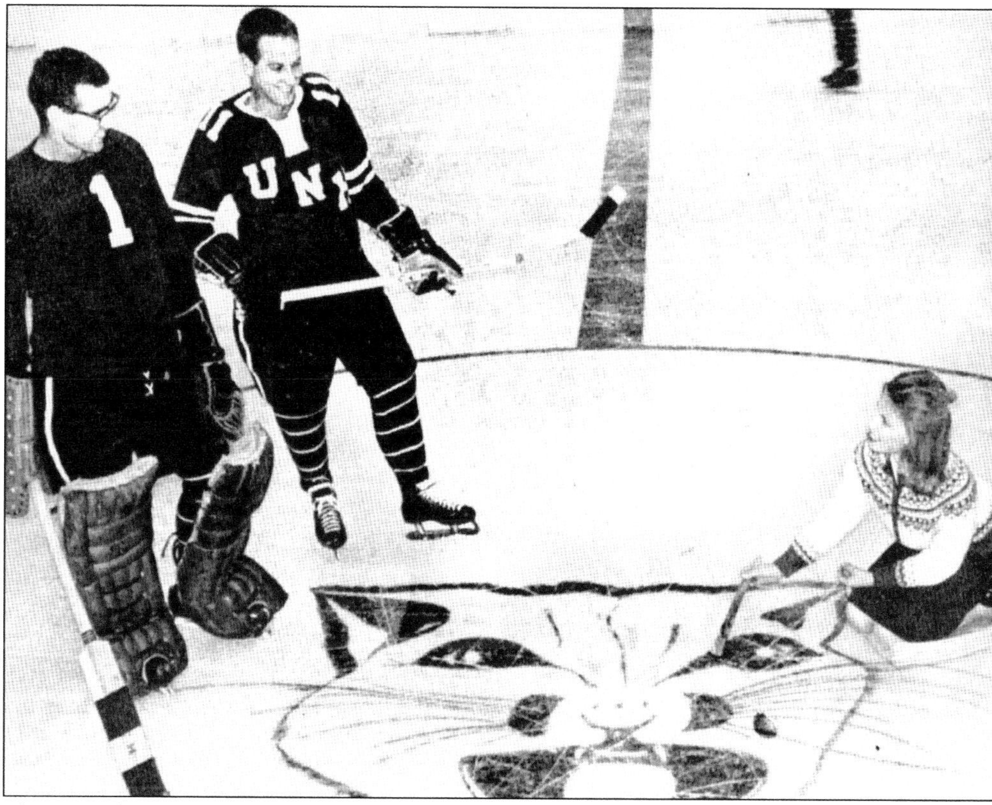
Players Colin Clark (left) and Dude Thorn watch as Jan Oliver puts the finishing touches on the Wildcat logo at mid-ice. (UNH Archives.)

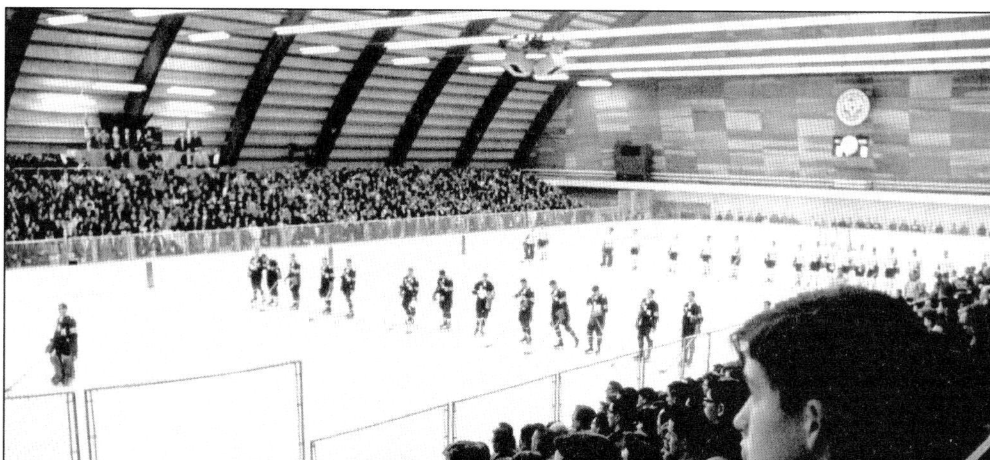
Rube Bjorkman, former head hockey coach at Rensselaer Polytechnic Institute (RPI), started coaching at UNH during the 1964–1965 season. The Wildcats began the season with 11 straight road games before returning home to a packed house at the newly completed Snively Arena. On February 13, 1965, the Wildcats lined up for a game against Norwich University. "Lively Snively" was born. (UNH Archives.)

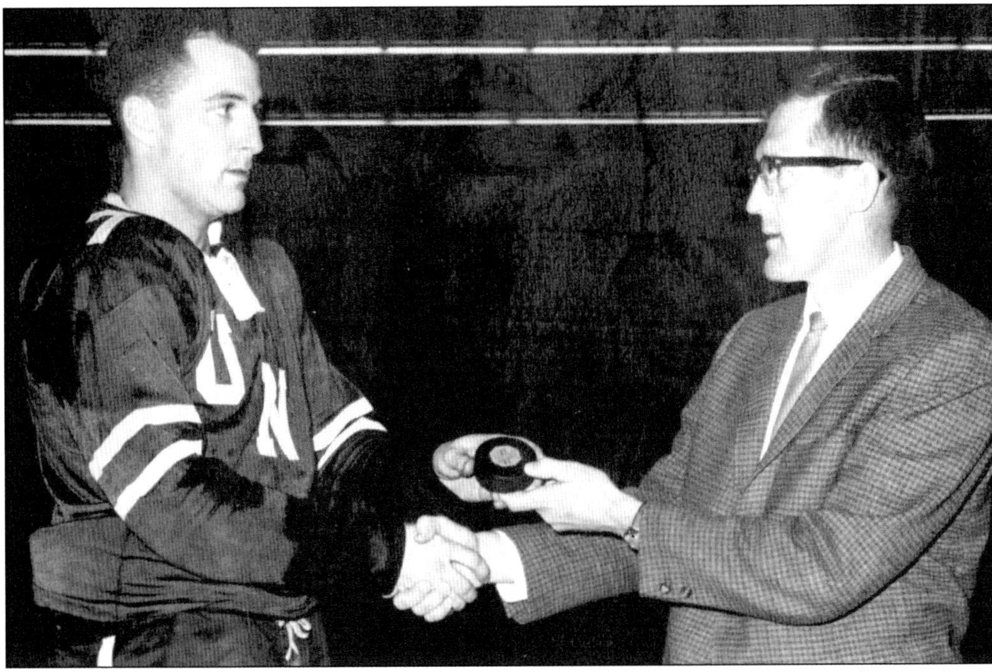

Brad Houston scored the first goal in Snively Arena. Play stopped so that Rube Bjorkman could present Houston with the puck. Norwich went on to a 4-3 overtime win. The Wildcats went 6-14 for the season and 6-9 in their first year of Eastern Collegiate Athletic Conference (ECAC) II play. The Wildcats stayed at the Collegiate level for two years before moving up to Division I. (UNH Archives.)

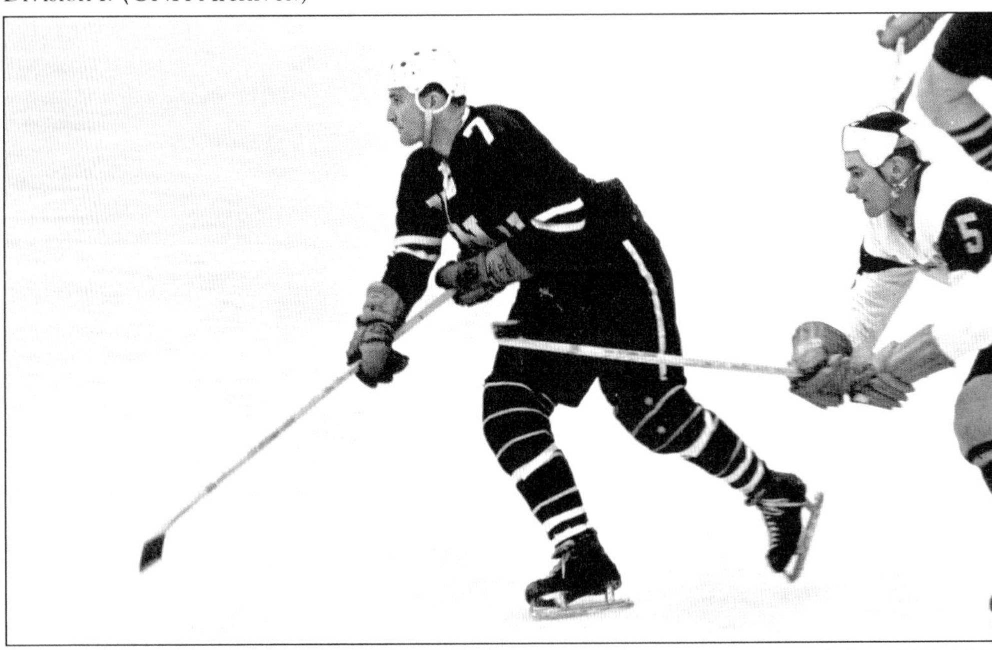

Defenseman Brad Houston skates away from his pursuers. Houston captained the 1965–1966 team that went 11-12 and improved to 11-5 in ECAC II play. He was named most valuable player for the season. (UNH Archives.)

This is the cover of the 1966 National Collegiate Athletic Conference (NCAA) *Ice Hockey Guide*, which features senior wing Bob McCarthy. Although UNH fared poorly against Division I opponents, they averaged seven goals a game against Division II teams and finished second in the ECAC Division II tournament. (Holt Archives of American Hockey, Milne Special Collections and Archives.)

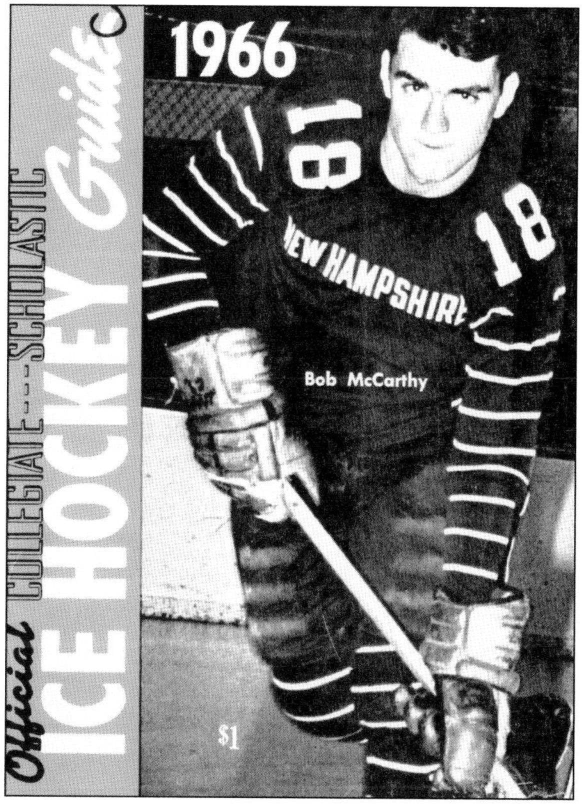

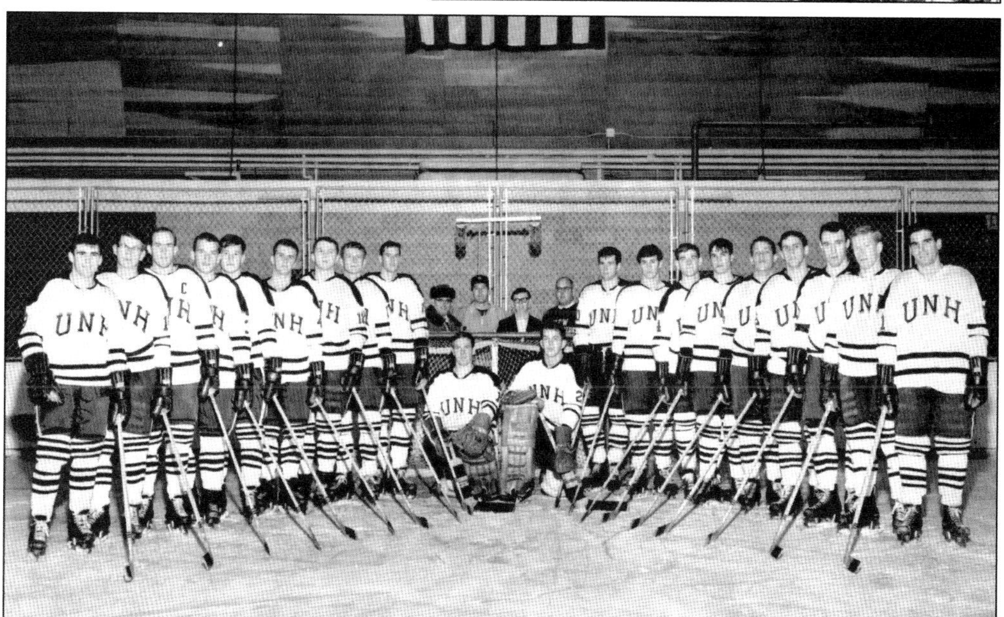

This is the 1966–1967 edition of the UNH Wildcats hockey team. In Rube Bjorkman's third year as head coach, UNH moved into Division I of the ECAC. With higher caliber teams coming into town, the crowds in Snively grew large and loud. During the season, the Wildcats were 9-2 at home and 18-7 overall. (UNH Archives.)

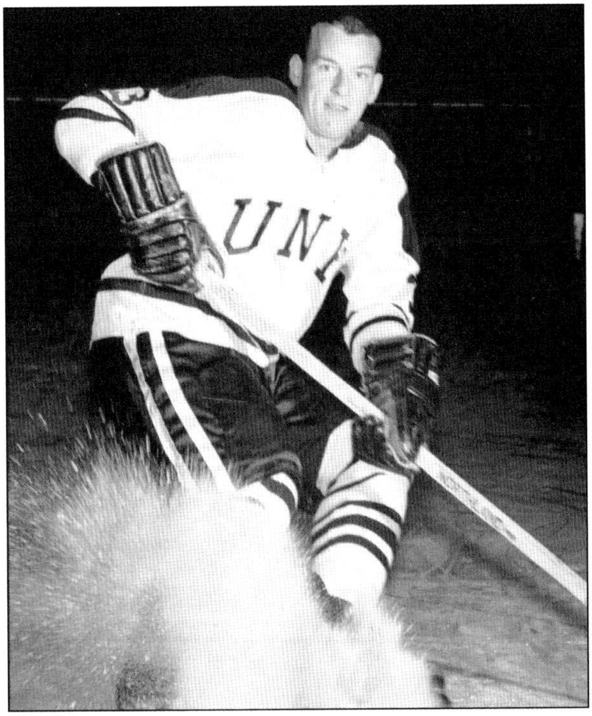

Defenseman Graham Bruder of Noranda, Quebec, was a two-time captain of the UNH ice hockey team. He helped lead the 1967–1968 team to a 22-7 record. Many thought the team's 7-6 record in ECAC play would result in an invitation to the ECAC Tournament, but none was forthcoming. (UNH Archives.)

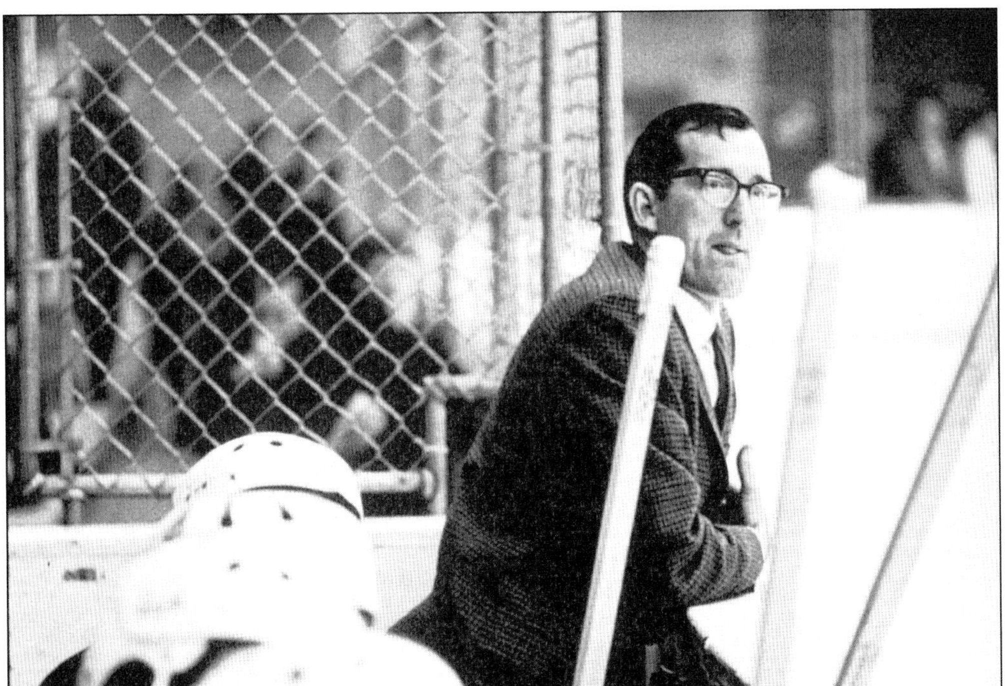

Coach Rube Bjorkman follows the action from the bench. Bjorkman's contacts in the Midwest and Canada expanded UNH recruiting and helped to usher in the era of big-time hockey at UNH. In 1966–1967 and 1967–1968, the Wildcats sported an impressive 40-14 overall record. (UNH Archives.)

Goalie Rick Metzer helped anchor the Wildcat defense from 1966 to 1969. Metzer still ranks in the top five for goals against average (2.89), career save percentage (.899), and season save percentage (91.56). (UNH Archives.)

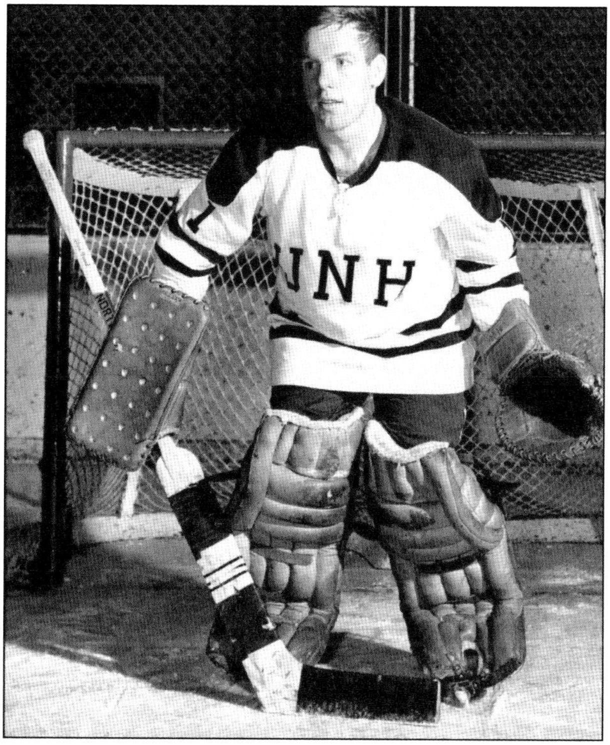

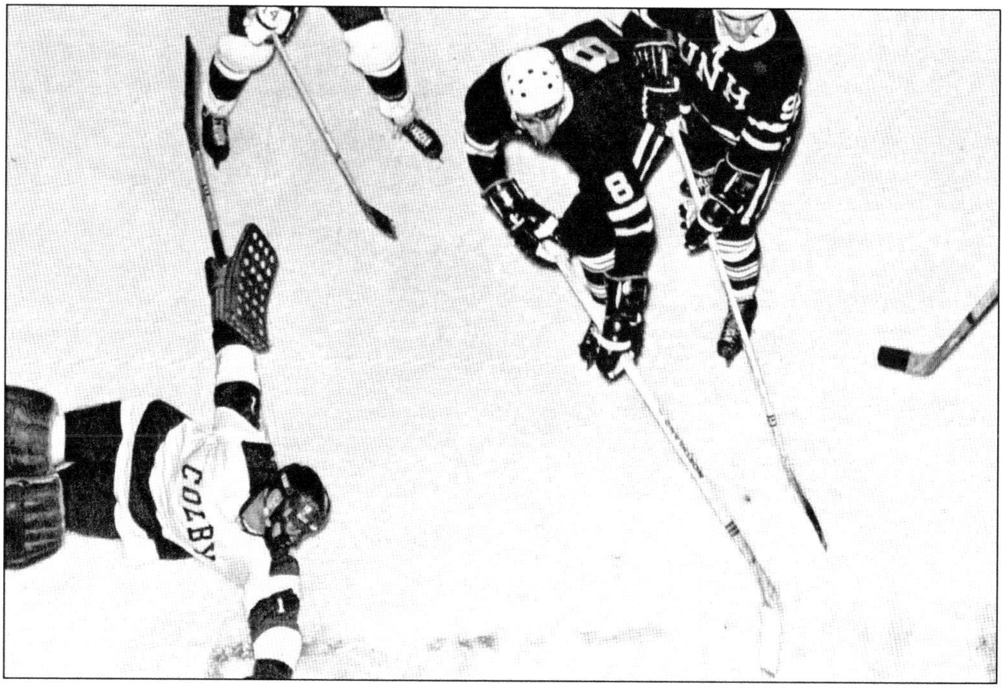

Mike Ontkean (No. 8) scores on a feed from Rich David (No. 9) against Colby College on January 13, 1968. Ontkean finished the season with 30 goals and 24 assists. He later exchanged his pads and stick for a career in Hollywood and, in 1977, the former UNH hockey star faced off against Paul Newman in the classic hockey movie *Slap Shot*. (UNH Archives.)

THE NEW HAMPSHIRE

VOL. 58 NO. 43 FRIDAY, MARCH 29, 1968 DURHAM, N.H.

Named N.E. Coach of Year

Bjorkman Resigns as UNH Hockey Coach

by John Donovan

Hockey coach Rube Bjorkman said yesterday that he is leaving UNH "to make a direct and meaningful contribution to a well-established youth hockey program in Grand Rapids, Minnesota."

Bjorkman's statement dispelled rumors, circulating in Durham yesterday, that he resigned because he was unhappy at UNH and dissatisfied with financial aid given him for recruiting hockey players.

"The past five years of college coaching have been very enjoyable for me, and I am grateful for the many fine associations I have formed," said Bjorkman. He also remarked that the UNH hockey program is off to a good start and will remain intact for two reasons.

"First, because the boys are excellent both as players and as gentlemen," said Bjorkman. "And second, because the community, especially the students, take great pride in the team."

"As far as UNH is concerned, I'm convinced that New Hampshire will remain a hockey power. If I thought my leaving would mean the death of UNH hockey, then I wouldn't go."

Rumors at the NCAA championships in Duluth, Minn., had Bjorkman "tired" of college hockey. "I just had to get back home to Minnesota," said Bjorkman. "It is something I have been thinking about for a couple of years. There was nothing wrong with the job at New Hampshire, and I am not looking for a college job elsewhere."

Bjorkman announced his resignation from UNH, effective June 30, 1968, at the New England Sportswriters and Hockey Coaches Luncheon at the Hotel Somerset in Boston, Wednesday night, where he received the "New England Coach of the Year" award.

Bjorkman's fellow New England coaches voted him the Clark Hudder plaque, symbolic of New England's outstanding coach. Boston University's Jack Kelley, last year's recipient, presented Bjorkman with the plaque which is named after a former Harvard hockey coach.

Bjorkman is the first hockey coach in New Hampshire history to receive the Hudder plaque. He is the second UNH coach honored by New England sportswriters and coaches this year. Former Wildcat coach, Joe Yukica of Boston College, was cited as "New England Football Coach of the Year" last fall.

"I feel that the Grand Rapids area presents an excellent opportunity for my particular family," explained

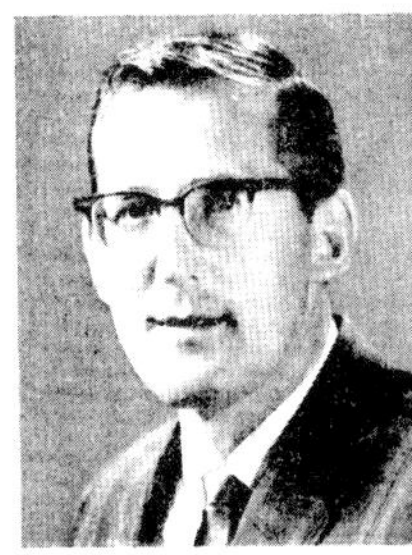

Rube Bjorkman

Bjorkman. "The job offers me a chance to create hockey players, or, at least work with them while they are developing, and I hope I can send some back here to New Hampshire."

UNH Director of Athletics, Andrew Mooradian, said yesterday that "New Hampshire is losing a fine person, as well as a great hockey coach, and we will always be indebted to Rube Bjorkman for the job he did with our hockey program. I enjoyed being around Rube, and hate to see him leave."

Bjorkman, 38, graduated from the University of Minnesota in 1952. He was a wing on the '48 and '52 Olympic teams, and captained the 1955 U.S. world team.

A native of Roseau, Minn., Bjorkman coached at Greenway High School, Coleraine, Minn., from 1955-63, before coming East to coach at Rensselaer Polytechnical Institute in Troy, N. Y.

He moved to UNH in 1964, and has compiled a record of 57 wins, 40 losses in four seasons with the Wildcats, including a 40-14 mark for the past two years, since New Hampshire moved into Division I of ECAC hockey league.

Cahill Takes Minnesota Post

Space Center Loses Director

by Ken Brown

Dr. Laurence J. Cahill, director of UNH's nationally famous Space Science Center, has resigned. He will accept a similar post with the University of Minnesota.

Rumors that Cahill's resignation resulted from dissatisfaction with the UNH space program are unfounded.

In a prepared statement, Cahill said, "There is no dissatisfaction, on my part, with the support of the UNH Space Science Center at the Department, College or University level."

Cahill said his decision to accept the Minnesota offer was based on the opportunity for "increased administrative responsibility" and "the challenge of contributing to the growth of a large multidisciplinary space research center."

Robert E. Houston, chairman of the Physics Department, indicated that UNH was not financially capable of providing an "integrated attack" which would deal with biological and mathematical problems of space science, as well as physics.

Robert N. Faiman,, vice-president for research, said, "We hope that the facilities of the space science program would still be appealing."

Faiman added that "ultimately we hope to provide adequate facilities" such as a building for the Space Science Center, which the University has contemplated at various times.

Cahill added, "The Center is presently in a strong position and is the largest, best supported group of its kind at any University of comparable size."

Houston said that other faculty members in the space science program were "not even considering" transferring to Minnesota with Cahill, contrary to rumors that followed Cahill's resignation.

Cahill said, "Two or three individuals in the Center may transfer to Minnesota with me." But, he added later, "No faculty are involved."

The people who might accompany him to Minnesota would be "engineers or technicians", according to Cahill, and the decision to leave is "completely up to them."

At UNH, Cahill has received several research grants from federal and private agencies to study space science problems, notably work on satellites.

Cahill estimated that he has been awarded about "$100,000" in contracts that will follow him to Minnesota, since

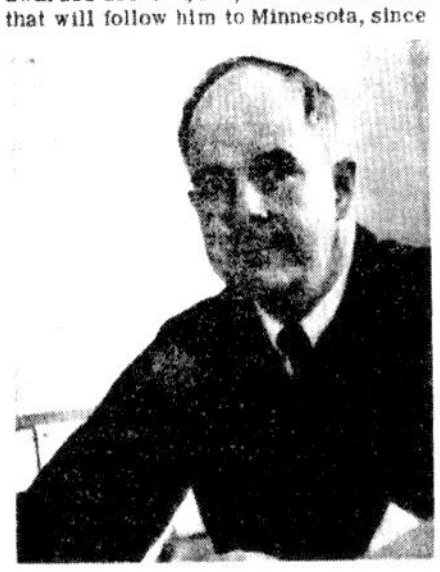

Dr. Laurence J. Cahill
(photo by Wallner)

he is the "principal investigator" in them.

Dale L. Chinburg, associate director of the Space Science Center, said the resignation of Cahill is "a great loss", but he felt other faculty will continue to receive important research grants.

Faiman was not certain what Cahill's resignation would mean to the University in research dollars, but, he said, "I'm sure it will hurt."

"Dr. Cahill was a most valuable leader," Faiman said.

"We will feel his loss significantly," said Houston. "There aren't too many people of his caliber around."

Senate Passes 4R Calendar

by Ed Brodeur

The University Senate adopted the 4R-4R calendar change by a three-fourths majority vote at a meeting Wednesday afternoon.

According to Arthur Grant, special assistant to President McConnell, the new plan is not really a calendar change.

"The 4R-4R plan calls for 13 weeks of instruction, two weeks of reading, and one six-day week of final exams. Final exams will still be given after Christmas vacation," Grant said.

At the Senate meeting, McConnell announced that the plan would not go into effect until September 1969. The reason for this is the problem of rescheduling classes.

"The rescheduling process will be tremendous," Grant said. Next semester's schedule has already been completed and the 1968-69 Catalogue has been printed. This, Grant said, was the cause of the delay.

Motions are now on the Senate floor pertaining to the course and credit aspect of the plan. One motion suggests that additional credits be added to the existing courses. This, for example, would give three credits to most two credit courses.

Other Senate members have suggested that some low credit courses be condensed into one quarter. This would make it possible to take two two-credit courses per semester.

Much of the opposition to the present calendar system arose mainly because of the two to three weeks of unproductive classes after Christmas vacation. "What we have done is to make this time into a reading period," Grant said. "Some people feel that it is unfortunate to shatter the sequence of learning by having four weeks without classes before finals, but almost everyone agrees that the reading period is better than having classes after Christmas," he said.

Student attitudes were taken into consideration before making the change. According to Grant, copies of the student opinion poll were sent to all University Senators and student opinions were voiced at Senate meetings.

Jeannette Roberts, co-chairman of The Student Senate Committee on Educational Policy, said a study would be made this weekend to determine what modifications students would like to see in the calendar change adopted by the University Senate. Ballots will be distributed to the housing units. Commuters may obtain them from the Student Senate Office.

Miss Roberts said that her committee would present the results of the survey to the University Senate task force before the Senate meeting Monday.

Paper Conducts Draft Poll

Students and faculty will be given a chance to express their views on the Draft beginning today. THE NEW HAMPSHIRE will conduct an opinion poll on the Selective Service System in the Memorial Union Lobby.

The table will be open today and Monday through Thursday of next week from 8:45 a.m. - 2 p.m. and from 8-9:30 p.m. The results of the poll will be printed in a special edition of THE NEW HAMPSHIRE concerning the Draft on April 17.

In March 1968, Rube Bjorkman shocked the university and the region when he resigned after four successful seasons at UNH. Fresh after being named New England Coach of the Year, Bjorkman announced his desire to return to the Midwest and direct a youth hockey program. He later took a head coaching job at the University of South Dakota. (UNH Archives.)

Three

The Charlie Holt Era

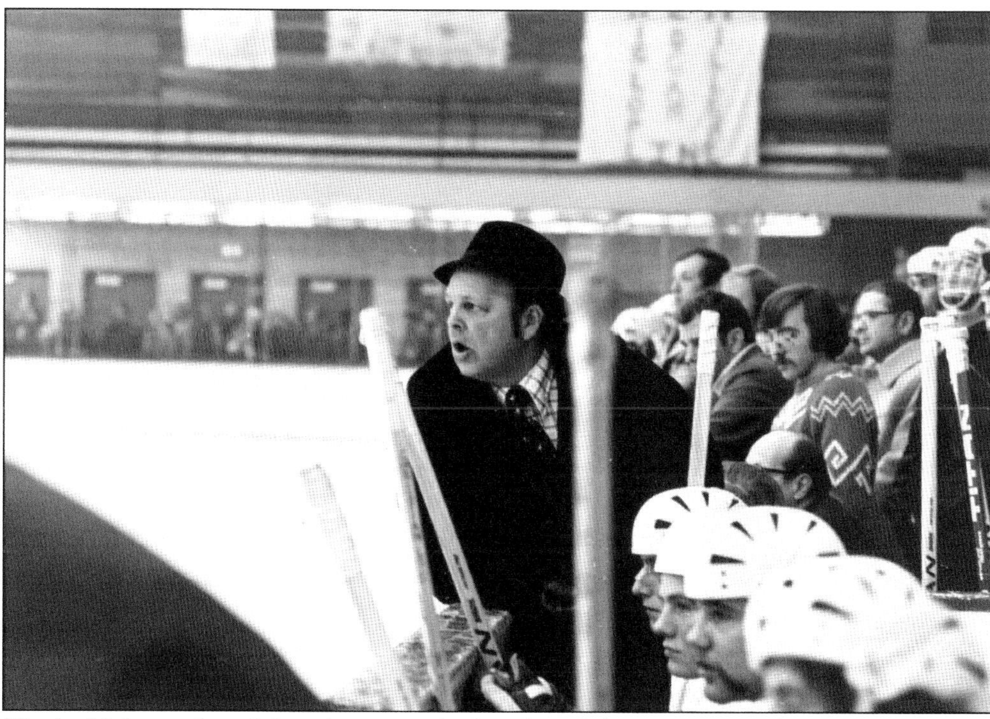

Charlie Holt stands with his players on the bench in February 1975. Holt was in his seventh season as the Wildcats' head coach. (UNH Archives.)

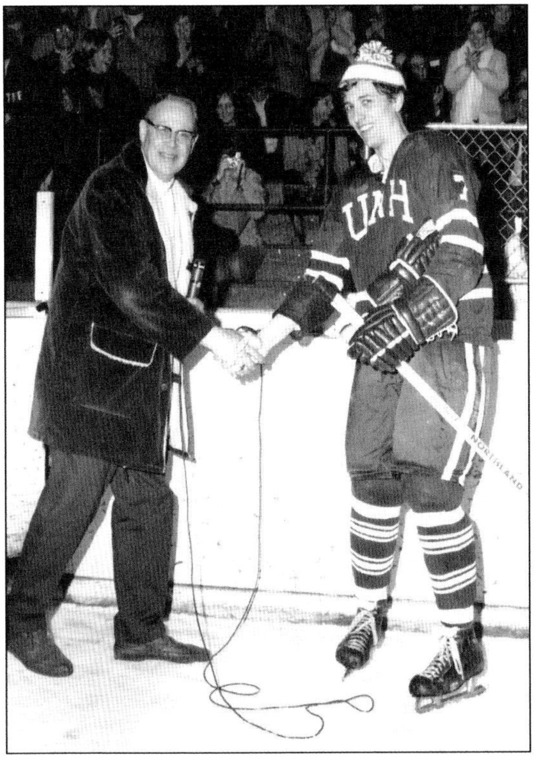

Dr. Eric Simmons gives Louis Frigon a hat in recognition of Frigon's hat trick in the final game of the 1969–1970 season. Frigon of Montreal, Quebec, was captain of the 1970–1971 team, which went 20-9. He stands sixth on the all-time scorers list, with 193 career points and 98 goals scored. (UNH Archives.)

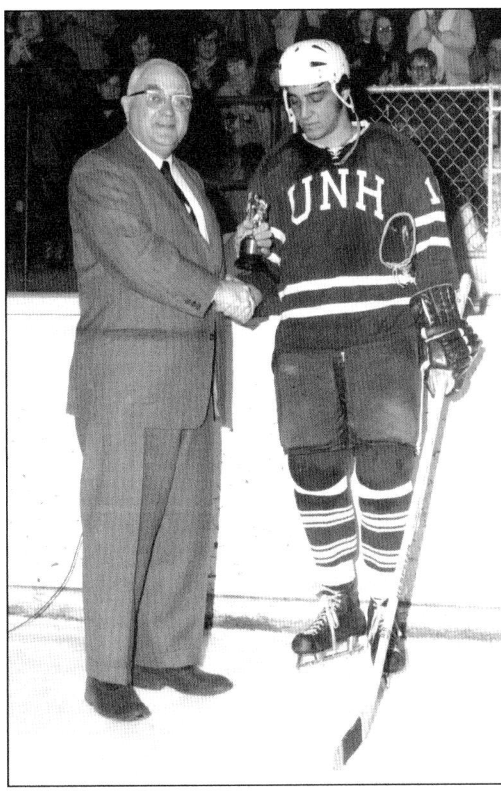

In 1970, Creely "Buck" Buchanan, the president of the UNH Alumni Association, presented Dick Umile with the Roger Leclerc Trophy. Umile finished his career with 144 points, placing him 27th in the Wildcat Century Club. The Wildcat Century Club includes players who have scored 100 points or higher in their career. (UNH Archives.)

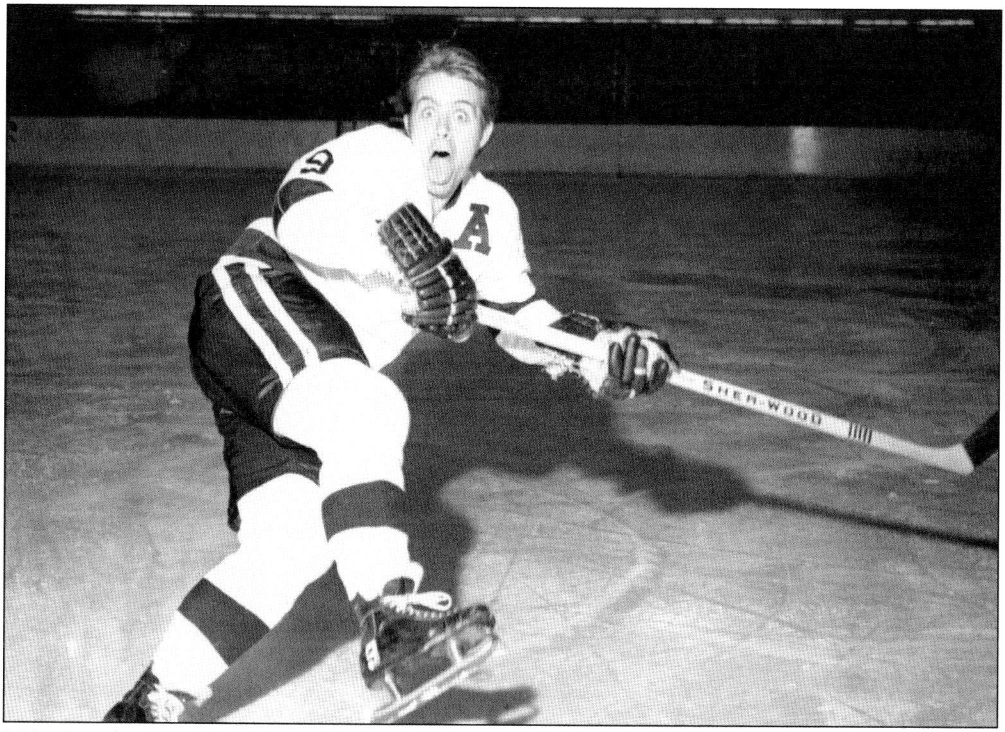

Mike McShane is shown in a light moment. McShane played for the Wildcats from 1968 to 1971 and ended his career with 139 points. He appears in the UNH top 10 list for both assists and penalty minutes. (UNH Archives.)

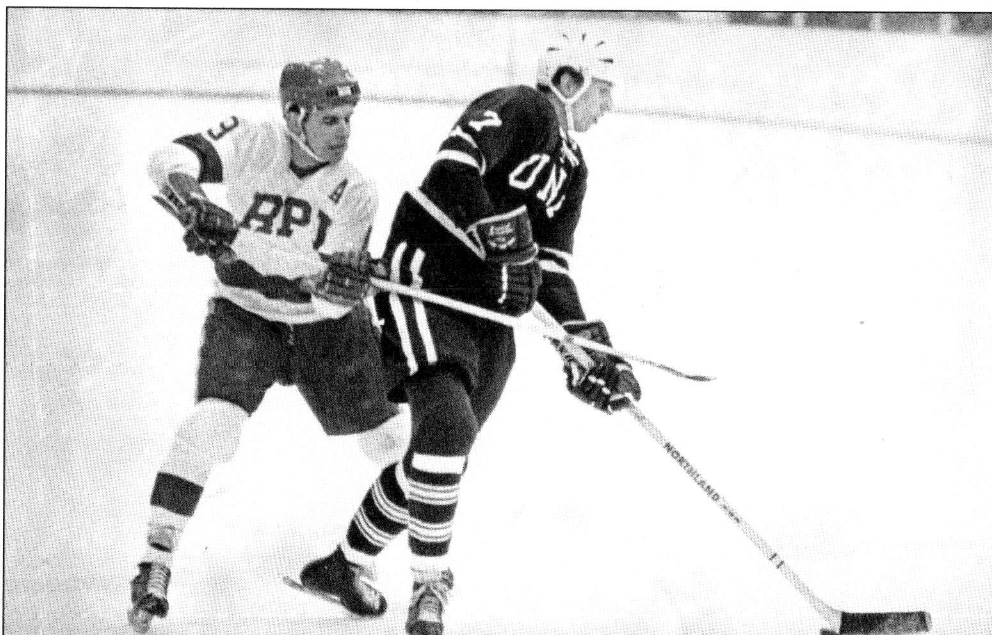

Louis Frigon is in action against RPI on March 6, 1971. Frigon had a goal and an assist in the Wildcats' 5-3 loss. (UNH Archives.)

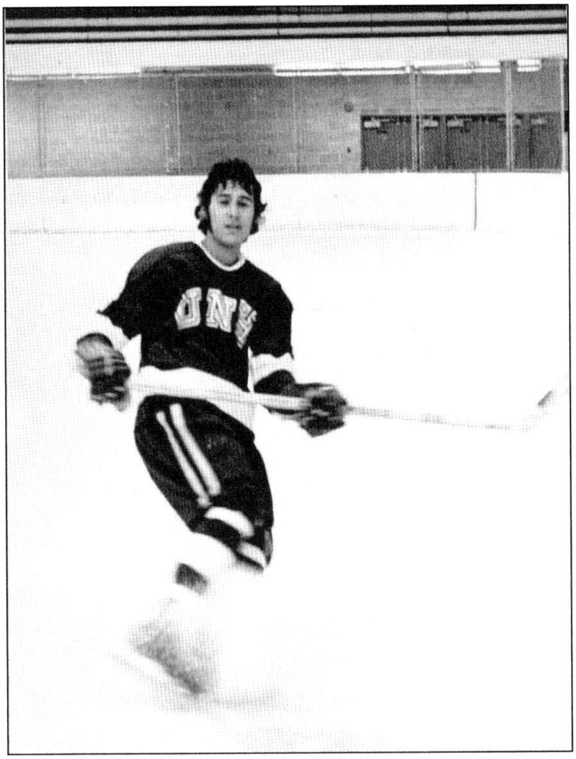

Guy Smith, with 153 career points, was an outstanding offensive player who was with the Wildcats from 1968 to 1972. The Best Offensive Player Award, given to a player voted on by teammates, was named in his honor after he passed away. (UNH Archives.)

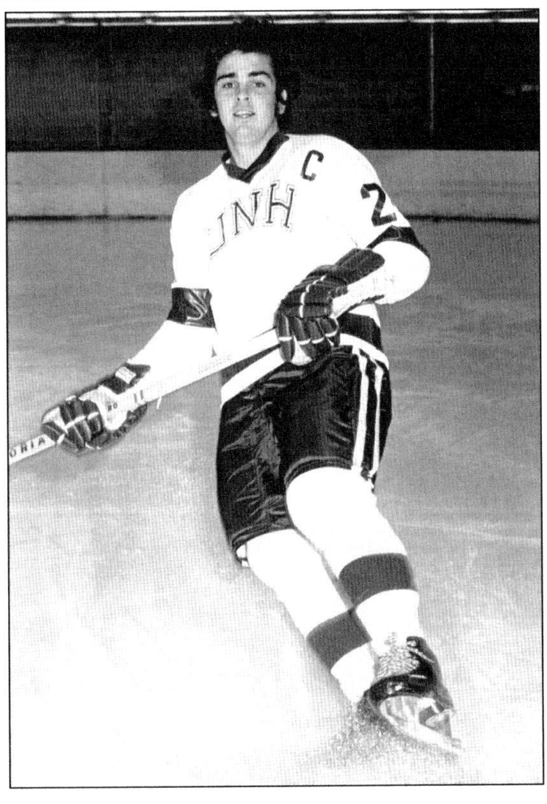

Center Bill Beaney of Lake Placid, New York, captained the 1972–1973 team, which finished with a 16-10-3 record. (UNH Archives.)

Gordie Clark (right) and Jere Chase attend an award ceremony at the end of the 1973–1974 season. Clark was a two-time All-American and was a recipient of the Roger Leclerc Trophy. He was the first UNH player to score more than 50 points three years in a row. (UNH Archives.)

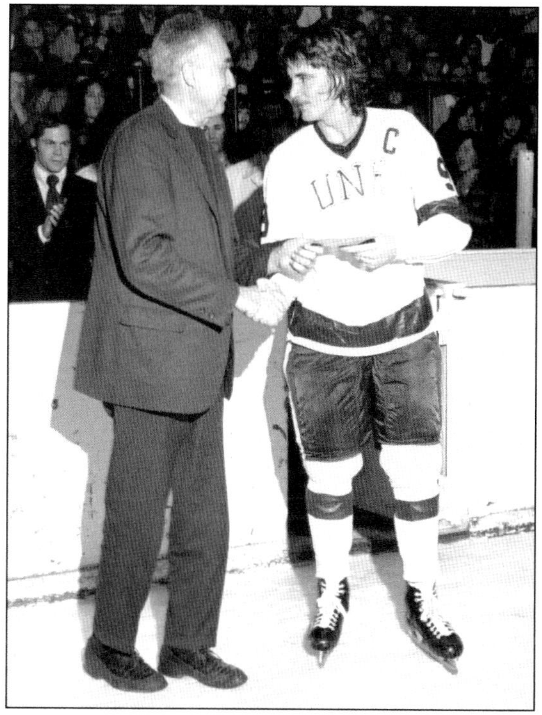

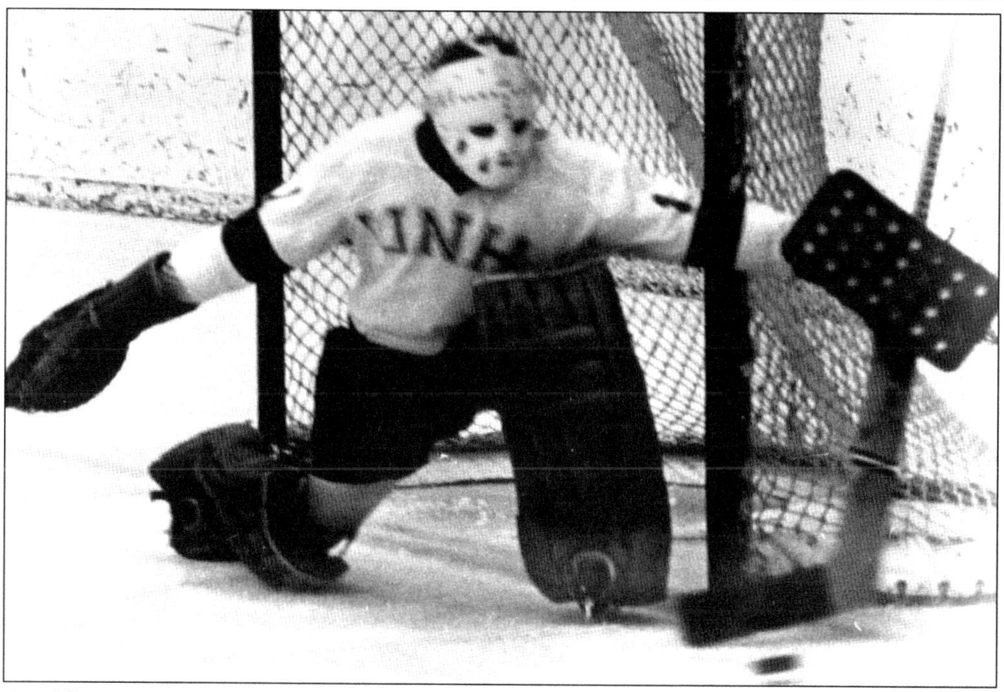

An All-American in 1974, Cap Raeder added to his save total during the 1974–1975 season. Raeder is fourth among the goalies with a career goals against average of 3.21, eighth with career saves (1, 861), eighth in career games played (68), and fifth in career wins. His record for season goals against average (2.64) for the 1973–1974 season stood for 24 years until surpassed by Sean Matile in 1997–1998. (UNH Archives.)

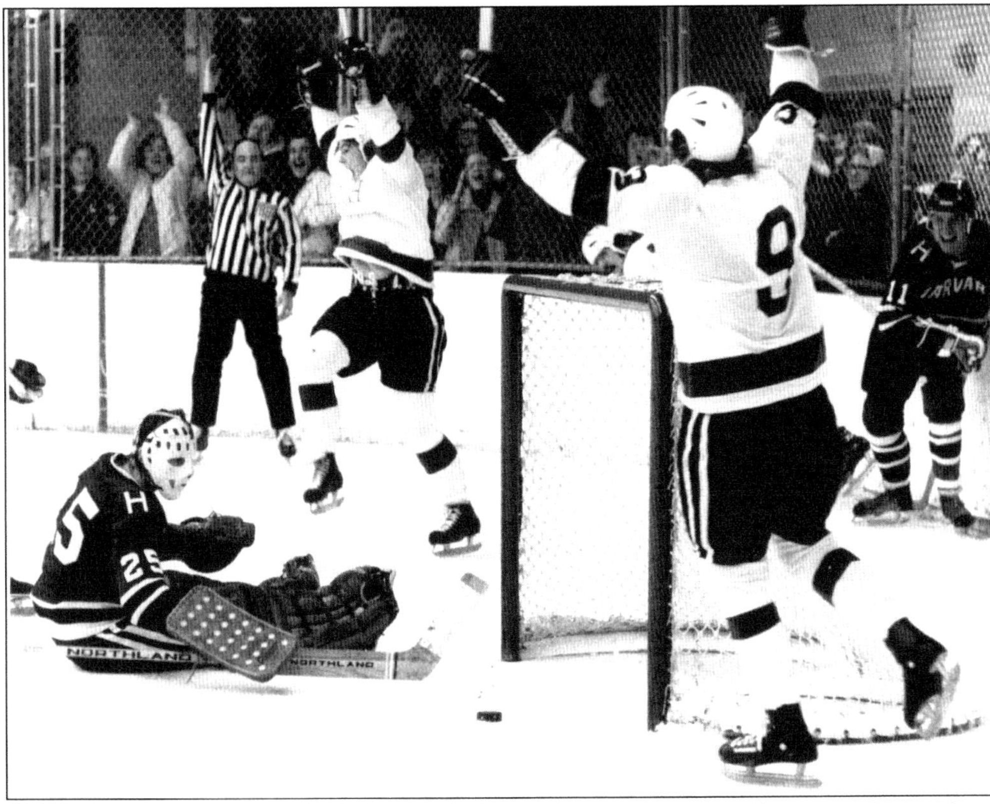

Jamie Hislop (No. 8) and Gordie Clark (No. 9) celebrate a goal against Harvard on November 28, 1973. Ed Freni is partially hidden behind the goal. UNH won the game 3-2. (UNH Archives.)

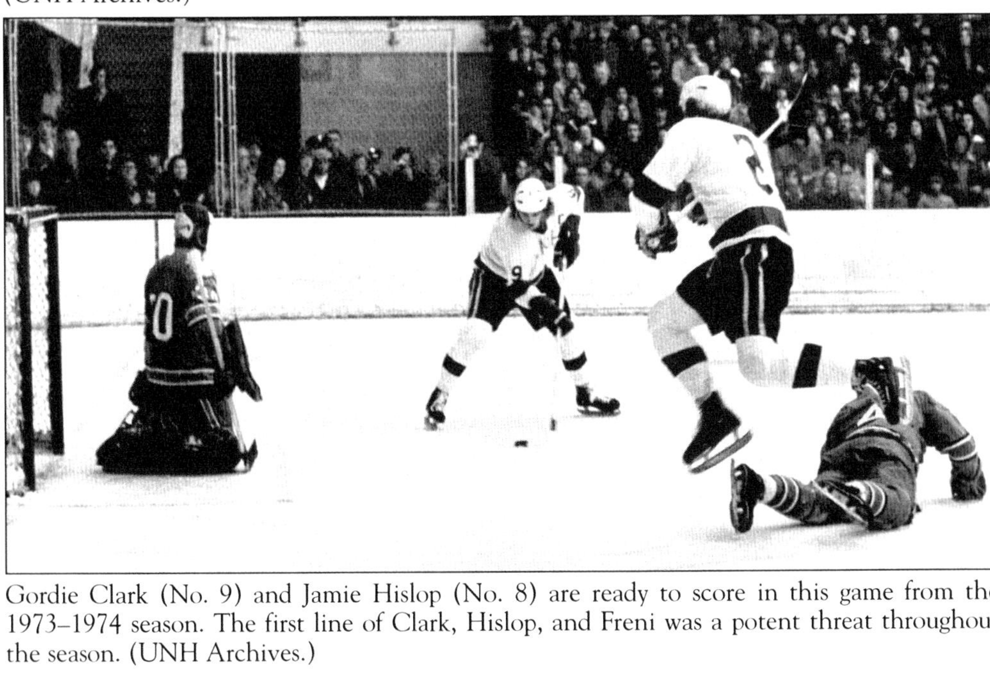

Gordie Clark (No. 9) and Jamie Hislop (No. 8) are ready to score in this game from the 1973–1974 season. The first line of Clark, Hislop, and Freni was a potent threat throughout the season. (UNH Archives.)

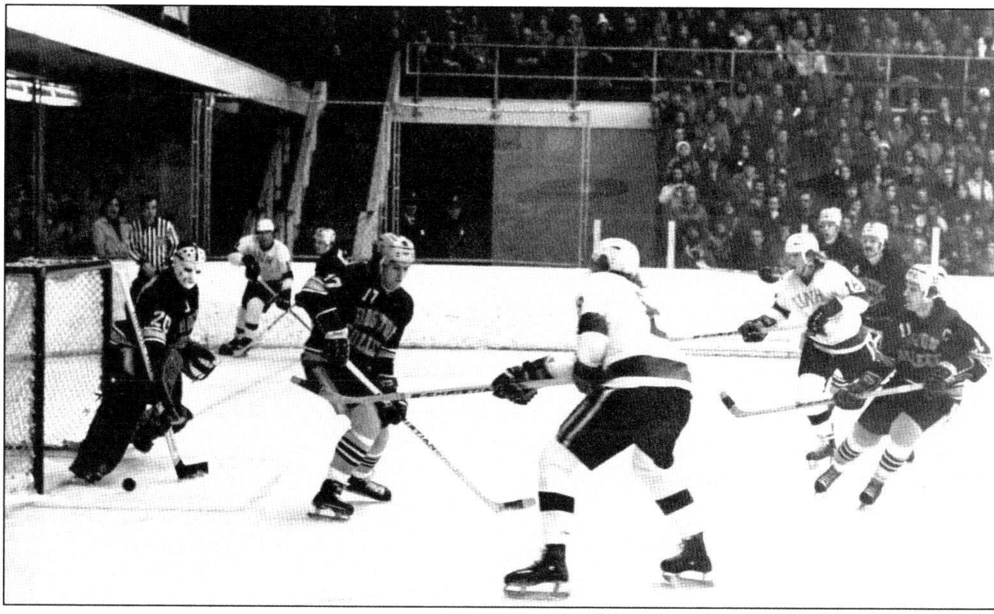

Jamie Hislop attempts a shot on goal against Boston College, with Cliff Cox following behind. Hislop and Cox both came to UNH in 1972, earned team-scoring titles, and were named All-Americans in 1976. It was the first time that two Wildcats were selected All-Americans in one year. (UNH Archives.)

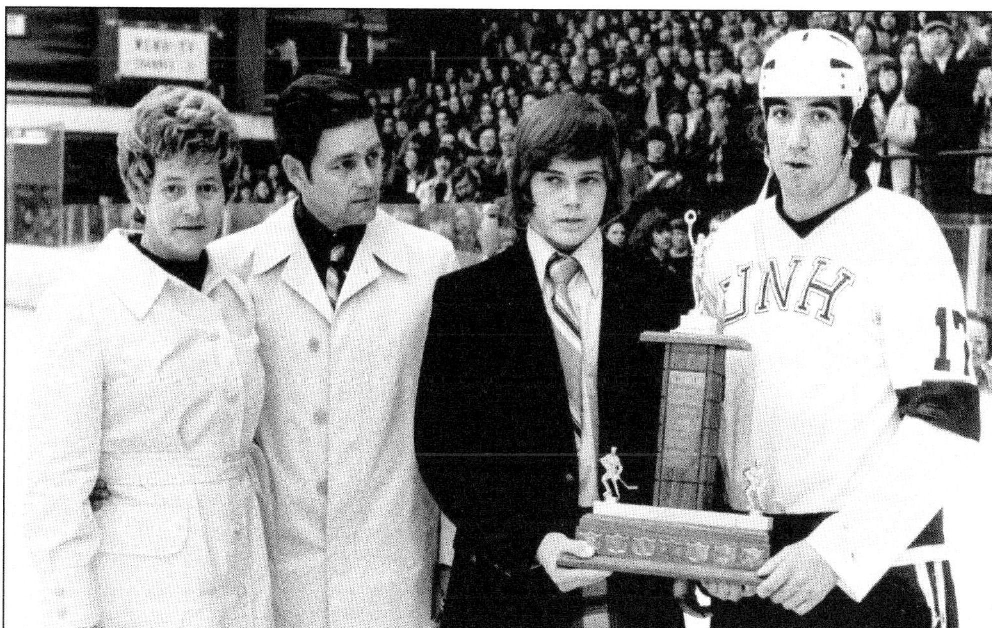

Warren Brown's family joins Dave Bertollo (right) at the first presentation of the Warren R. Brown Memorial Trophy in February 1974. Warren Brown died in a car accident in December 1973. The trophy named in his honor was given to the most outstanding left wing. Dave Bertollo, one of the survivors of the car accident, was the first to receive the trophy in 1974. Since 1991, the Warren Brown Trophy has been given to the best defensive forward. (UNH Archives.)

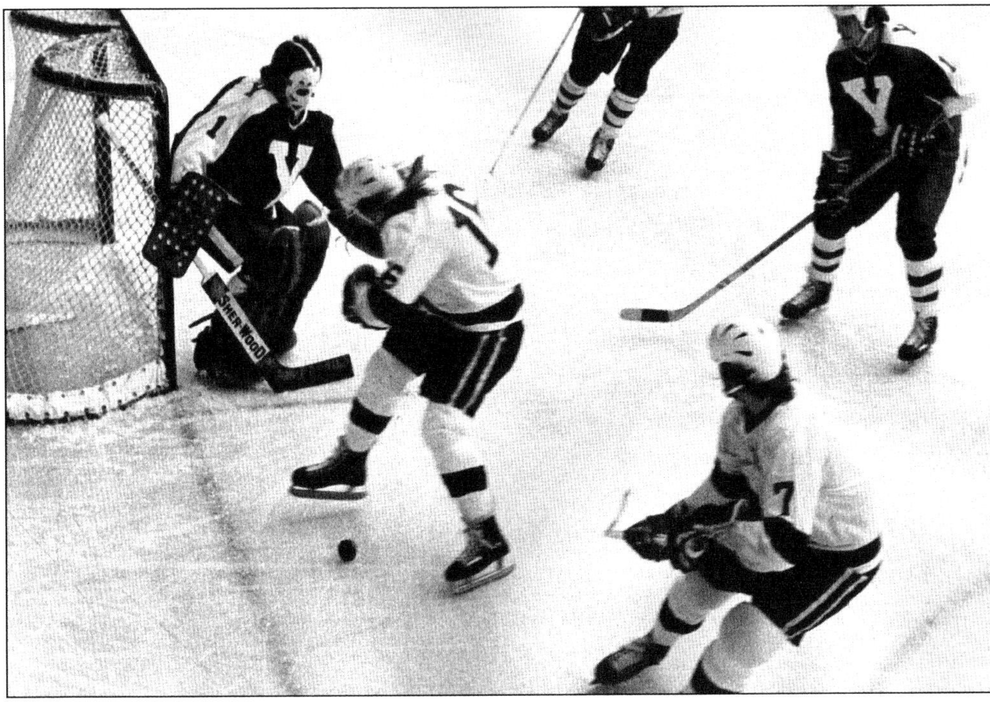

Cliff Cox (No. 16) and Mike Burkhart (No. 7) skate against Yale in this December 15, 1973 game. UNH won 6-1. Cox, one of the great offensive players of the 1970s, amassed a career total of 175 points. He was awarded the Most Exciting Player Award in 1974 and 1975. Burkhart was captain of the 1974–1975 team. (UNH Archives.)

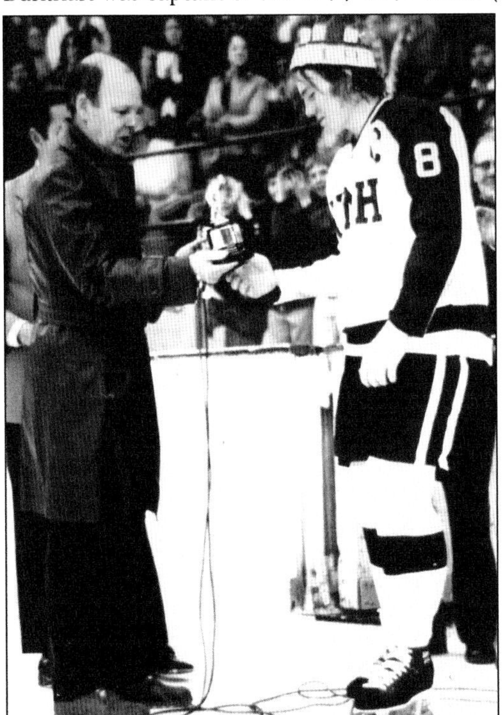

Jamie Hislop receives the first of his two Roger Leclerc Trophies in 1975. He received the trophy again in 1976. Hislop is one of only four Wildcats to score 200 points. He also holds the school record for points scored in the most consecutive games: 31, from February 15, 1974, through February 18, 1975. (UNH Archives.)

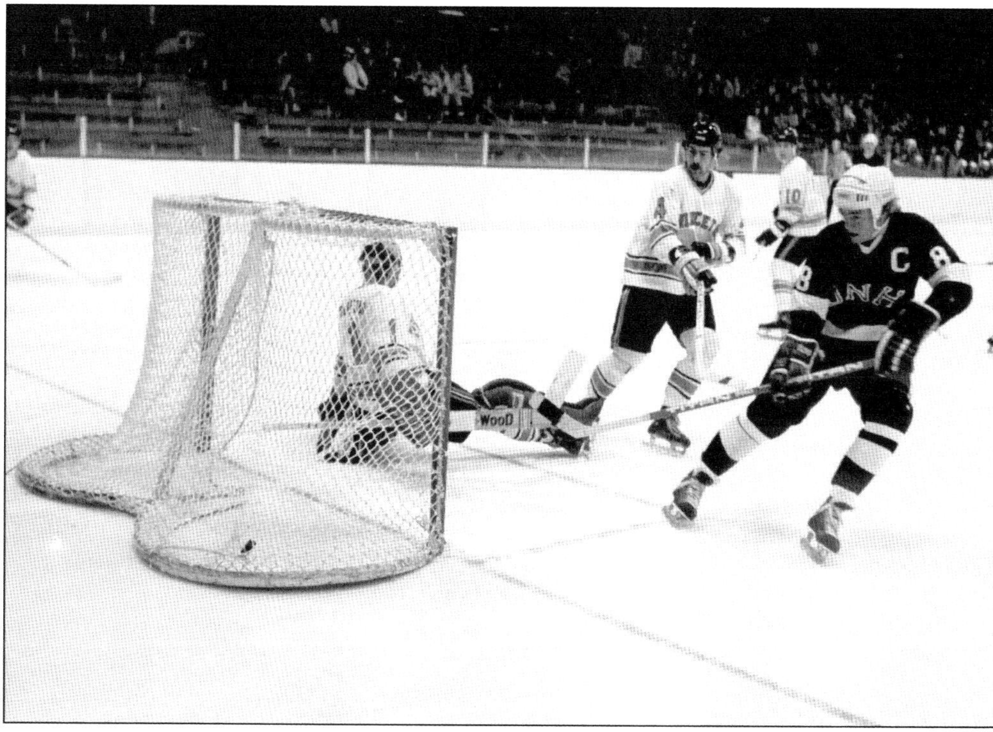

Jamie Hislop scores a goal against Princeton in the 1976 Yale-Saab Invitational. UNH went on to win 11-2. (S. Frinzi photograph. UNH Archives.)

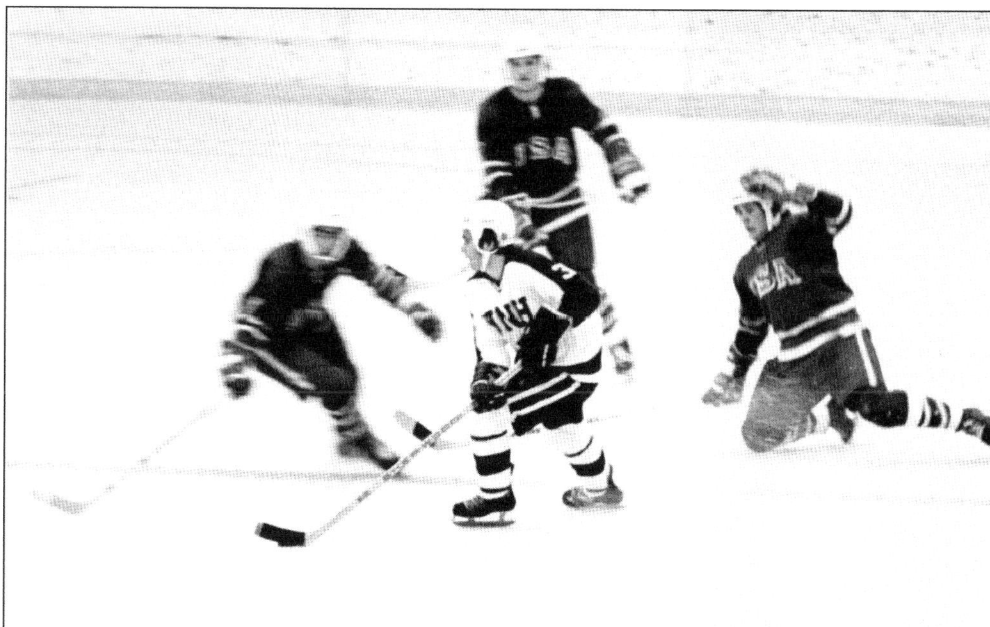

Paul Powers skates by Team USA in an exhibition game with the United States National Team in November 1975. UNH men's ice hockey has produced four Olympians: Bob Miller in 1976, Ralph Cox in 1980, Steve Leach in 1988, and Jeff Lazaro in 1992. (Jack Adams photograph. UNH Archives.)

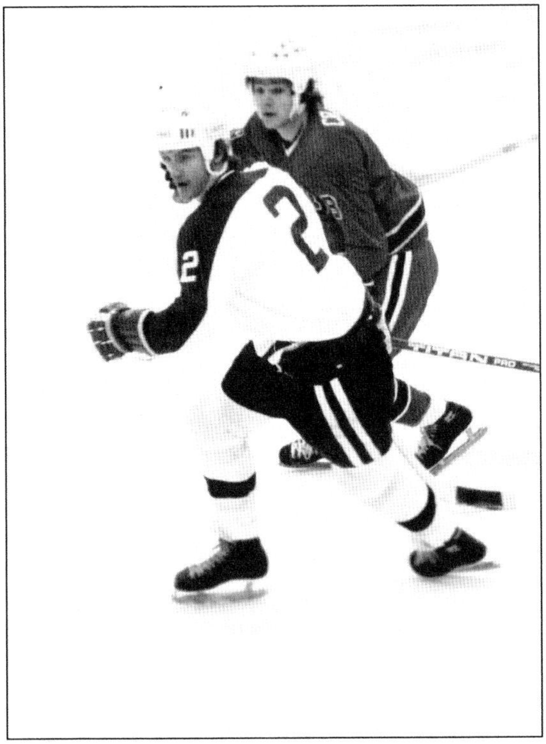

Rod Langway shows his ability that eventually earned him two Norris Trophies in the National Hockey League (NHL). Langway was a member of the 1976–1977 team that sent eight players to the National Hockey League. (Jack Adams photograph. UNH Archives.)

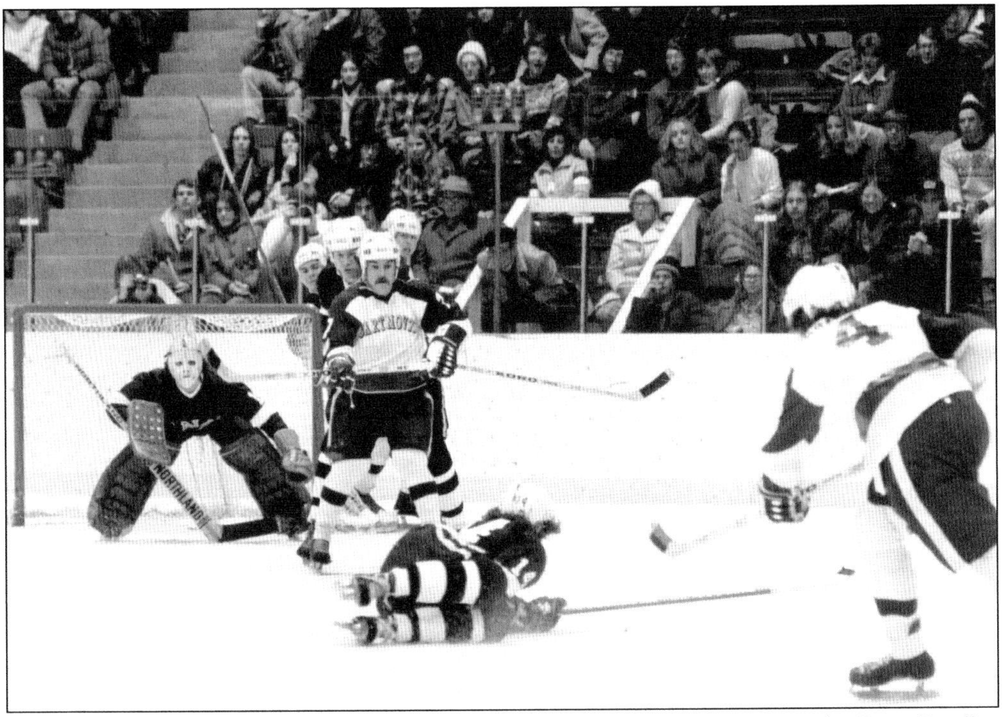

With Dan Magnarelli in goal, Dave Lumley blocks a goal attempt by Dartmouth's Doug Bradley in the final of the Blue-Green Invitational in January 1976. UNH won the game 6-3 and the tournament. (UNH Archives.)

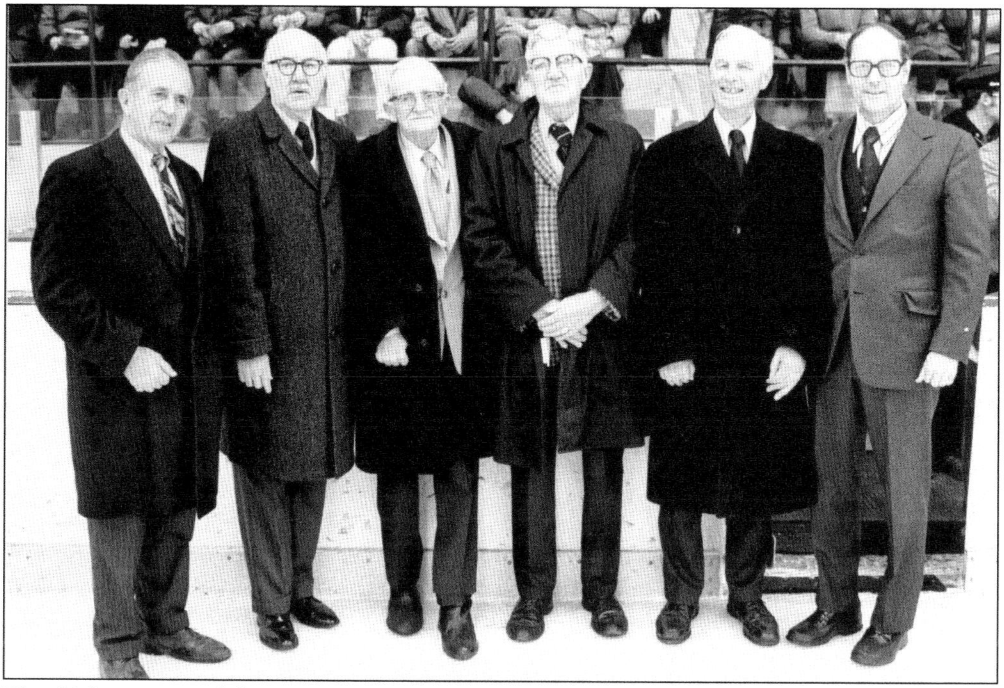

The 50th reunion of the 1925 hockey team was in January 1975. Of the original eleven team member, five came to Snively to watch UNH defeat Bates College 2-1. From left to right are John O. Morton, Edward Y. Blewett, Frank W. Bartlett, Searls Dearington, Bill Sayward (captain), and Eugene S. Mills (UNH president). (UNH Archives.)

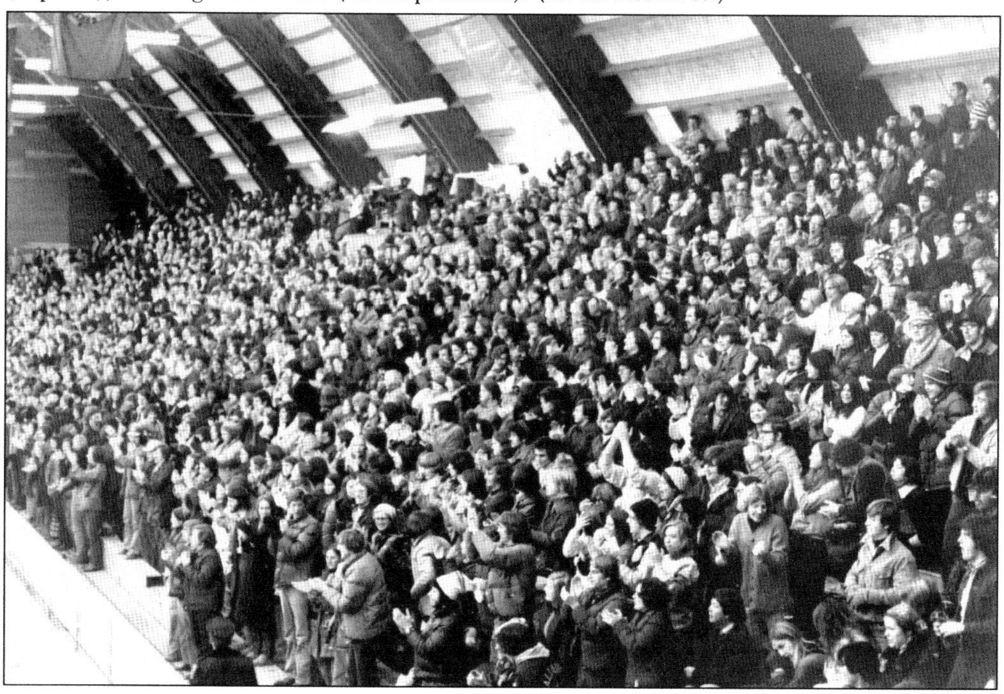

Fans enjoy a game in Snively Arena c. February 1975. Their enthusiasm and love of UNH hockey gave rise to the nickname Lively Snively, the "barn with attitude." (UNH Archives.)

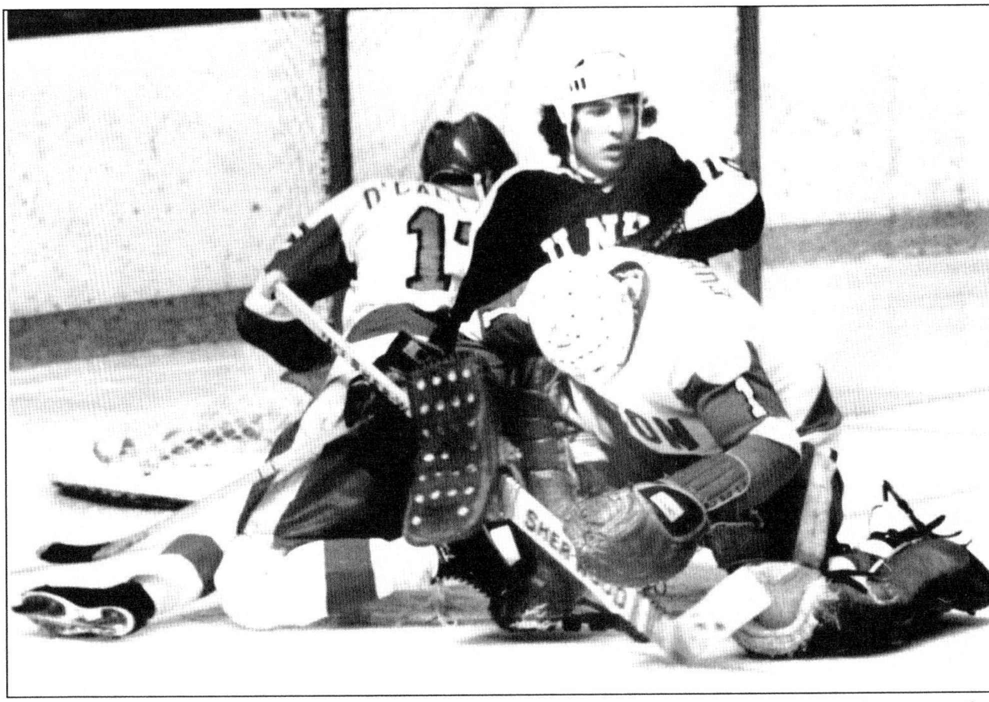

Jon Fontas, captain of the 1977–1978 team, is trapped by Boston University players in this December 4, 1976 game. The Wildcats won 5-3 over the Terriers. Fontas caught fire in the 1977–1978 season, setting a school record for most goals in a single period (4, in February 1978 against Colby). He scored 12 goals in three games that February. He is a member of the Wildcat Century Club, with his career 174 points. (UNH Archives.)

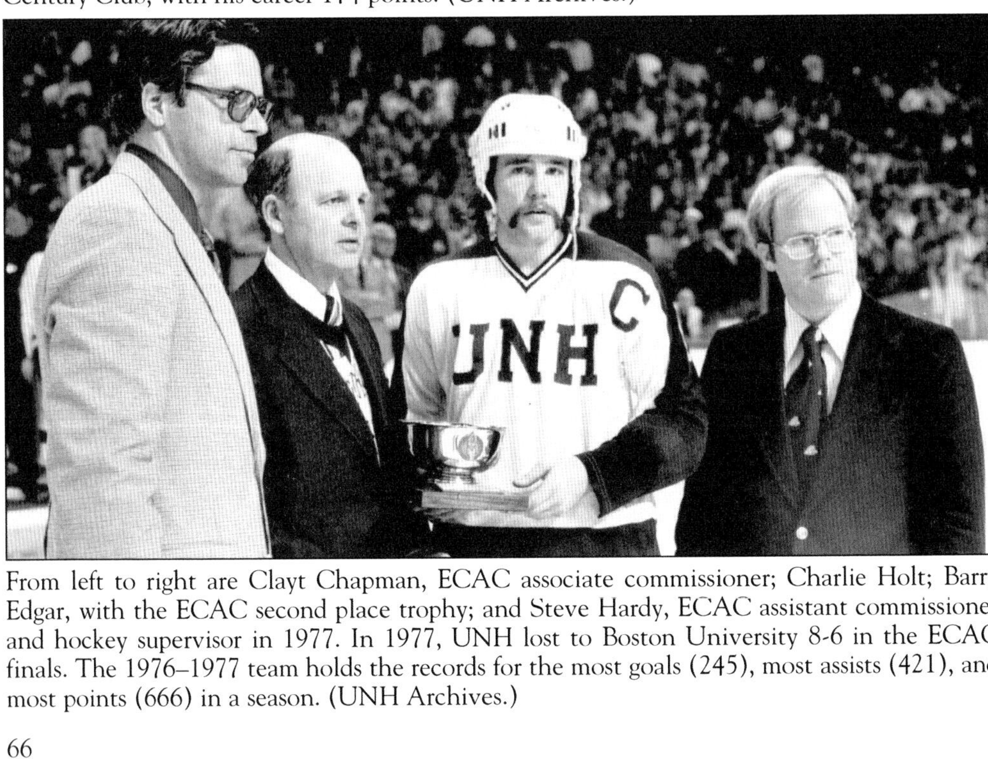

From left to right are Clayt Chapman, ECAC associate commissioner; Charlie Holt; Barry Edgar, with the ECAC second place trophy; and Steve Hardy, ECAC assistant commissioner and hockey supervisor in 1977. In 1977, UNH lost to Boston University 8-6 in the ECAC finals. The 1976–1977 team holds the records for the most goals (245), most assists (421), and most points (666) in a season. (UNH Archives.)

This is the program from the third annual Blue-Green Invitational in 1977. UNH hosted the invitational and beat Providence 6-4 to win the tournament on January 3, 1977. UNH and Dartmouth hosted the Blue-Green Invitational sporadically during the 1970s. (UNH Archives.)

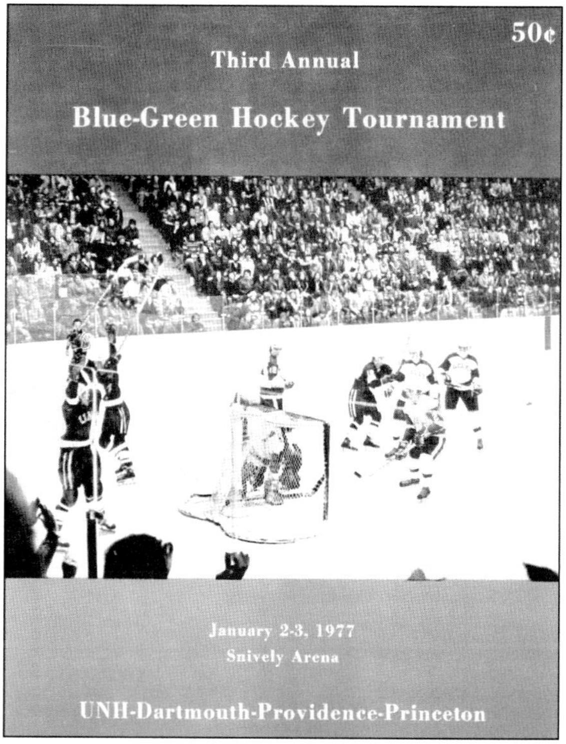

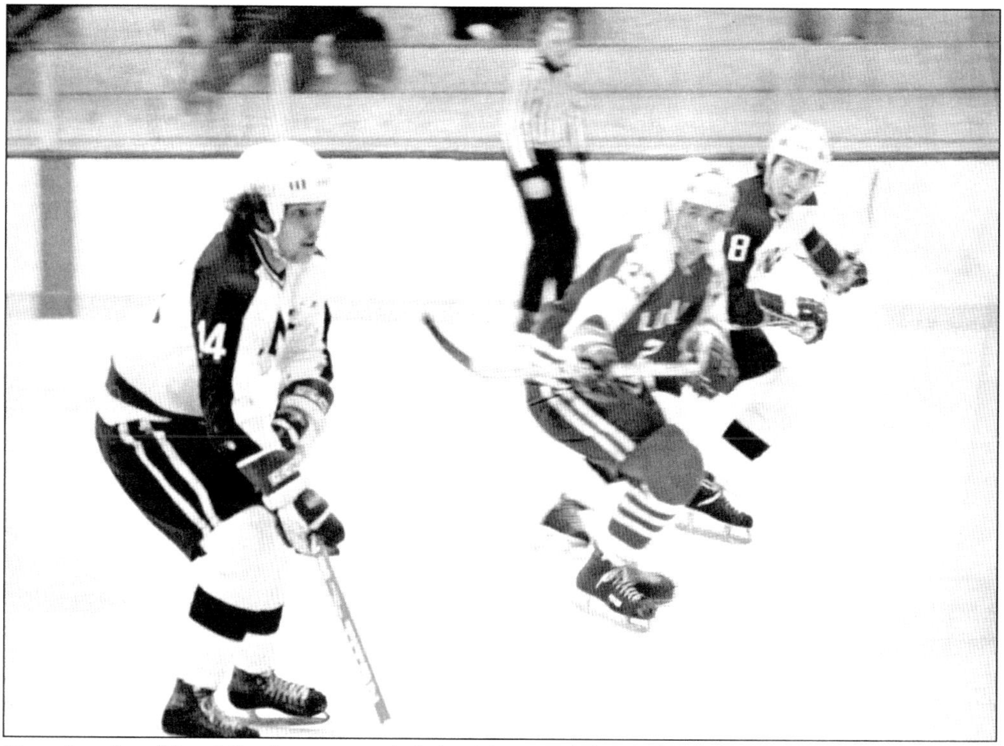

Dave Lumley (No. 14) advances with John Normand (No. 8) on the opponent in this game from the 1976–1977 season. (UNH Archives.)

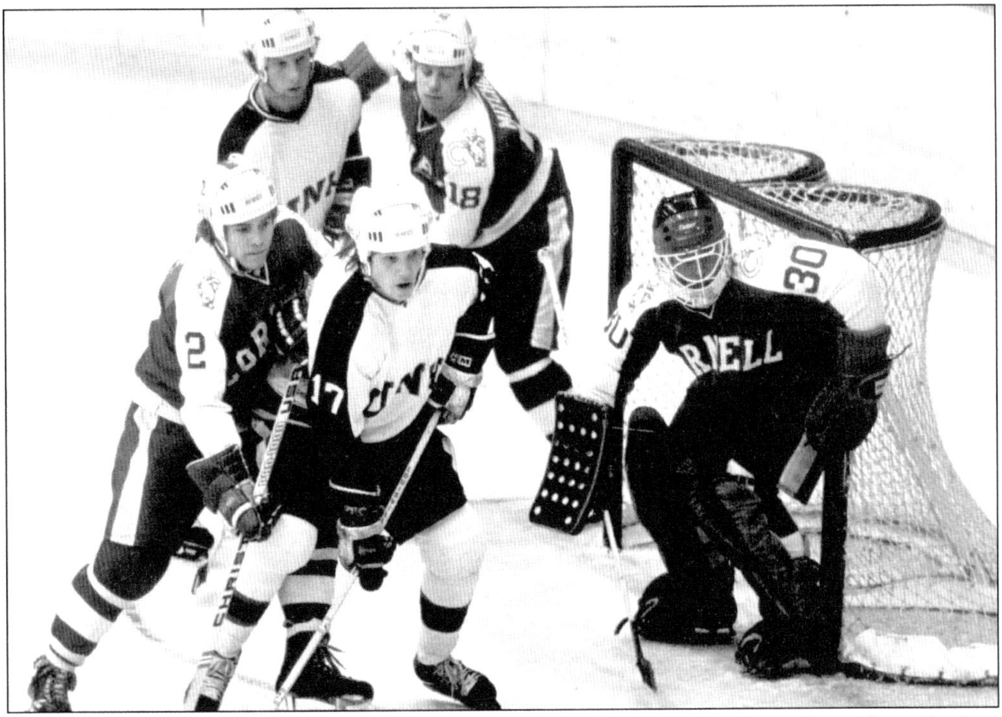

Bob Gould and Bruce Crowder await the puck in this home game against Cornell in the late 1970s. (UNH Archives.)

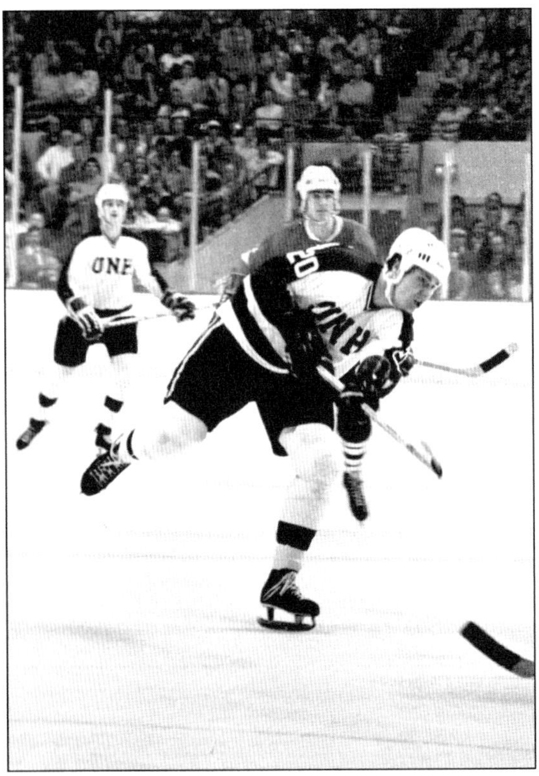

Tim Burke and 1976–1977 teammate Rod Langway were named All-Americans in 1977, the second time two Wildcats were named to the same All-American team. In 1977, Burke was the school's all-time highest scoring defenseman, with 140 career points. (UNH Archives.)

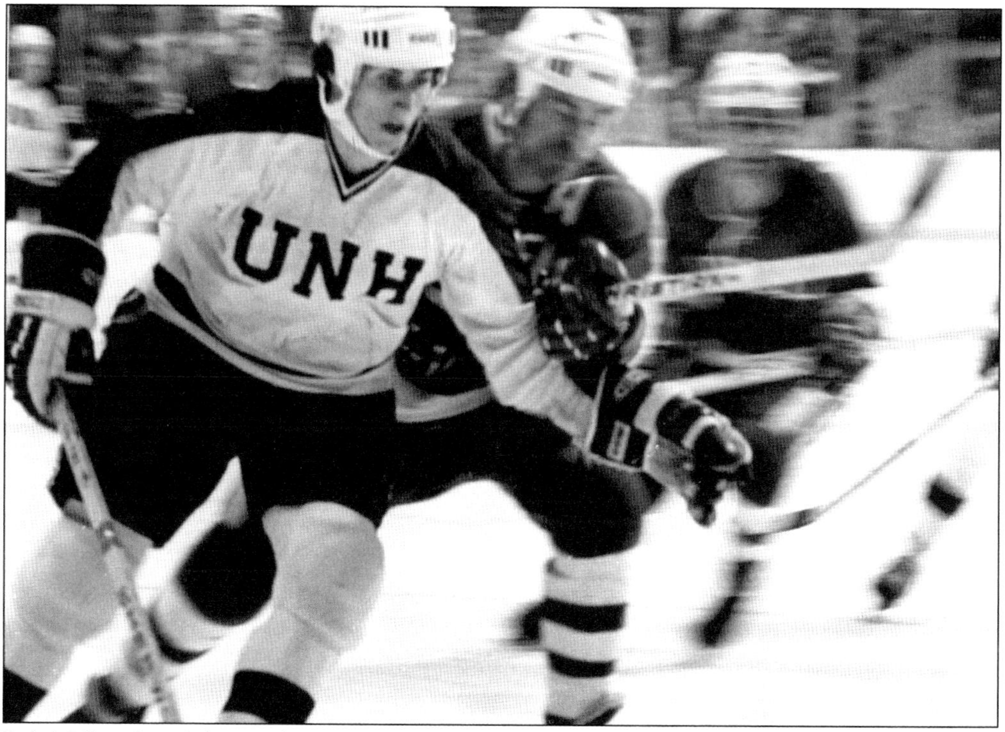

Bob Miller played during the 1976–1977 season. He was named to the Olympic Team in 1976, named an All-American in 1977, and is a member of the Wildcat Century Club, with 148 career points. He holds season records for assists (59), points (89), and the all-time record for points per game (2.28). (UNH Archives.)

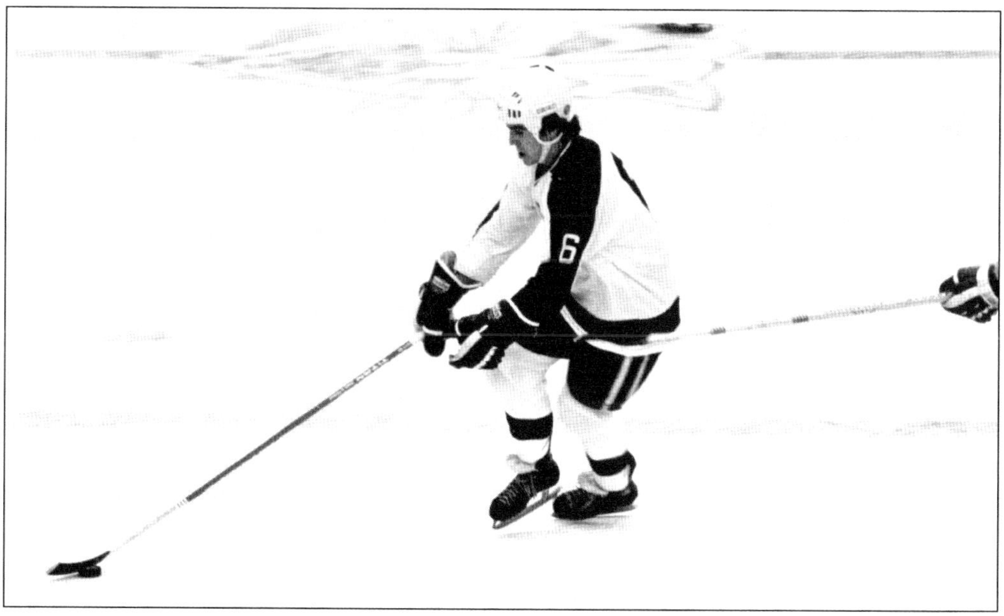

Peter Noonan skates past the Wildcat in Batchelder Rink in a game from the 1976–1977 season. Noonan played for the Wildcats from 1972 through 1977 and, in 1975, was awarded the Most Improved Player Award, as voted by the players. (UNH Archives.)

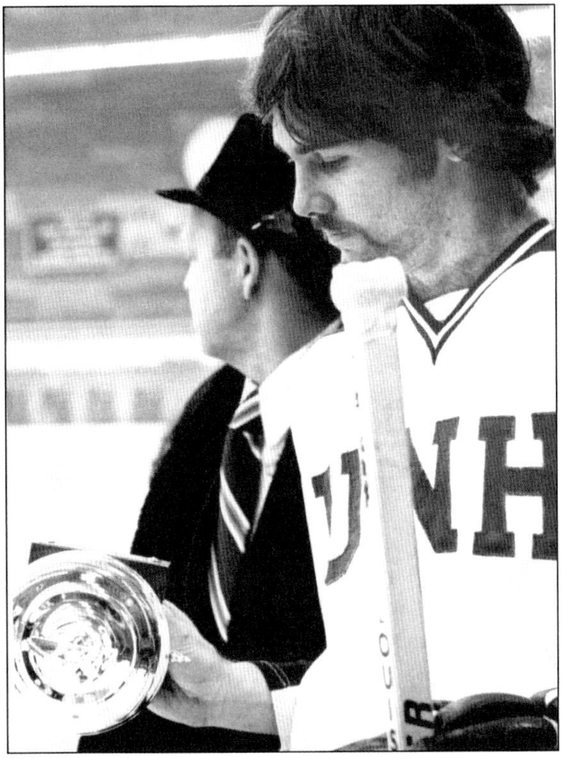

Ralph Cox contemplates his Most Valuable Player award from the Blue-Green Invitational Tournament in 1977. Cox was the first player to score more than 200 career points (243) and more than 100 goals (127), thus earning him the top spot on the all-time top scorers list. He was named to the All-American team twice in 1978 and in 1979. Cox was also UNH's lone representative on the 1980 Olympic men's hockey team. No other players came close to his numbers until Jason Krog and Darren Haydar came along. (UNH Archives.)

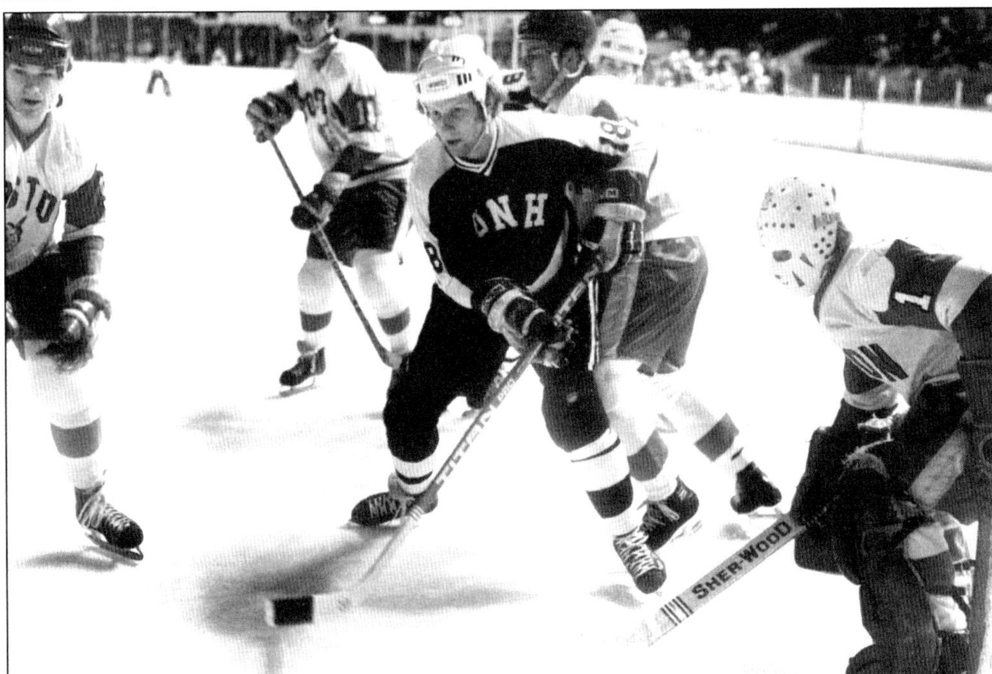

Bruce Crowder, who had 133 career points, tries to score on Boston University in the ECAC championship game on March 12, 1977. The Terriers went on to win 8-6. UNH and Boston University met in the consolation game of the Frozen Four two weeks later. (UNH Archives.)

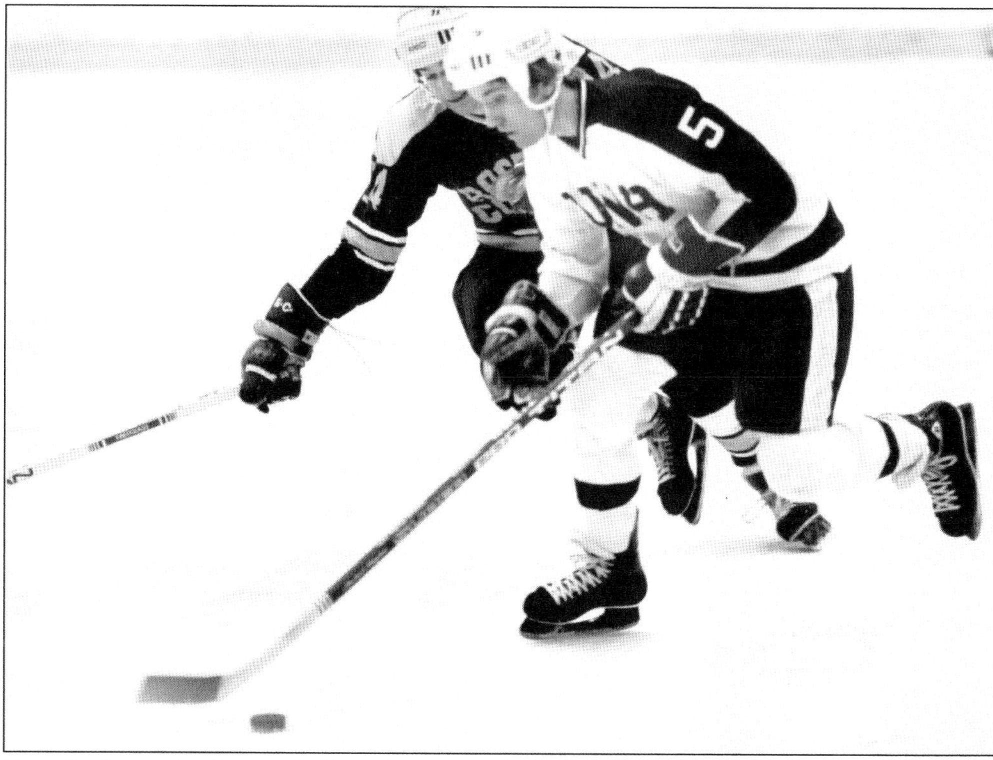

Dana Barbin and a Boston College skater race for the puck in December 1978. The Eagles fell to the Wildcats 7-5. Barbin earned the Unsung Hero Award in 1981. (UNH Archives.)

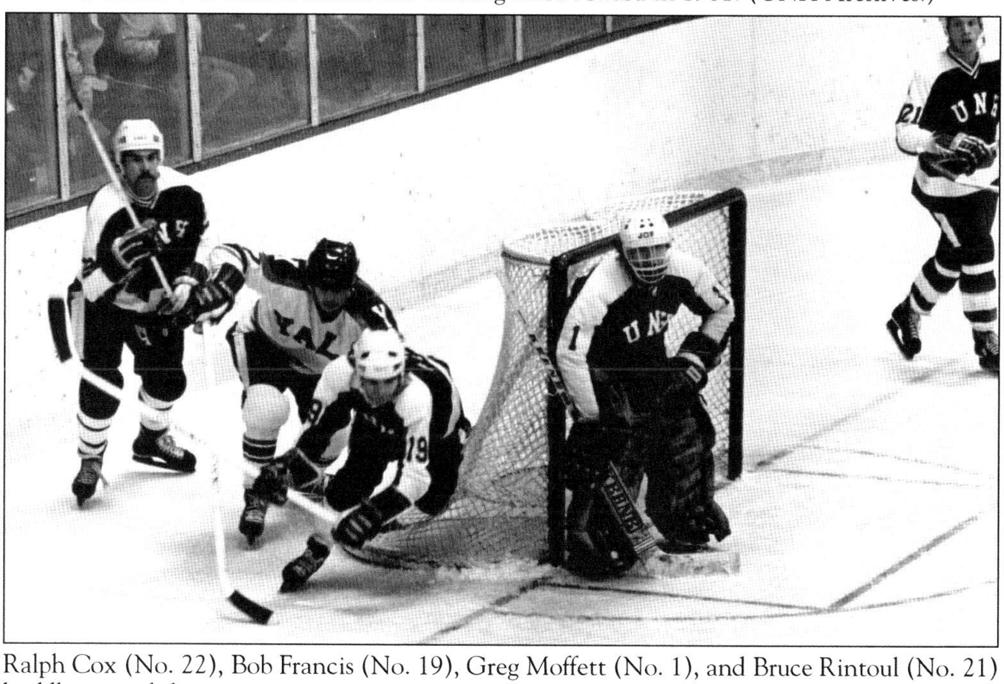

Ralph Cox (No. 22), Bob Francis (No. 19), Greg Moffett (No. 1), and Bruce Rintoul (No. 21) huddle around the net in action against Yale in the last game of the 1978–1979 regular season. UNH beat Yale 9-2 and finished the year with a 22-10-3 record. (UNH Archives.)

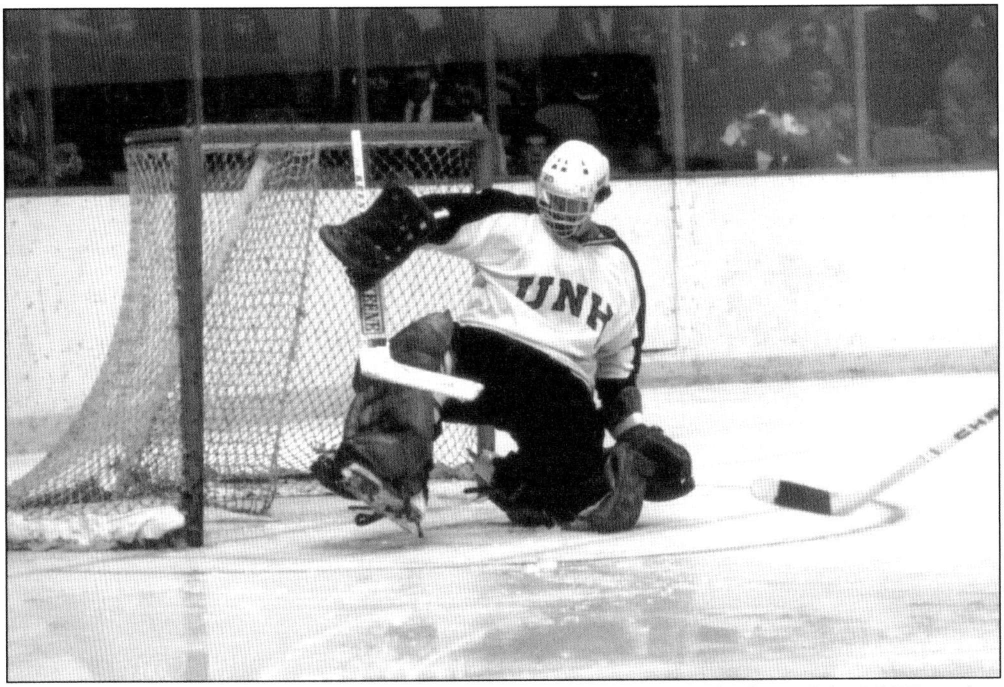

Greg Moffett reaches for a shot between the goal posts. Moffett ranks first of the UNH goalies in career saves with 2,602. (UNH Archives.)

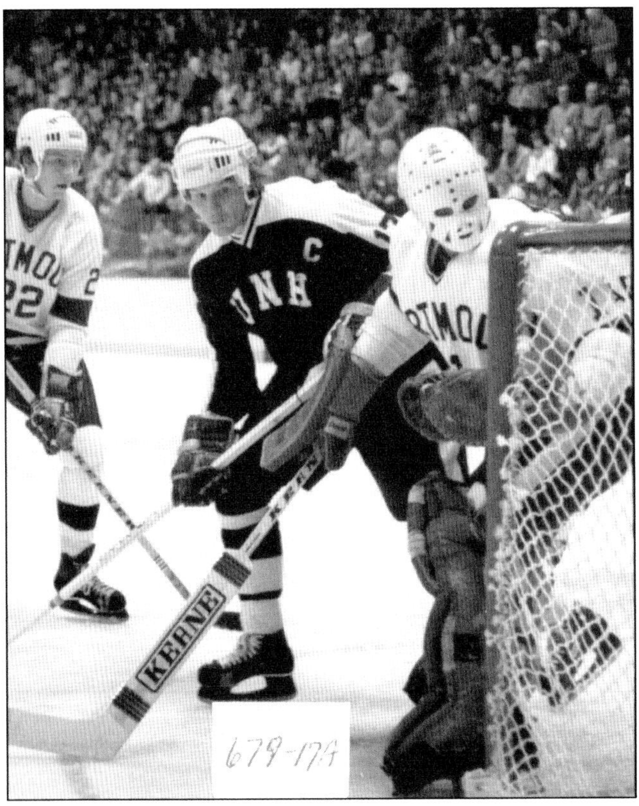

Bob Gould, captain of the 1978–1979 team, waits in front of the Dartmouth net during the 1979 ECAC championship game. Gould is the eighth all-time scorer, with 192 career points. (UNH Archives.)

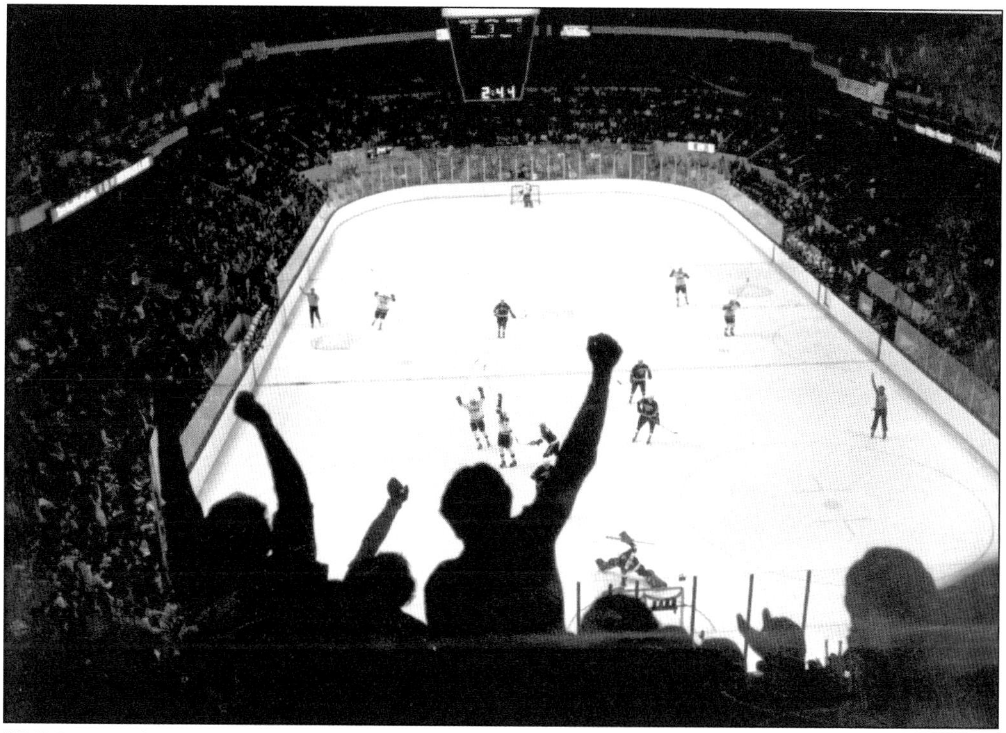

UNH won the 1979 ECAC Division I Championship over Dartmouth. Bob Gould, on a pass from Paul Surdam, scored this goal in the third period. The final score was 3-2. (UNH Archives.)

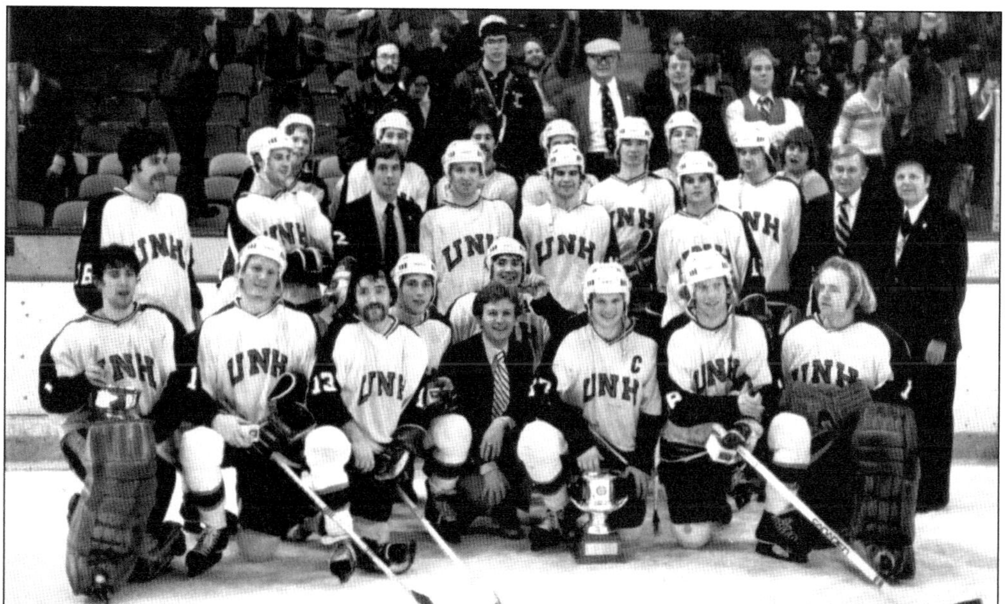

The 1978–1979 Wildcats pose with the ECAC trophy after their championship win. UNH went to the ECAC Tournament 15 times but won the championship only once. The team went on to the NCAA Frozen Four but ultimately lost to Dartmouth 7-3. (UNH Archives.)

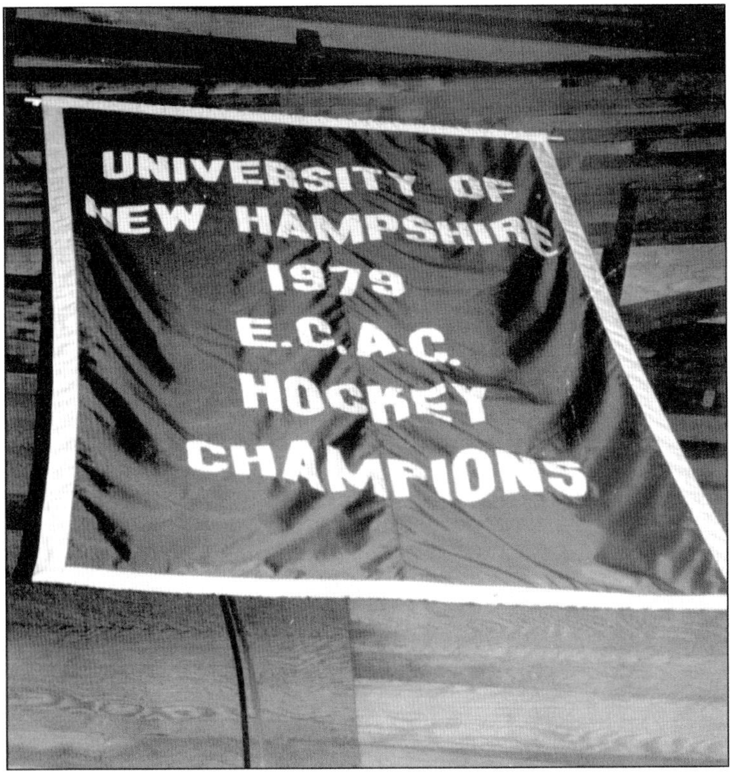

The 1979 ECAC championship banner hangs in Snively Arena. (UNH Archives.)

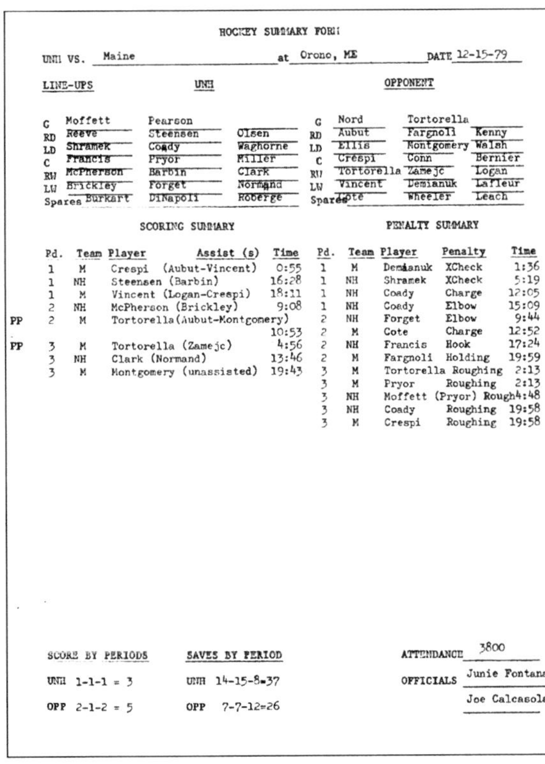

HOCKEY SUMMARY FORM

UNH VS. Maine at Orono, ME DATE 12-15-79

LINE-UPS	UNH			OPPONENT		
G	Moffett	Pearson		Nord	Tortorella	
RD	Reeve	Steensen	Olsen	Aubut	Fargnoli	Kenny
LD	Shramek	Coady	Waghorne	Ellis	Montgomery	Walsh
C	Francis	Pryor	Miller	Crespi	Conn	Bernier
RW	McPherson	Barbin	Clark	Tortorella	Zamejc	Logan
LW	Brickley	Forget	Normand	Vincent	Demianuk	Lafleur
Spares	Burkart	DiNapoli	Roberge	Cote	Wheeler	Leach

SCORING SUMMARY

	Pd.	Team	Player	Assist (s)	Time
	1	M	Crespi	(Aubut-Vincent)	0:55
	1	NH	Steensen	(Barbin)	16:28
	1	M	Vincent	(Logan-Crespi)	18:11
	2	NH	McPherson	(Brickley)	9:08
PP	2	M	Tortorella	(Aubut-Montgomery)	10:53
PP	3	M	Tortorella	(Zamejc)	4:56
	3	NH	Clark	(Normand)	13:46
	3	M	Montgomery	(unassisted)	19:43

PENALTY SUMMARY

Pd.	Team	Player	Penalty	Time
1	M	Demianuk	XCheck	1:36
1	NH	Shramek	XCheck	5:19
1	NH	Coady	Charge	12:05
1	NH	Coady	Elbow	15:09
2	NH	Forget	Elbow	9:44
2	M	Cote	Charge	12:52
2	NH	Francis	Hook	17:24
2	M	Fargnoli	Holding	19:59
3	M	Tortorella	Roughing	2:13
3	M	Pryor	Roughing	2:13
3	NH	Moffett (Pryor)	Rough	4:48
3	NH	Coady	Roughing	19:58
3	M	Crespi	Roughing	19:58

SCORE BY PERIODS
UNH 1-1-1 = 3
OPP 2-1-2 = 5

SAVES BY PERIOD
UNH 14-15-8=37
OPP 7-7-12=26

ATTENDANCE 3800
OFFICIALS Junie Fontana, Joe Calcasola

This is the hockey summary from the game against the University of Maine at Alford Arena in Orono on December 15, 1979. This was the first time that the Wildcats played the Black Bears, who joined the ECAC Division I in the 1979–1980 season. UNH lost 3-5. (UNH Archives.)

This hockey program is from the second game against Maine in the 1979–1980 season. UNH lost again 6-5, and the rivalry between the two schools intensified. (UNH Archives.)

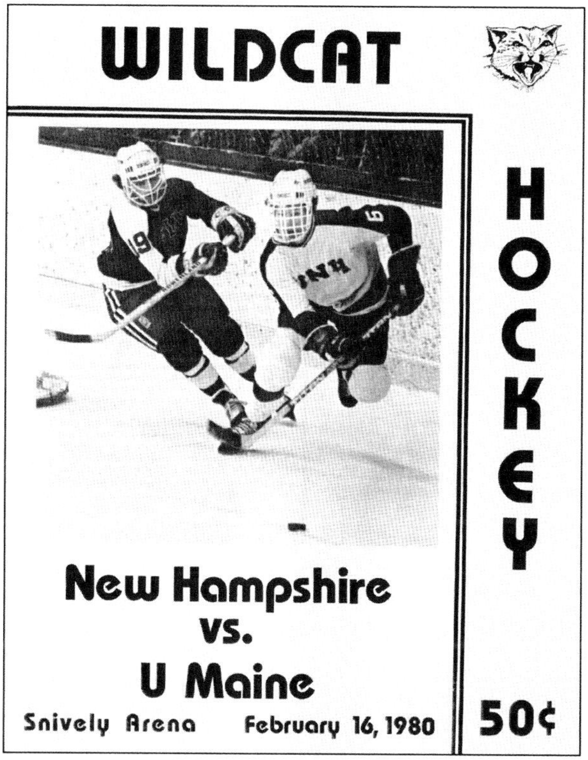

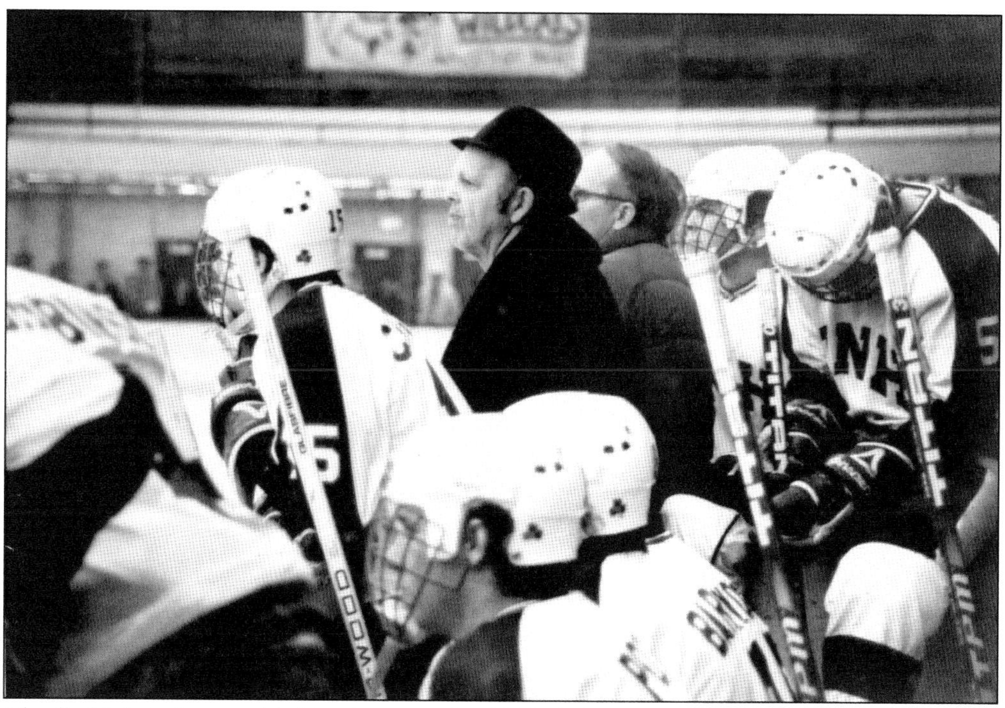

Charlie Holt is shown with his players in the 1980–1981 season. (UNH Archives.)

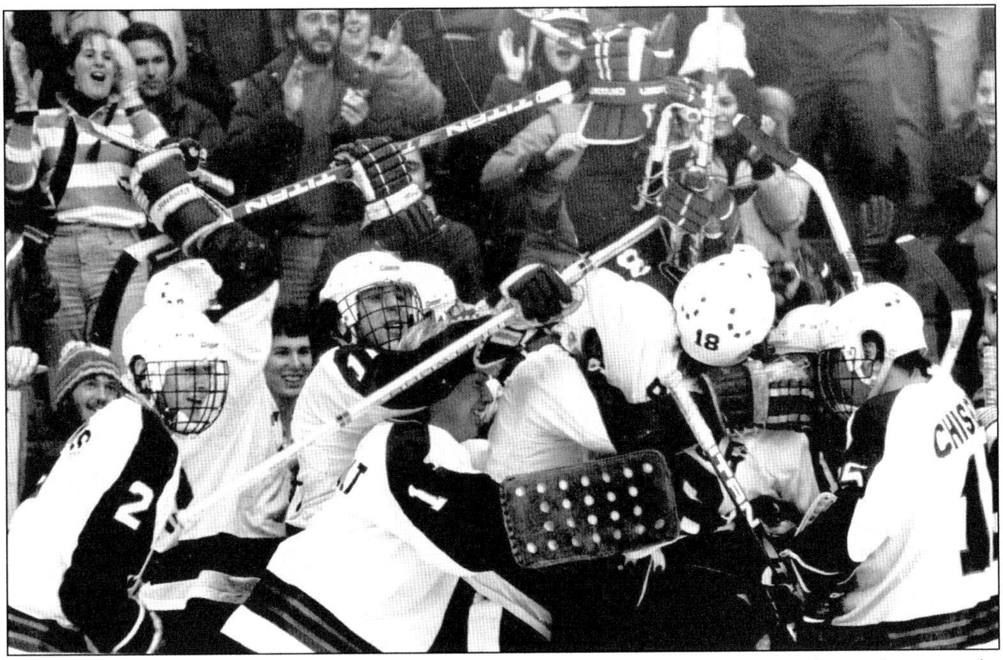

The Wildcats celebrate during the 1980–1981 season. (Henri Barber photograph. UNH Archives.)

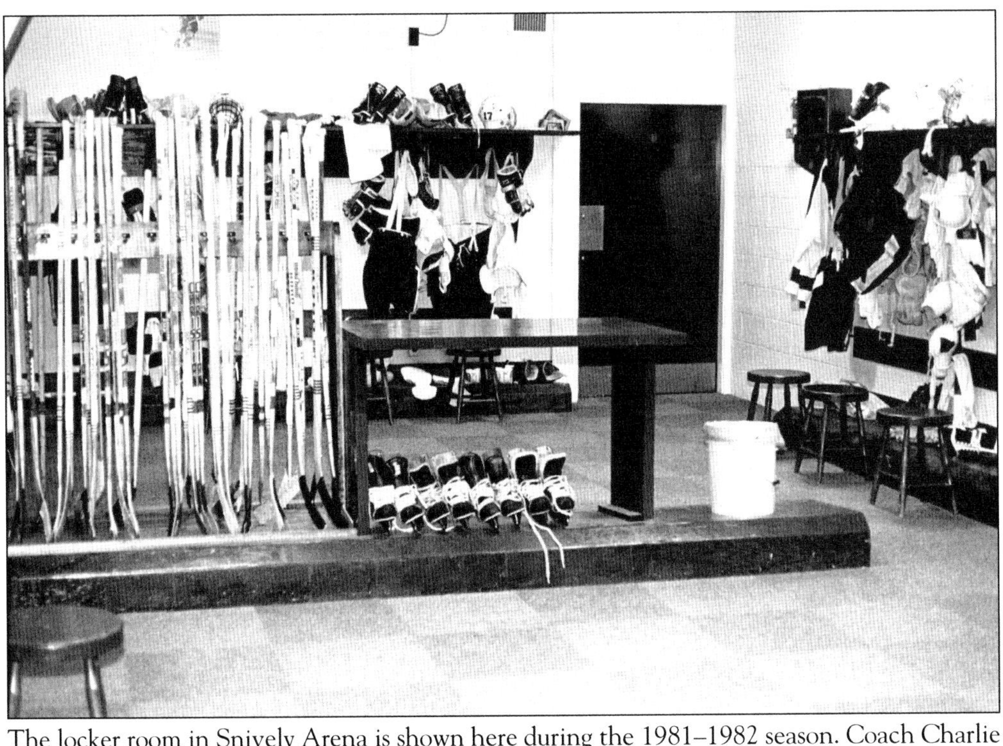

The locker room in Snively Arena is shown here during the 1981–1982 season. Coach Charlie Holt insisted that the players leave the locker room neat and orderly after practices and games. (UNH Archives.)

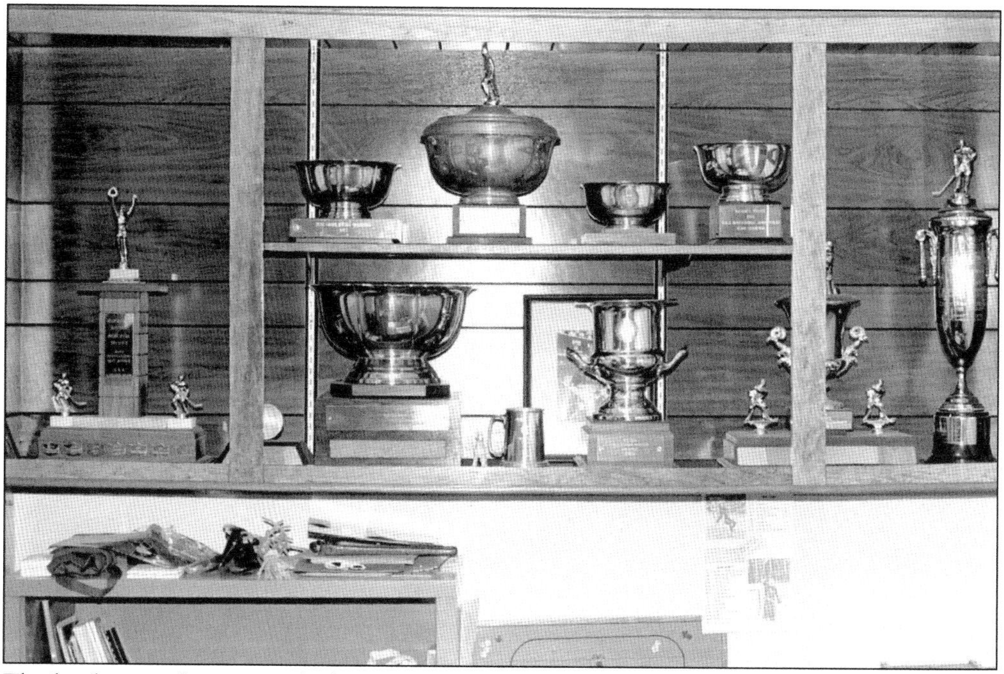

The hockey trophy case with the ECAC championship cup is shown in Charlie Holt's office in 1981. (UNH Archives.)

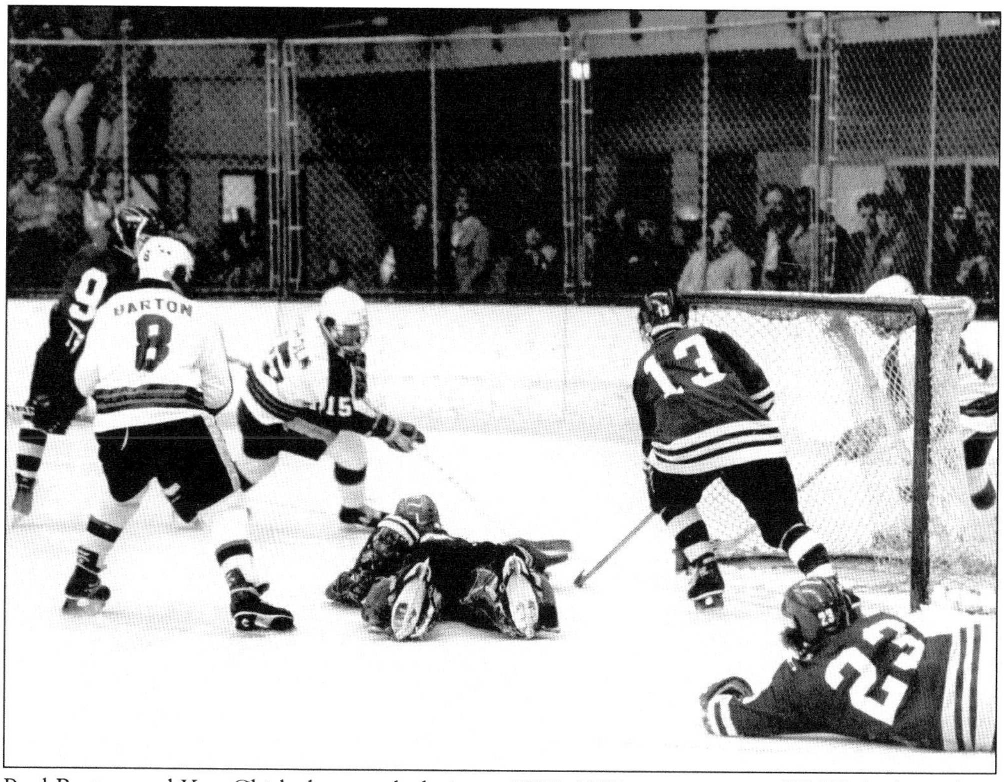

Paul Barton and Ken Chisholm attack during a 1980–1981 season game. (UNH Archives.)

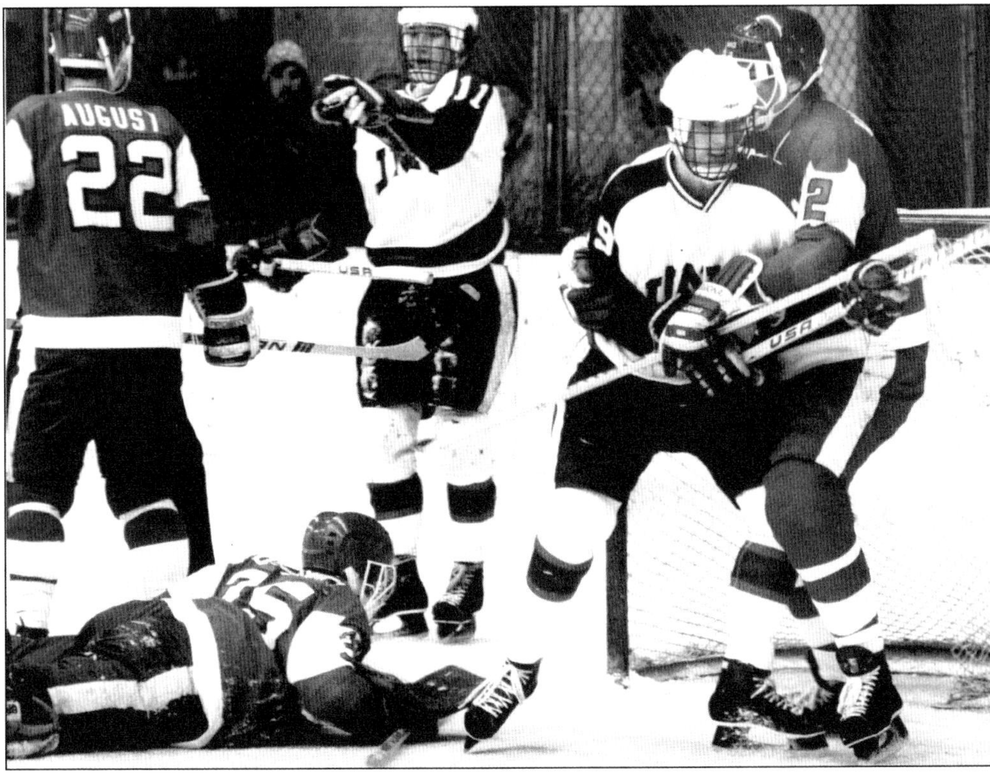

Dan Potter (No. 11) and Steve Lyons (No. 9) are shown in action during the 1980–1981 season. The season ended with a 19-31-1 record. (UNH Archives.)

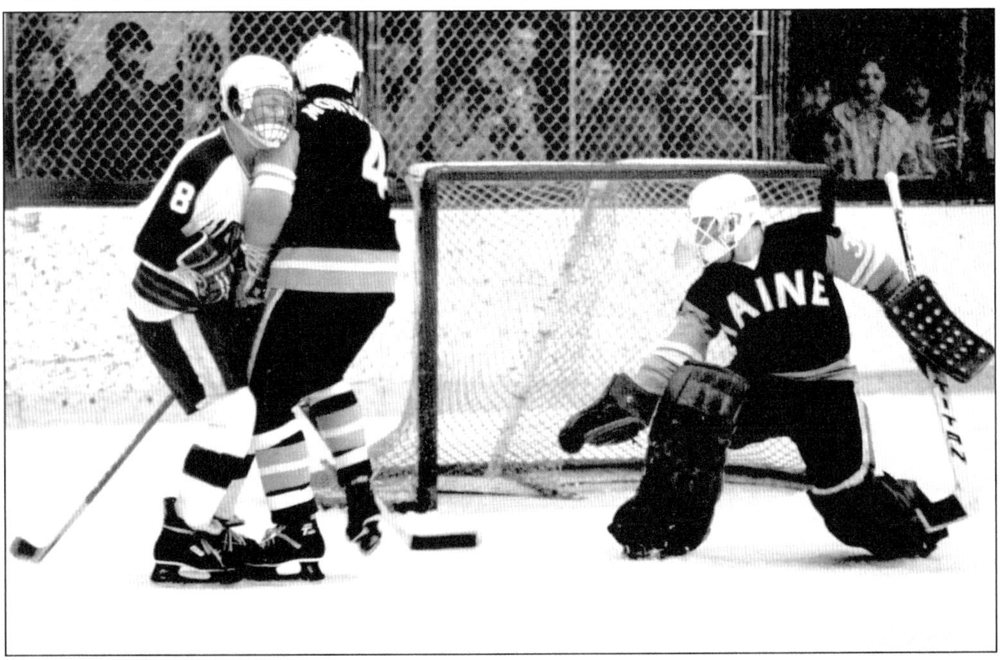

Paul Barton and Maine defenders tangle in a February 1982 game. UNH defeated Maine 8-5. The Wildcats had a 22-14 season and a trip to the NCAA quarterfinals. (UNH Archives.)

Goalie Todd Pearson rests on the bench. In the UNH record books, Pearson ranks fourth for career saves (2,178) and second for season saves (1,028). (UNH Archives.)

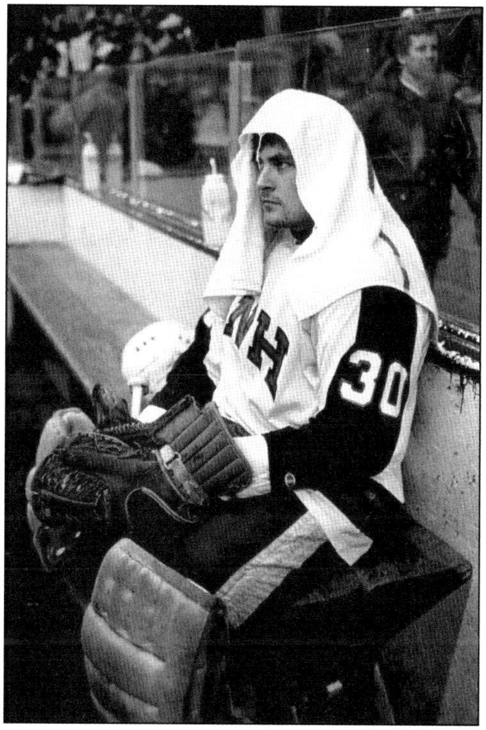

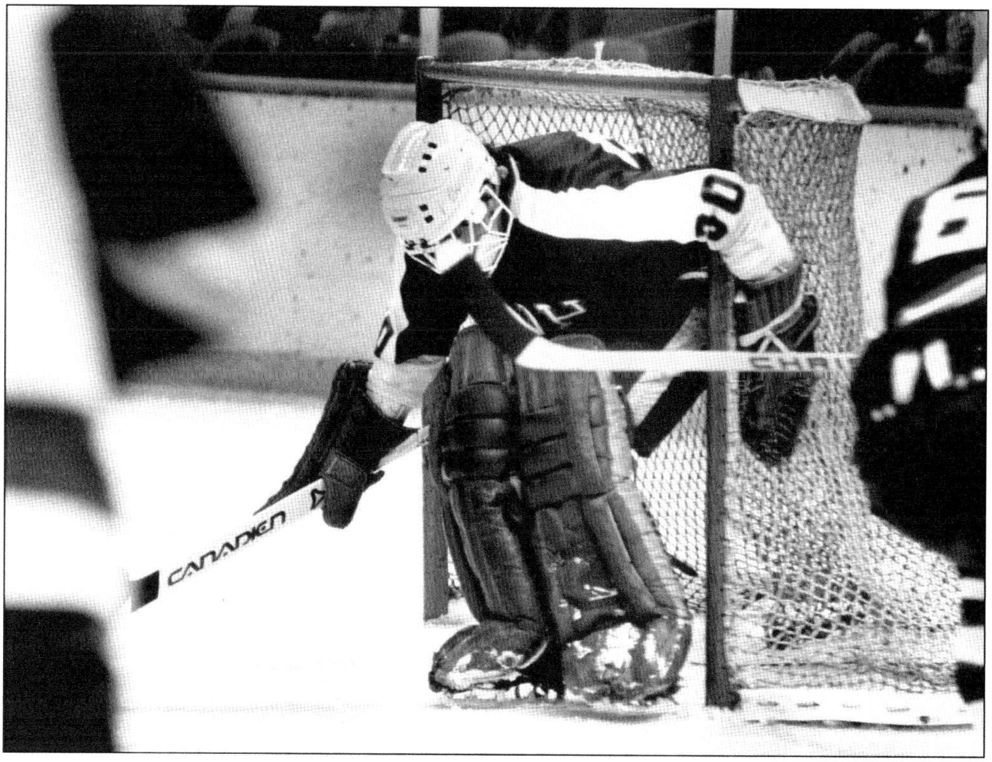

Todd Pearson makes a save in the 1982 NCAA quarterfinal game against the Wisconsin Badgers. UNH lost the game 5-0. (UNH Archives.)

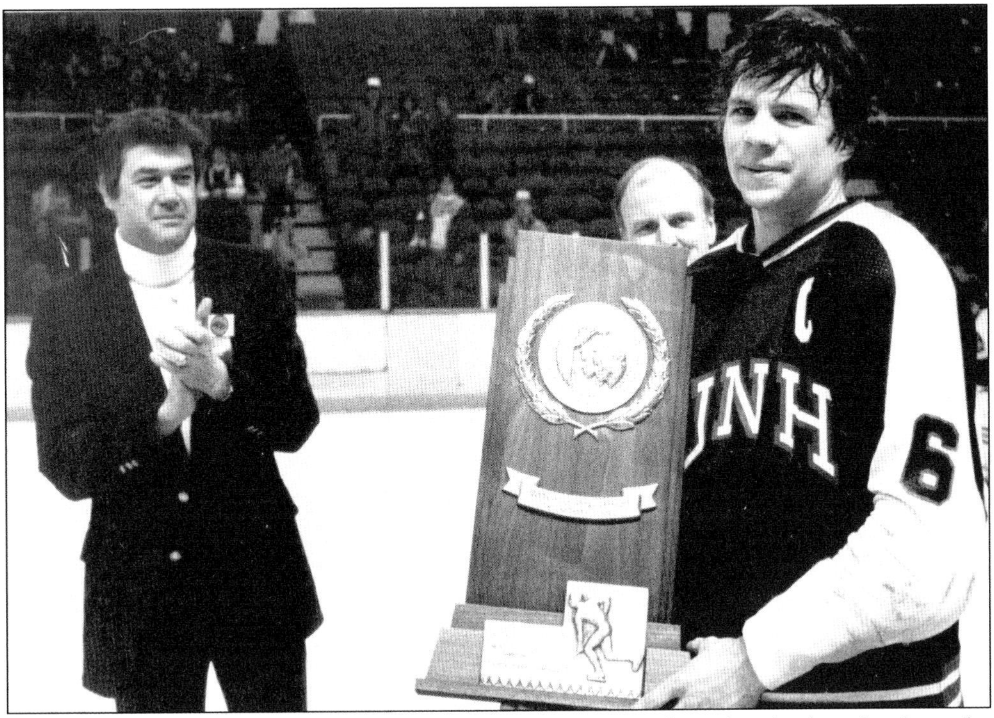

Ed Olsen, captain of the 1981–1982 team, holds the trophy for a fourth-place finish in the 1982 NCAA Tournament. The Wildcats have been to the NCAA championships 12 times and appeared in the Frozen Four 6 times. The closest UNH has come to a NCAA championship title is when they lost in the 1999 finals game to Maine. (Henri Barber photograph. UNH Archives.)

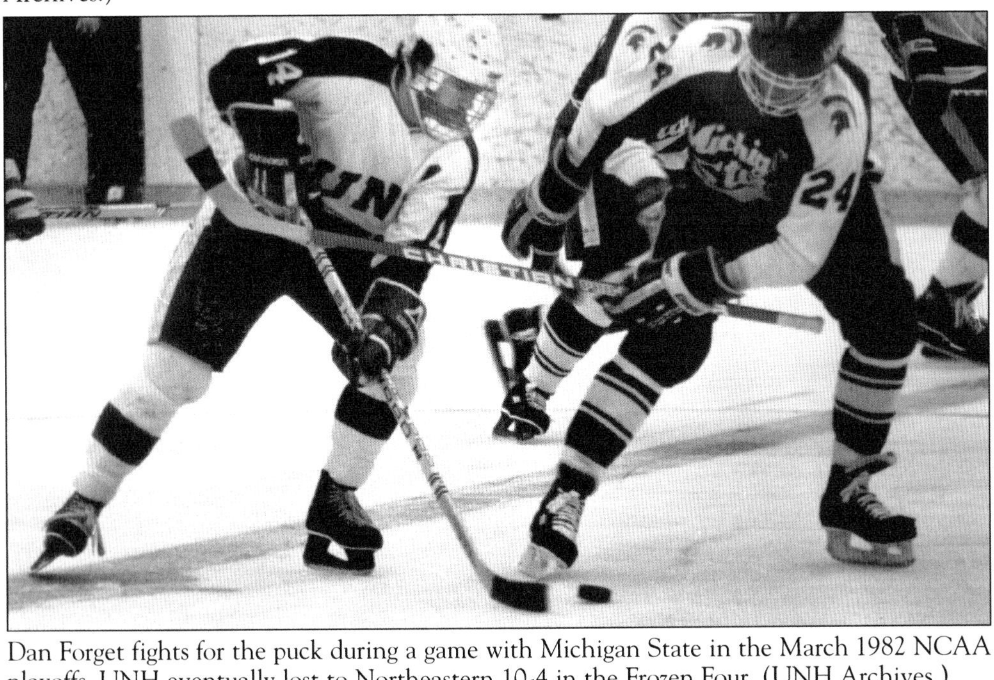

Dan Forget fights for the puck during a game with Michigan State in the March 1982 NCAA playoffs. UNH eventually lost to Northeastern 10-4 in the Frozen Four. (UNH Archives.)

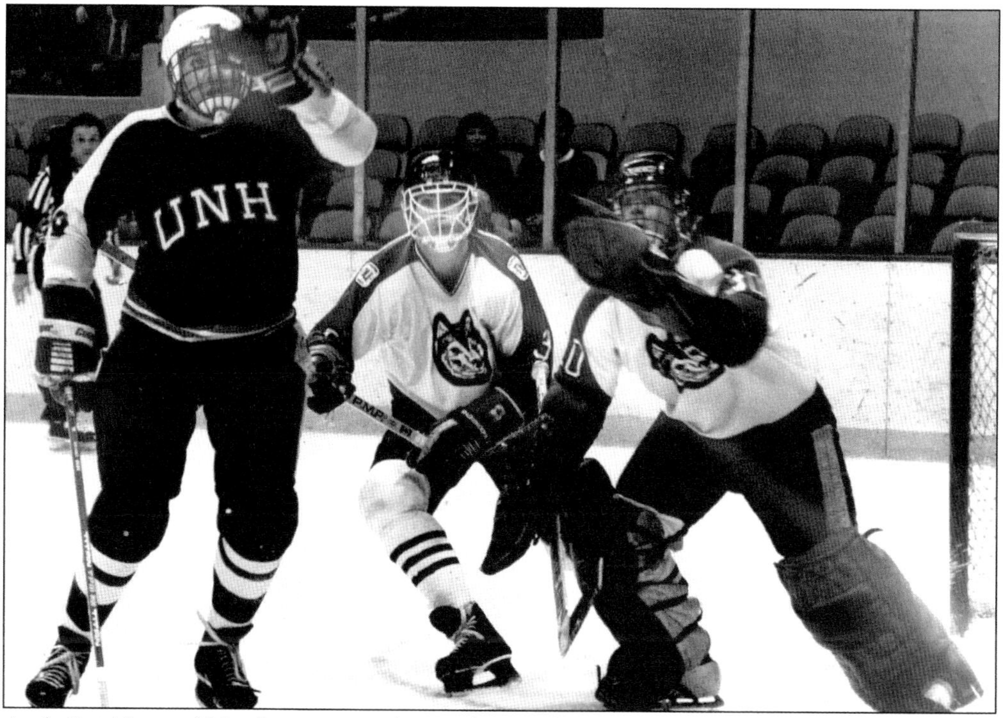

Andy Brickley and Northeastern goalie Mark Davidson compete for a loose puck in the 1982 NCAA semifinal. UNH lost 10-4. Andy Brickley was UNH's ninth All-American hockey player. (UNH Archives.)

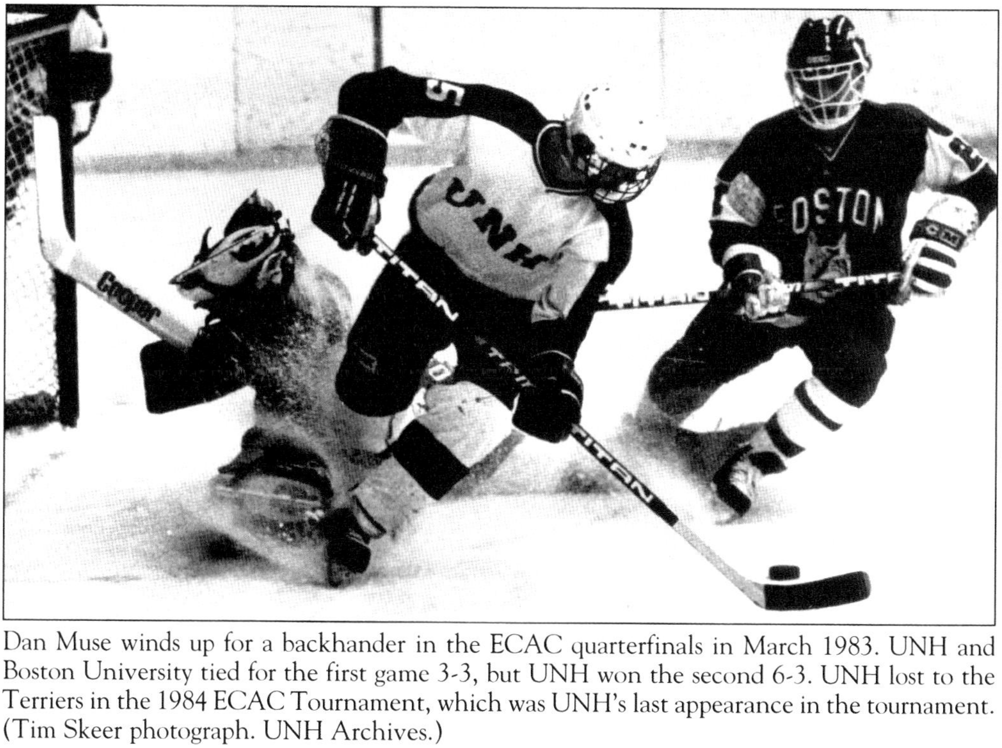

Dan Muse winds up for a backhander in the ECAC quarterfinals in March 1983. UNH and Boston University tied for the first game 3-3, but UNH won the second 6-3. UNH lost to the Terriers in the 1984 ECAC Tournament, which was UNH's last appearance in the tournament. (Tim Skeer photograph. UNH Archives.)

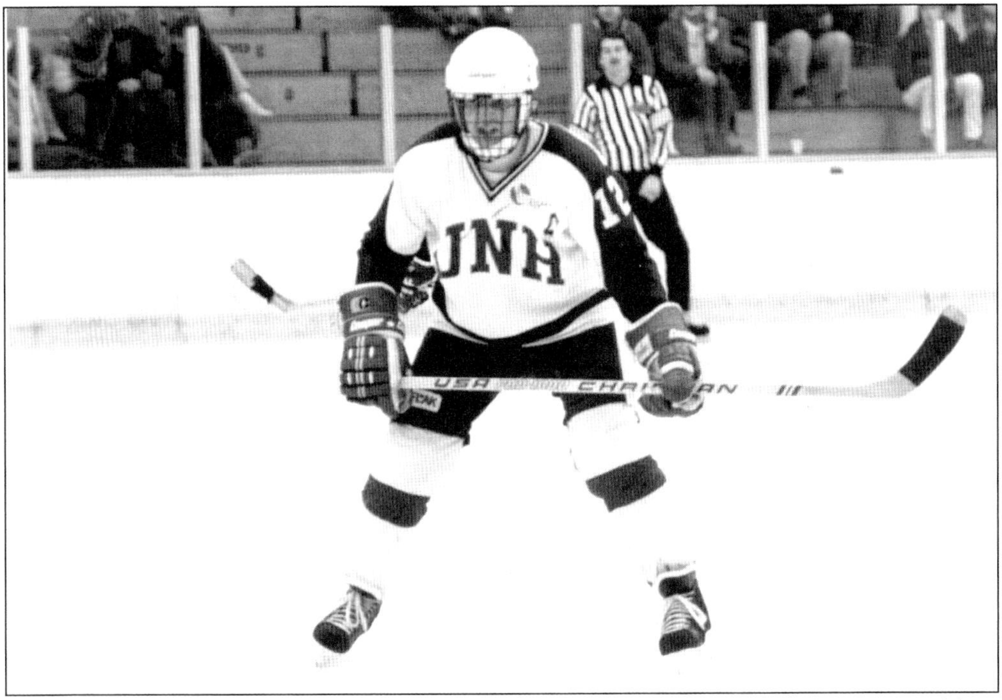

Ralph Robinson from the 1984–1985 season wears a uniform with the Hockey East emblem. (Hank Ellsmore photograph. UNH Archives.)

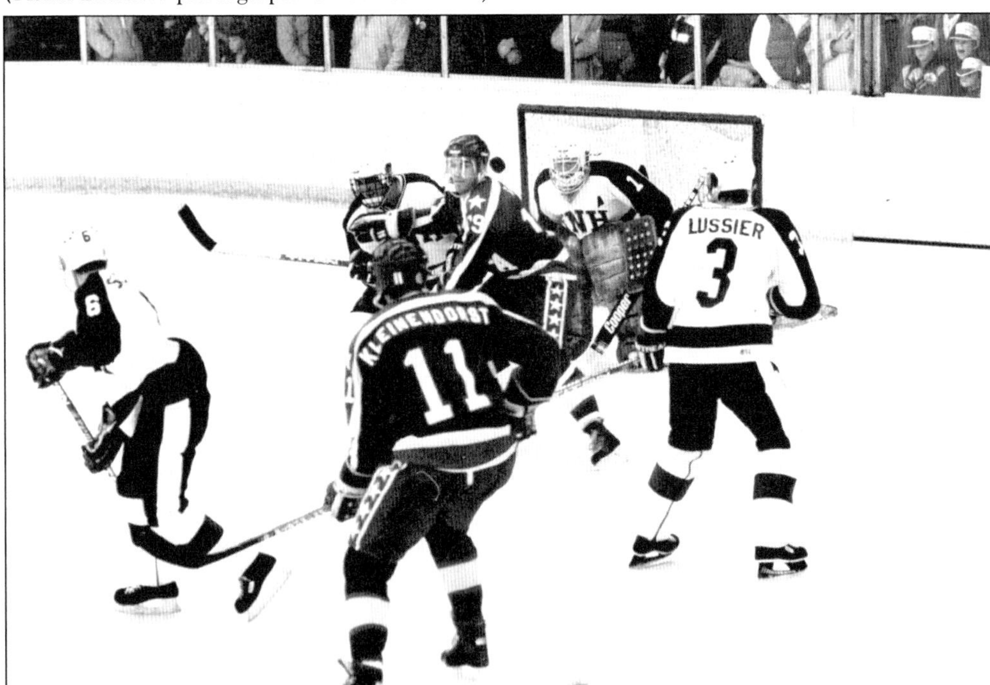

Bruce Gillies played during an exhibition game with the U.S. Olympic team. On the Wildcats team from 1982 to 1985, he had a total of 71 career games. (Hank Ellsmore photograph. UNH Archives.)

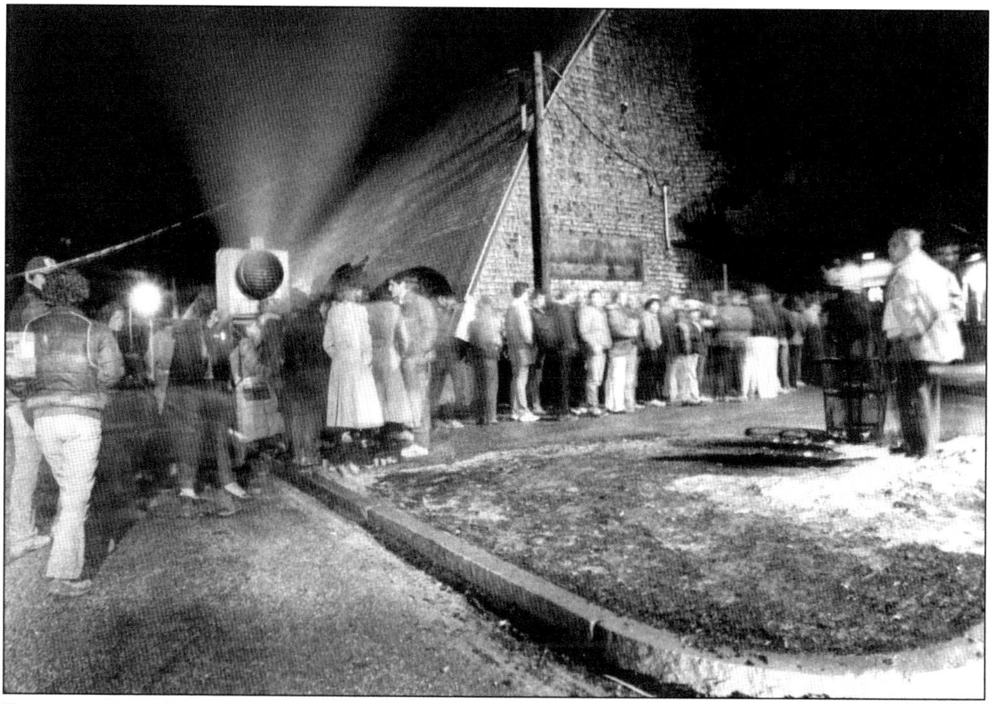

Fans wait outside Snively Arena during the 1983–1984 season. (UNH Archives.)

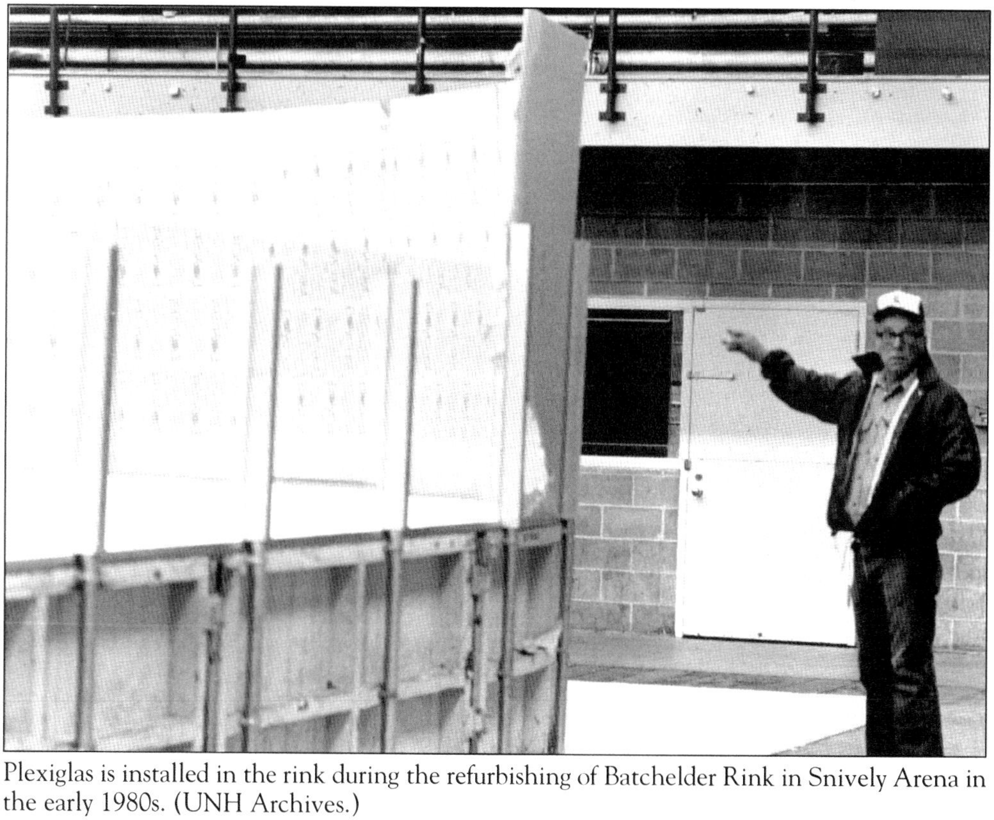

Plexiglas is installed in the rink during the refurbishing of Batchelder Rink in Snively Arena in the early 1980s. (UNH Archives.)

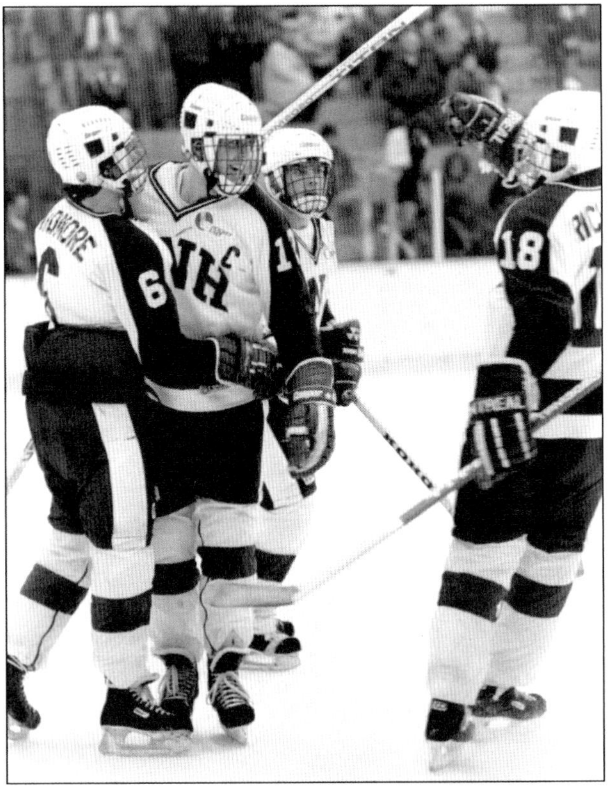

Shane Skidmore (No. 6), co-captain Ralph Robinson (No. 12), and James Richmond (No. 18) huddle on the ice during the 1984–1985 season. The season ended with a 16-26-01 record. (UNH Archives.)

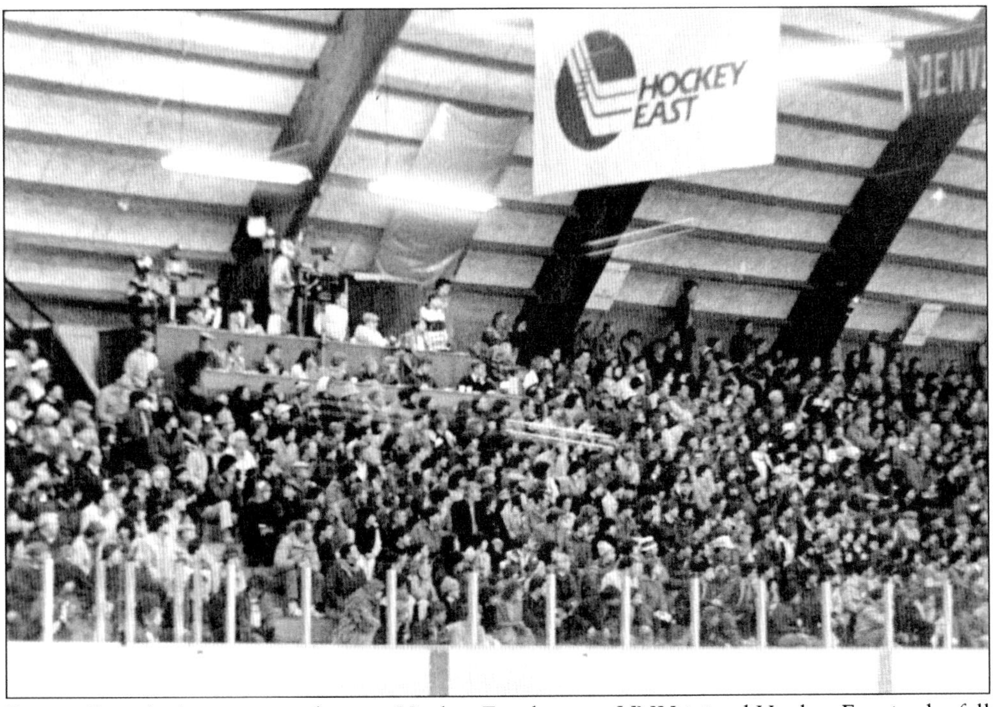

Fans in Snively Arena enjoy the new Hockey East banner. UNH joined Hockey East in the fall of 1984. (UNH Archives.)

Players congregate on the bench with Bob Kullen in the 1980s. (Hank Ellsmore photograph. UNH Archives.)

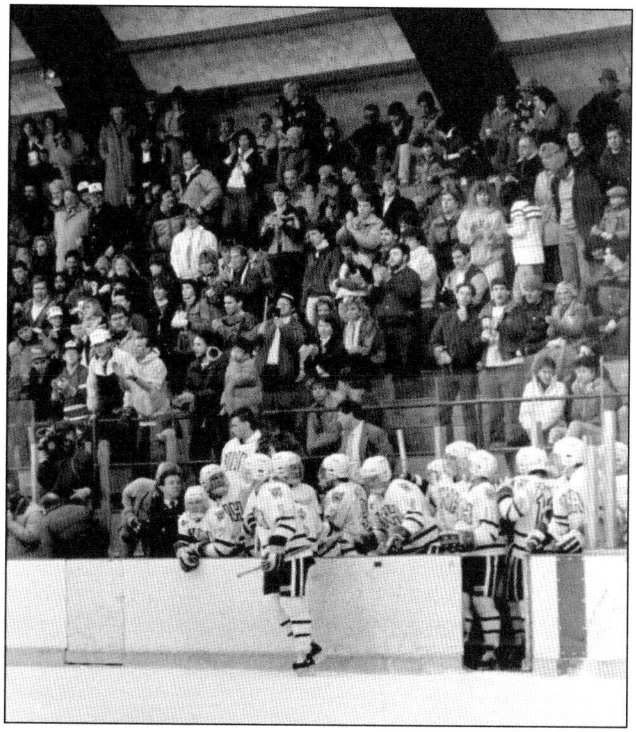

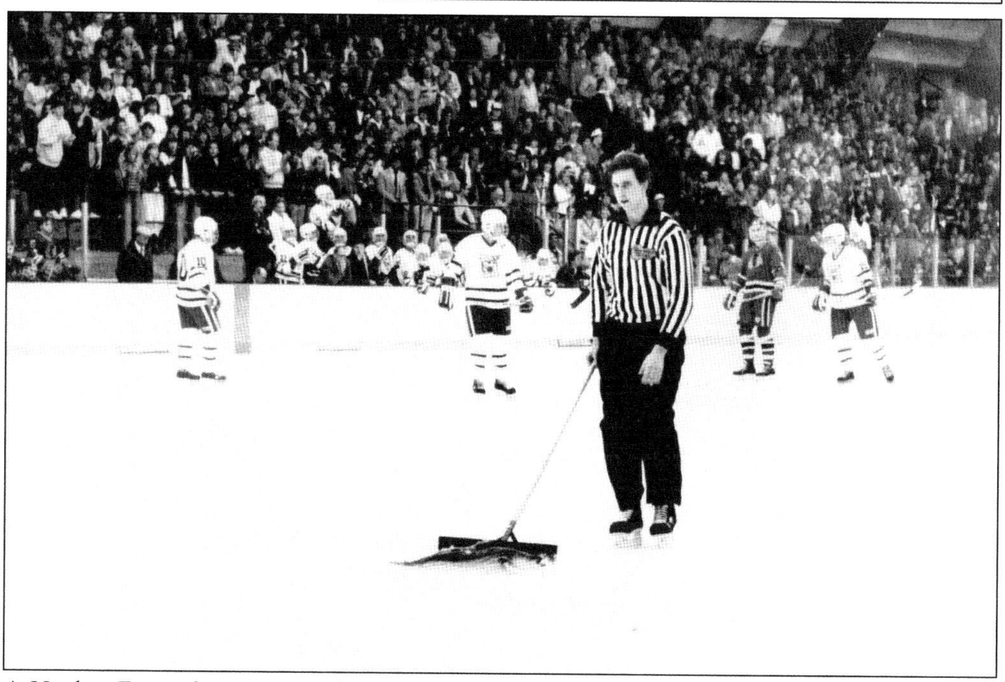

A Hockey East referee scrapes the fish off the rink. A long-lasting UNH tradition with murky beginnings, the fish is thrown out after the first goal scored by a UNH player. One story is that the tradition started in a game against ECAC Division II Bowdoin College in the 1970s. The UNH fans threw out a small fish, naming it a Division II fish after Bowdoin. (Paul Chalue photograph. UNH Archives.)

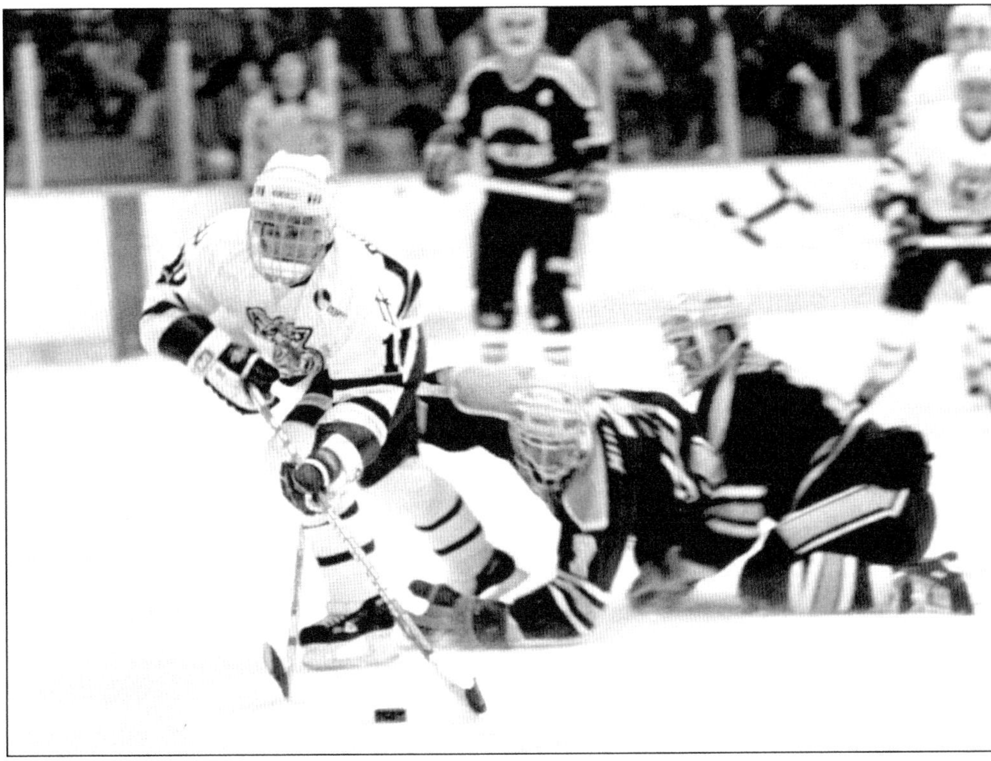

Mike Rossetti escapes from Boston College players in an eventual 8-4 UNH loss in December 1986. (UNH Archives.)

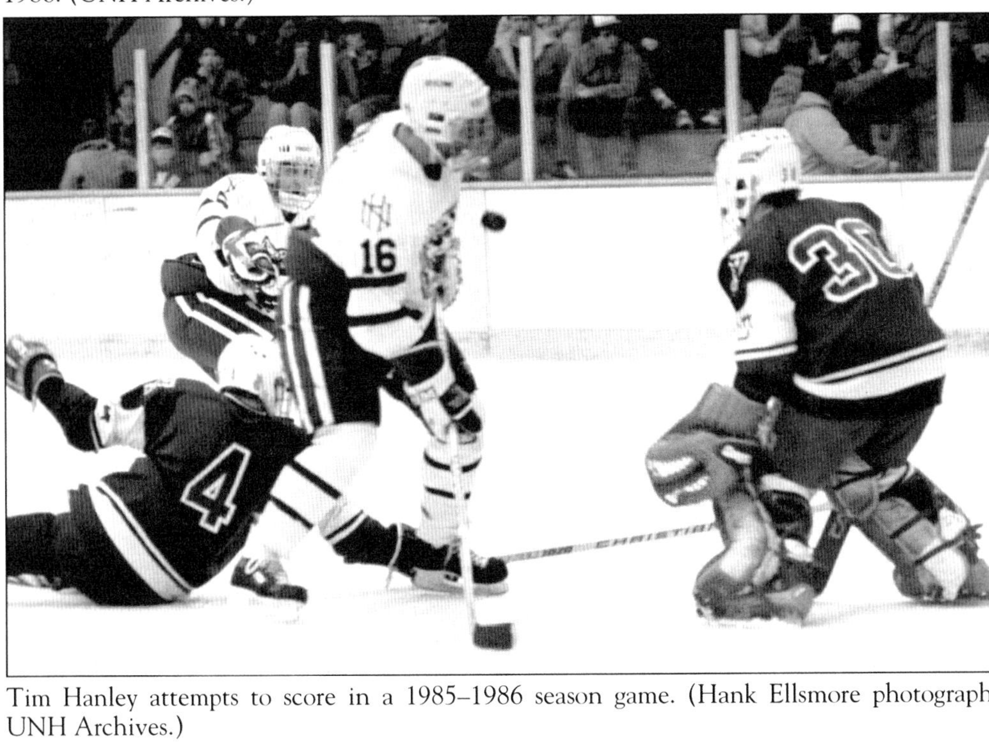

Tim Hanley attempts to score in a 1985–1986 season game. (Hank Ellsmore photograph. UNH Archives.)

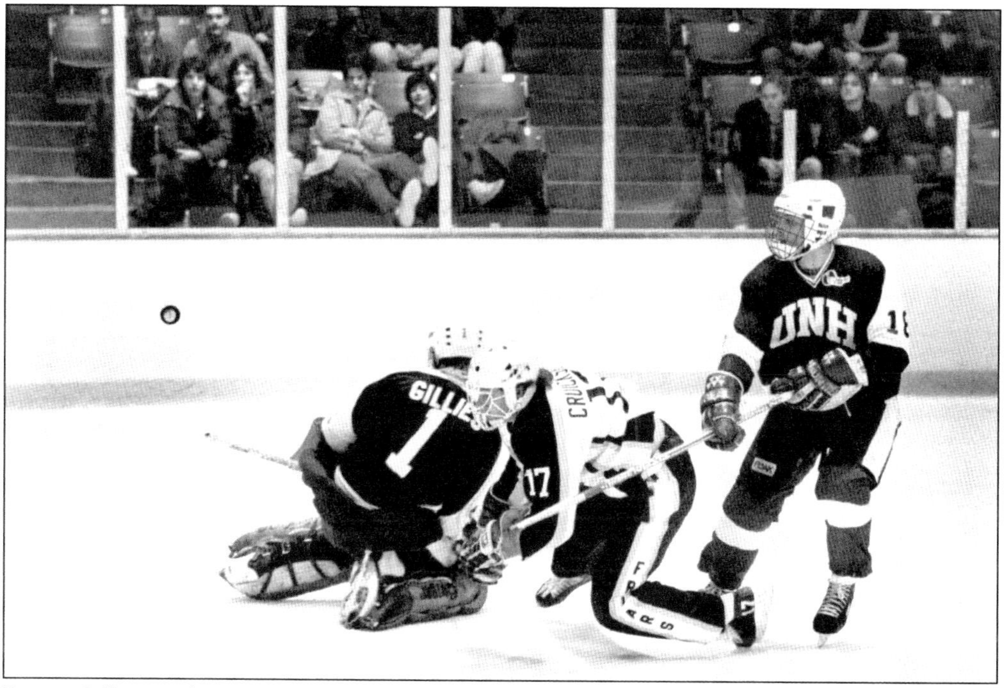

Bruce Gillies and James Richmond tangle with a Friar in a game at Providence College. The Wildcats lost 4-2. Charlie Holt's last season closed with a 5-29-3 record. (Tom Maguire photograph. UNH Archives.)

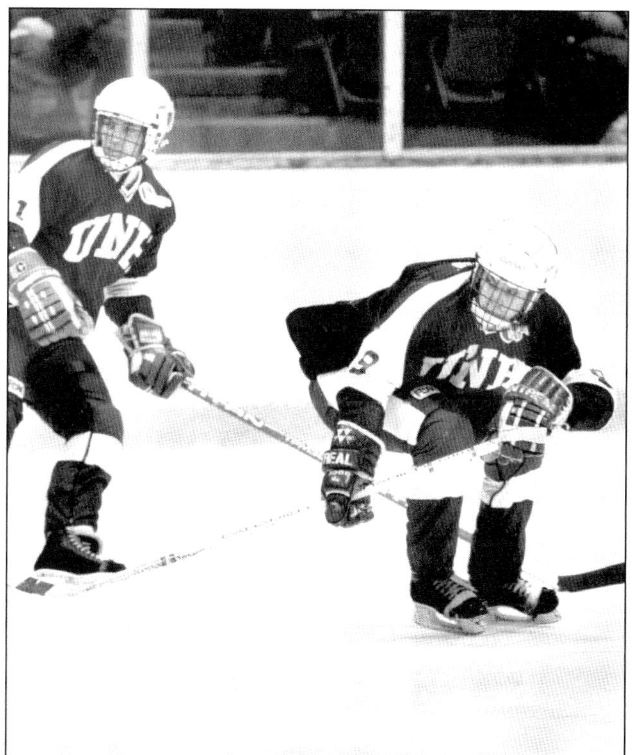

Peter Hermes (No. 9) and Steve Leach (No. 11) skate during the 1984–1985 season. Leach was on the 1988 Olympic team. (Tom Maguire photograph. UNH Archives.)

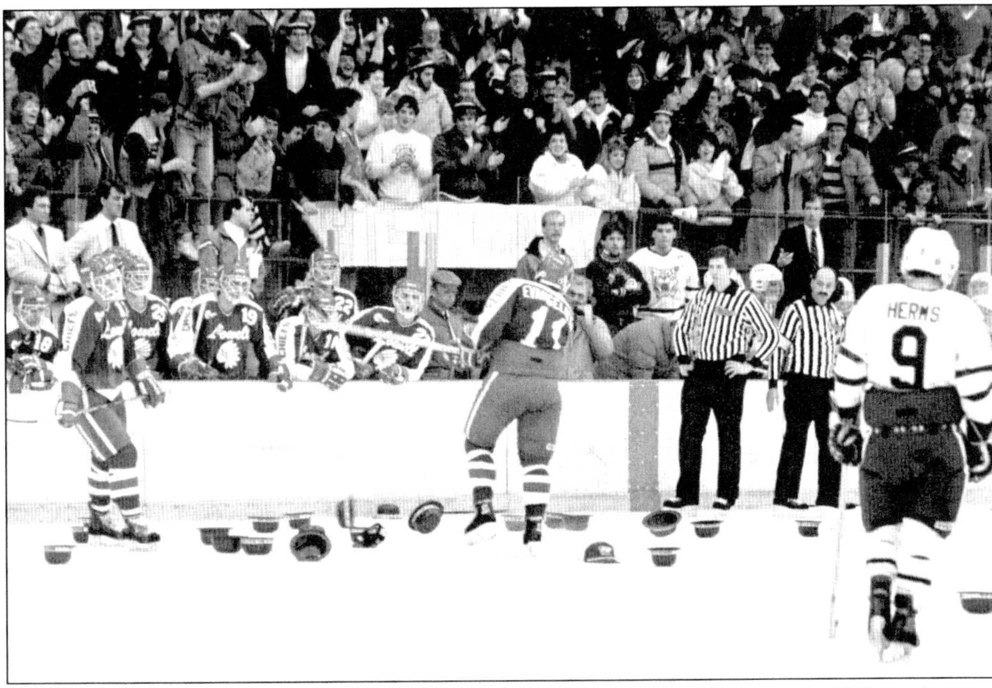

Hats go off to Charlie Holt on March 3, 1986. UNH beat the University of Massachusetts, Lowell, 7-4. Holt retired with a record of 347-232-18 (.596), as a three-time winner of the Spencer T. Penrose Award, and with an ECAC championship. During this game, Mike Rossetti scored a hat trick and all the plastic fedoras were thrown to the ice in honor of Charlie Holt. (Hank Ellsmore photograph. UNH Archives.)

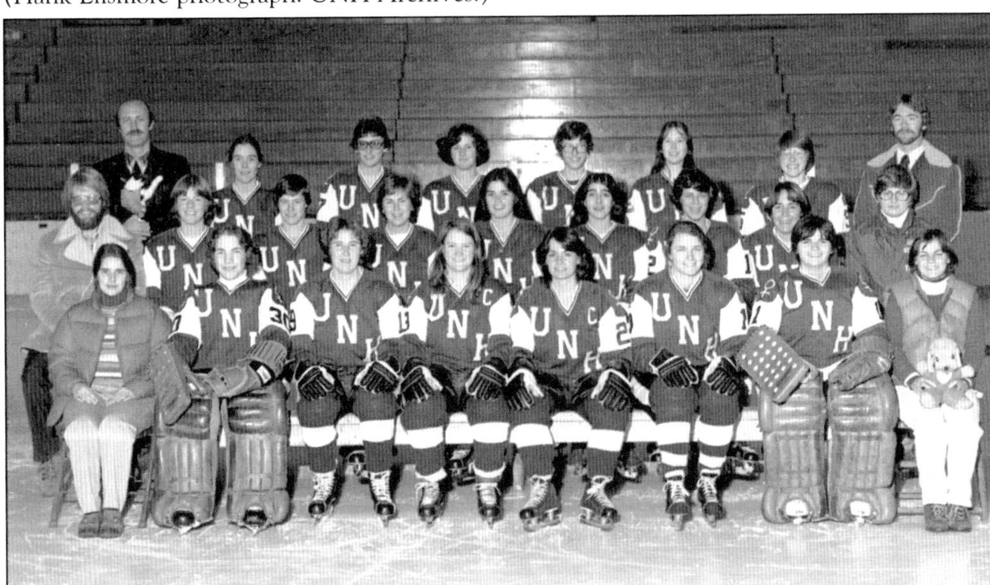

Women began playing ice hockey in the fall of 1977. Included in this 1977–1978 team photograph are Kathy Bryant, Melissa White, and Gail Griffith. Bryant has the second highest career score with 255 points. White and Bryant share a record for most goals in a single period (three), set at the same game against Boston University. (UNH Photographic Services.)

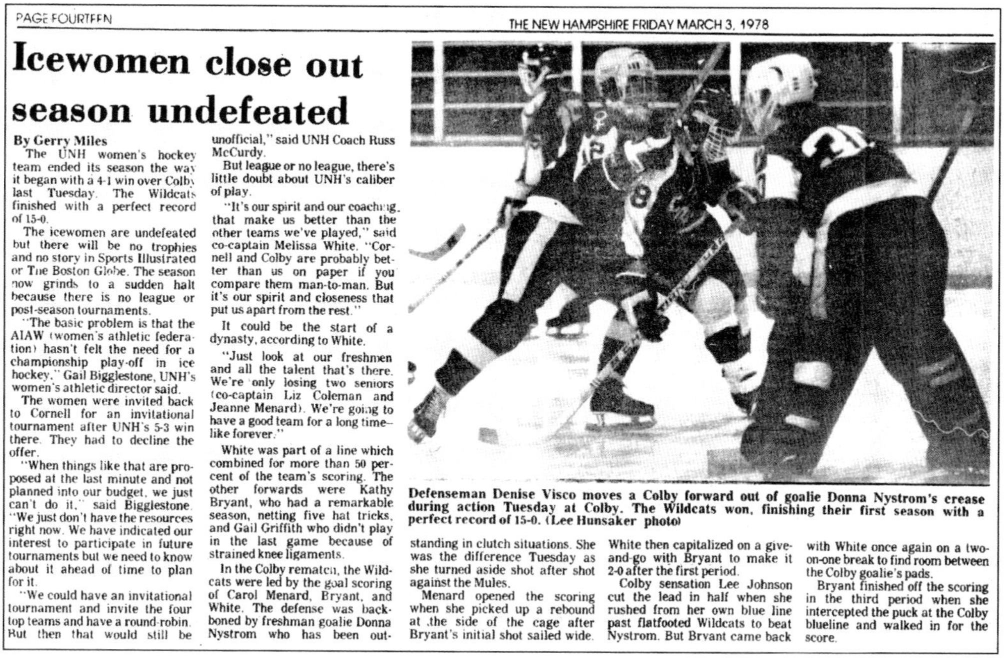

PAGE FOURTEEN THE NEW HAMPSHIRE FRIDAY MARCH 3, 1978

Icewomen close out season undefeated

By Gerry Miles

The UNH women's hockey team ended its season the way it began with a 4-1 win over Colby last Tuesday. The Wildcats finished with a perfect record of 15-0.

The icewomen are undefeated but there will be no trophies and no story in Sports Illustrated or The Boston Globe. The season now grinds to a sudden halt because there is no league or post-season tournaments.

"The basic problem is that the AIAW (women's athletic federation) hasn't felt the need for a championship play-off in ice hockey," Gail Bigglestone, UNH's women's athletic director said.

The women were invited back to Cornell for an invitational tournament after UNH's 5-3 win there. They had to decline the offer.

"When things like that are proposed at the last minute and not planned into our budget, we just can't do it," said Bigglestone. "We just don't have the resources right now. We have indicated our interest to participate in future tournaments but we need to know about it ahead of time to plan for it.

"We could have an invitational tournament and invite the four top teams and have a round-robin. But then that would still be unofficial," said UNH Coach Russ McCurdy.

But league or no league, there's little doubt about UNH's caliber of play.

"It's our spirit and our coaching that make us better than the other teams we've played," said co-captain Melissa White. "Cornell and Colby are probably better than us on paper if you compare them man-to-man. But it's our spirit and closeness that put us apart from the rest."

It could be the start of a dynasty, according to White.

"Just look at our freshmen and all the talent that's there. We're only losing two seniors (co-captain Liz Coleman and Jeanne Menard). We're going to have a good team for a long time—like forever."

White was part of a line which combined for more than 50 percent of the team's scoring. The other forwards were Kathy Bryant, who had a remarkable season, netting five hat tricks, and Gail Griffith who didn't play in the last game because of strained knee ligaments.

In the Colby rematch, the Wildcats were led by the goal scoring of Carol Menard, Bryant, and White. The defense was backboned by freshman goalie Donna Nystrom who has been outstanding in clutch situations. She was the difference Tuesday as she turned aside shot after shot against the Mules.

Menard opened the scoring when she picked up a rebound at the side of the cage after Bryant's initial shot sailed wide. White then capitalized on a give-and-go with Bryant to make it 2-0 after the first period.

Colby sensation Lee Johnson cut the lead in half when she rushed from her own blue line past flatfooted Wildcats to beat Nystrom. But Bryant came back with White once again on a two-on-one break to find room between the Colby goalie's pads.

Bryant finished off the scoring in the third period when she intercepted the puck at the Colby blueline and walked in for the score.

Defenseman Denise Visco moves a Colby forward out of goalie Donna Nystrom's crease during action Tuesday at Colby. The Wildcats won, finishing their first season with a perfect record of 15-0. (Lee Hunsaker photo)

The *New Hampshire* reports the women's undefeated season in March 1978. The first women's hockey team at UNH went 15-0 for its first season, a very auspicious start for the program. (UNH Archives.)

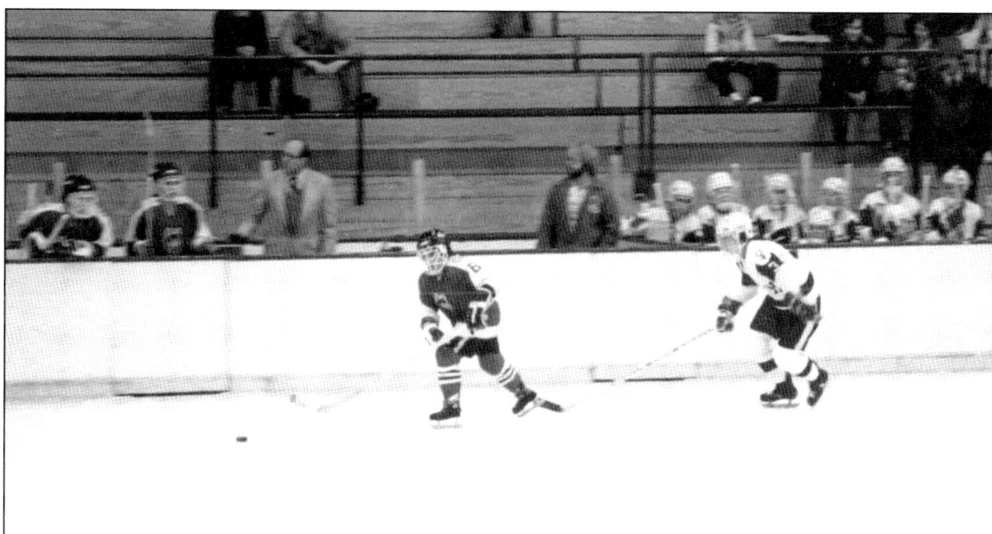

Cindy McKay chases down a Northeastern player in November 1979. UNH won 8-1. McKay is the women's third all-time scorer on defense, with 100 career points. (Ron Bergeron photograph. UNH Archives.)

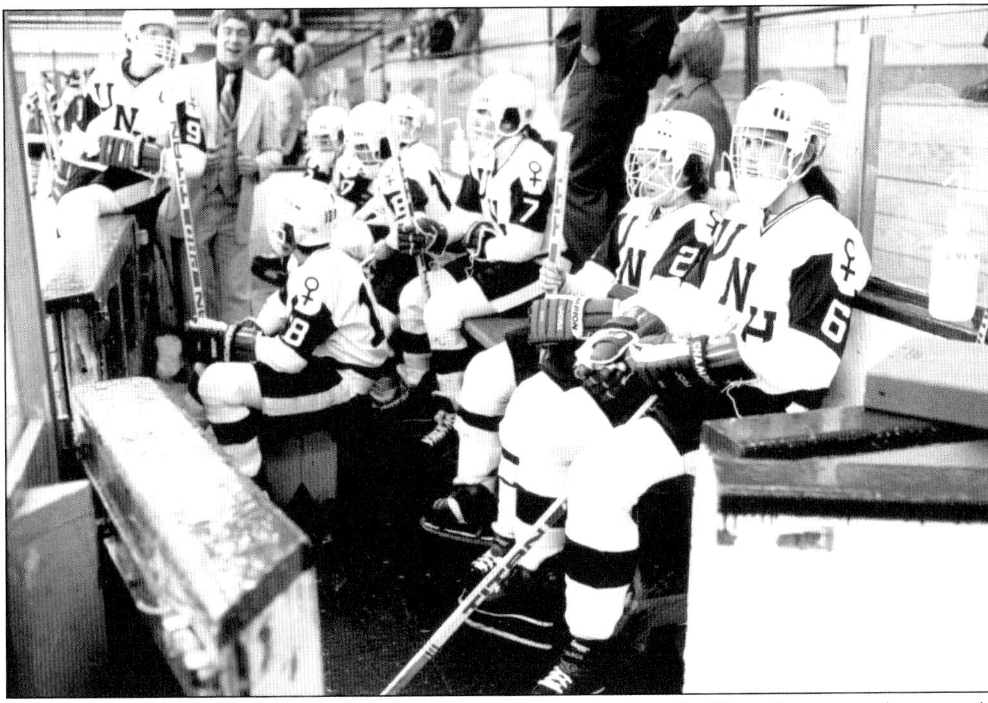

Players on the 1979–1980 UNH women's team rest on the bench. (Ron Bergeron photograph. UNH Archives.)

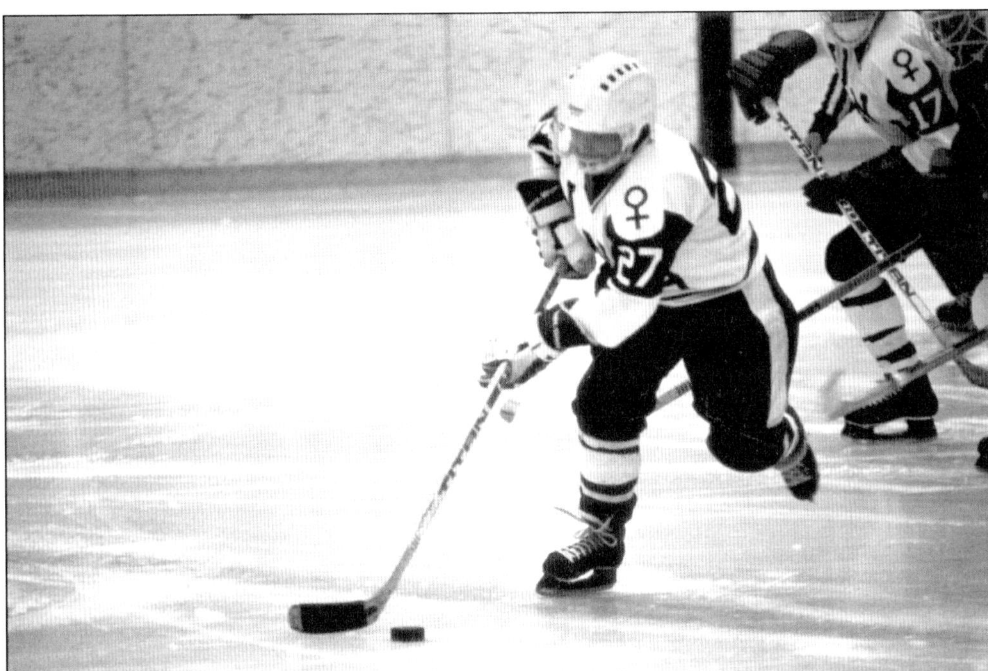

Diane Langlais takes the puck during the 1978–1979 season. Langlais has 149 career points. (UNH Archives.)

This is the program for the 1980–1981 Women's Ice Hockey Championship held at Snively Arena. The UNH women were four-time Eastern Association for Intercollegiate Athletics for Women (EAIAW) champions between 1980 and 1983 and appeared in every ECAC Tournament from 1984 through 2001. They have won the ECAC championship five times. (UNH Archives.)

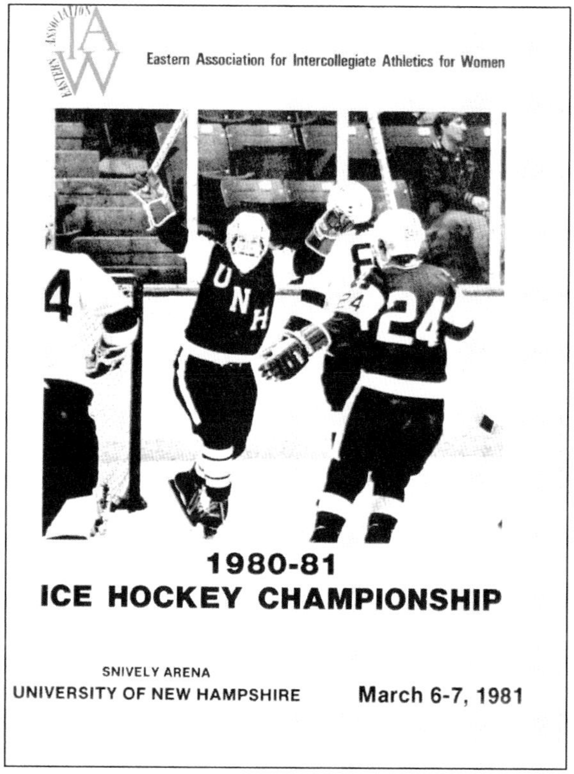

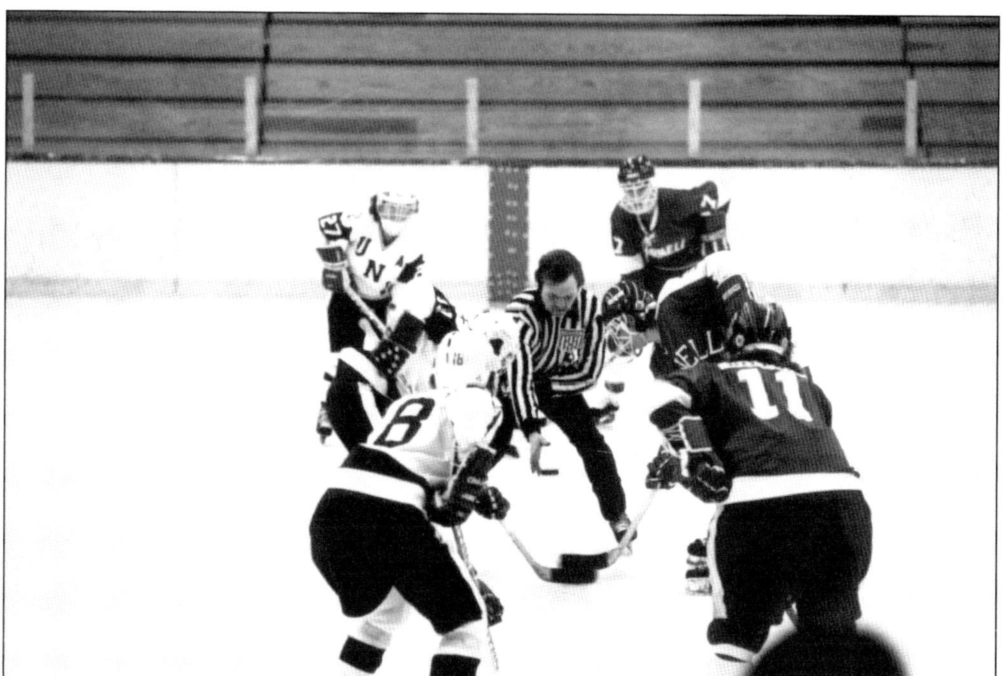

Diane Langlais, Robin Balducci, and Kip Porter face-off against Cornell in January 1982. (John Bardwell photograph. UNH Archives.)

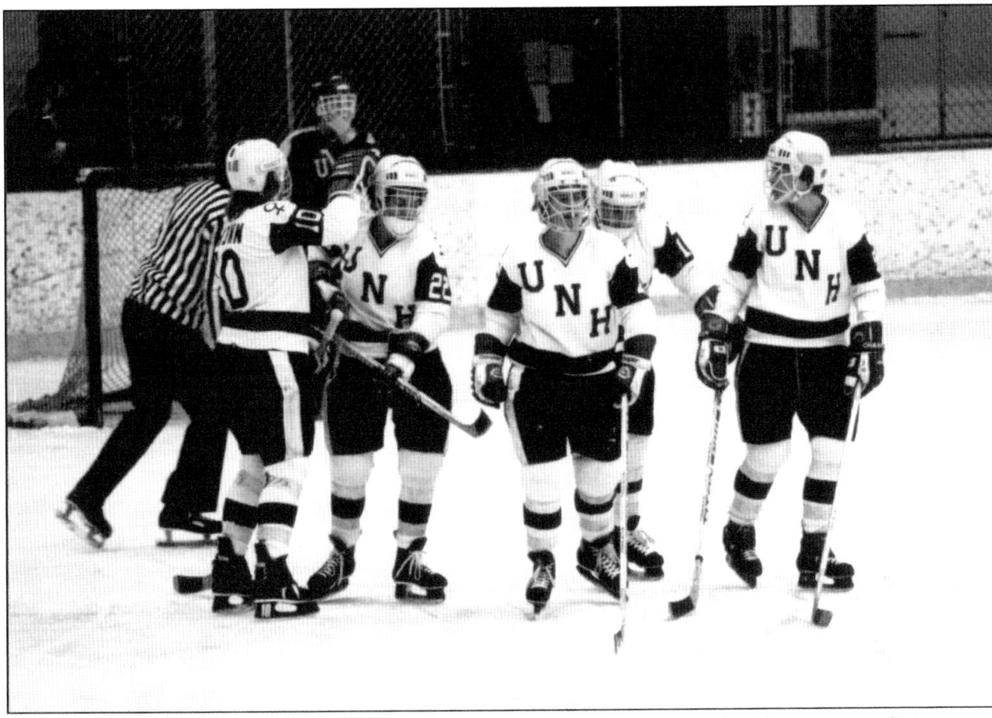

The women gather on the ice during a February 1982 game against the University of Vermont, in which they shutout Vermont 6-0. (John Bardwell photograph. UNH Archives.)

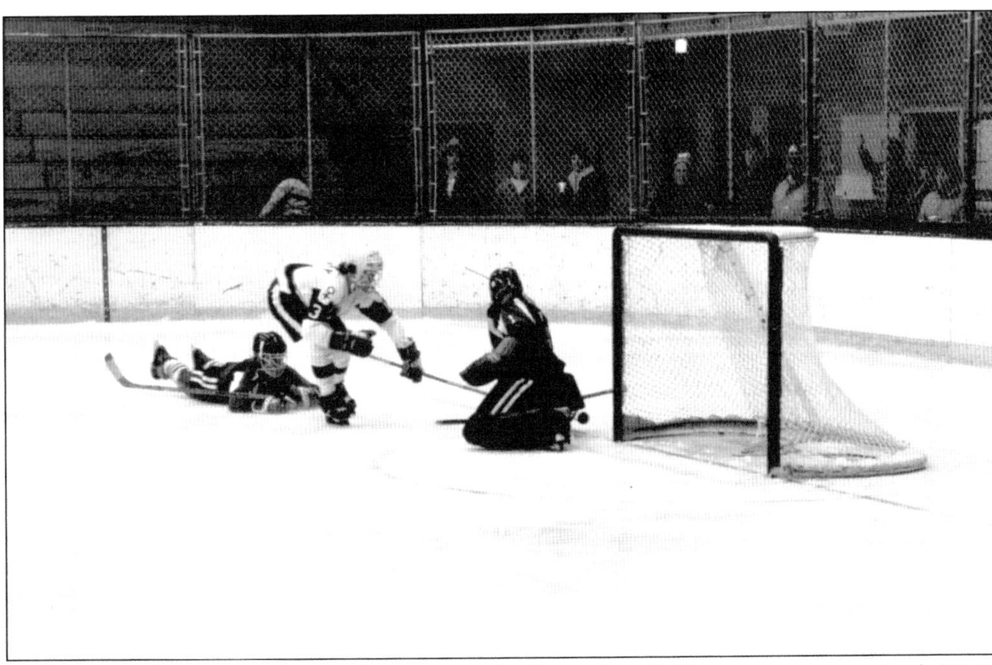
Cindy McKay scores against Northeastern in the December 1982 season opener, which UNH won. (Dwight Bardwell photograph. UNH Archives.)

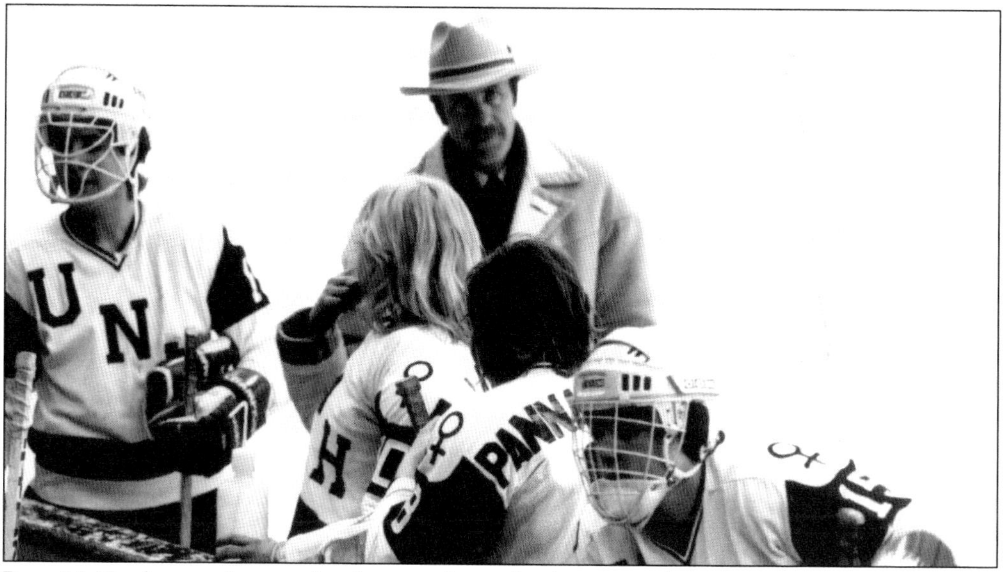

Russ McCurdy was the coach of women's ice hockey team from 1977 to 1992. His record was 264-36-10, and included four EAIAW championships, four ECAC championships, and numerous appearances in ECAC tournaments. The blonde woman next to McCurdy is Kathy Kazmaier, the sister of Patty Kazmaier, for whom the USA Hockey Foundation national women's ice hockey award is named. (UNH Archives.)

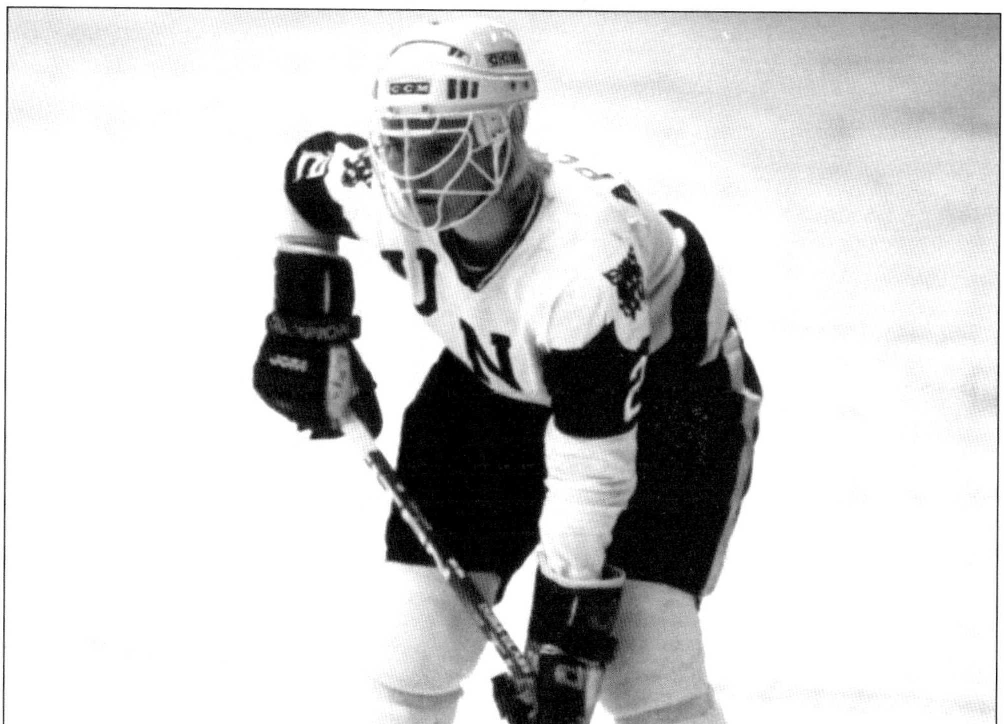

Lauren Apollo has 105 career points and holds the record for most penalties in a single game. She earned four in a February 1985 game against Northeastern. (John Bardwell photograph. UNH Archives.)

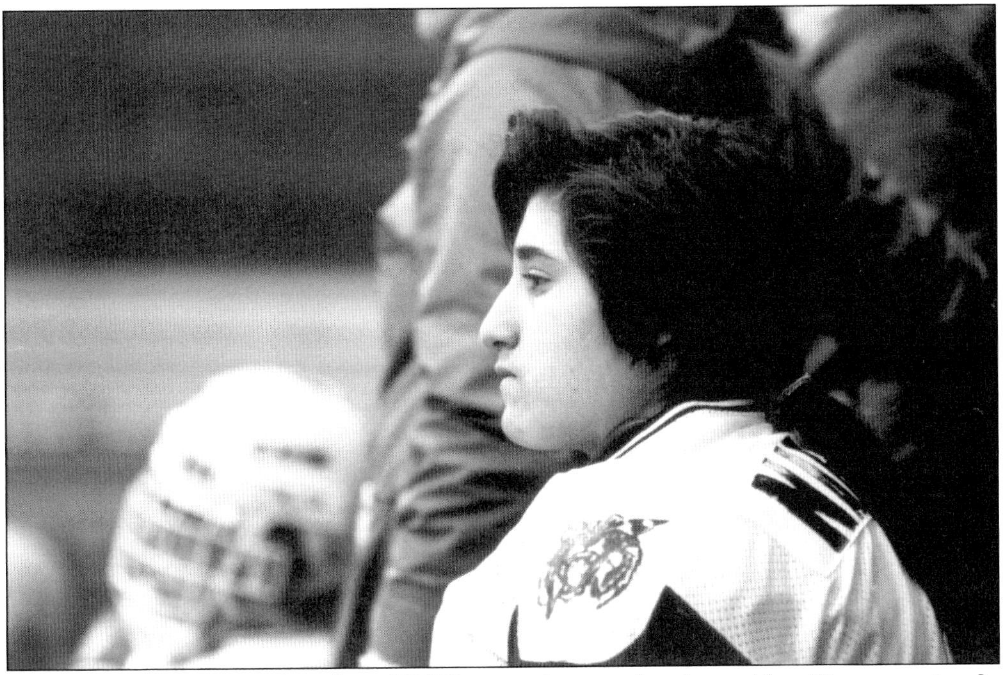

Cathy Narsiff (1983–1987) ranks as UNH's second top goaltender and has 52 career wins. In addition, she has the most career shutouts (16). (John Bardwell photograph. UNH Archives.)

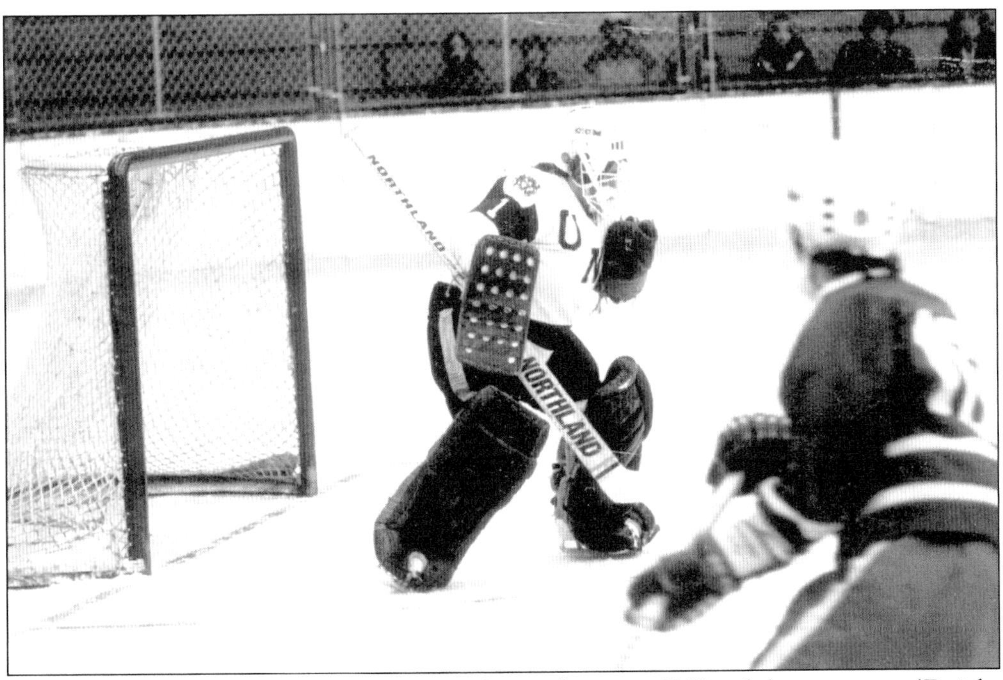

Cathy Narsiff defends the goal against Assabet Valley in a 1983 exhibition game. (Dwight Bardwell photograph. UNH Archives.)

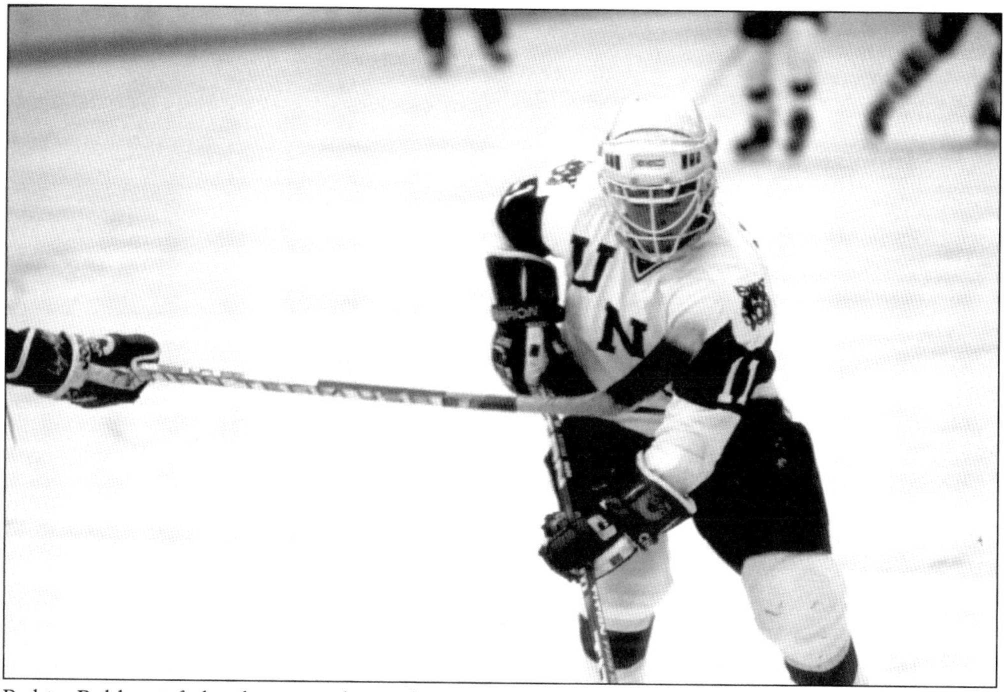

Robin Balducci fights her way down the ice. Balducci had a career-point total of 180. (John Bardwell photograph. UNH Archives.)

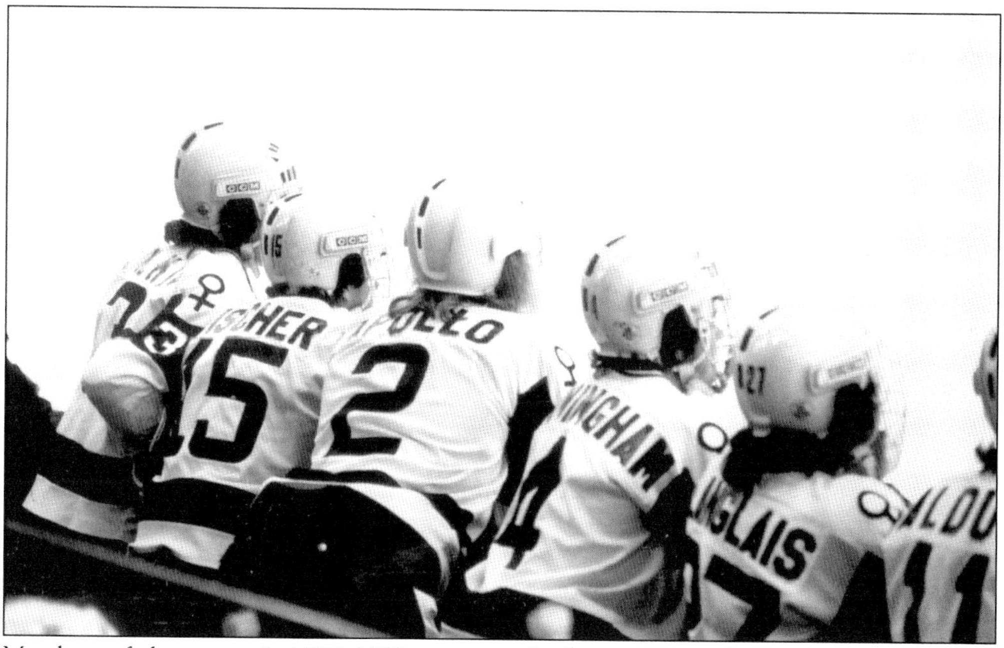

Members of the women's 1982–1983 team watch the ice action from the bench during a February 1983 game against Princeton. (UNH Archives.)

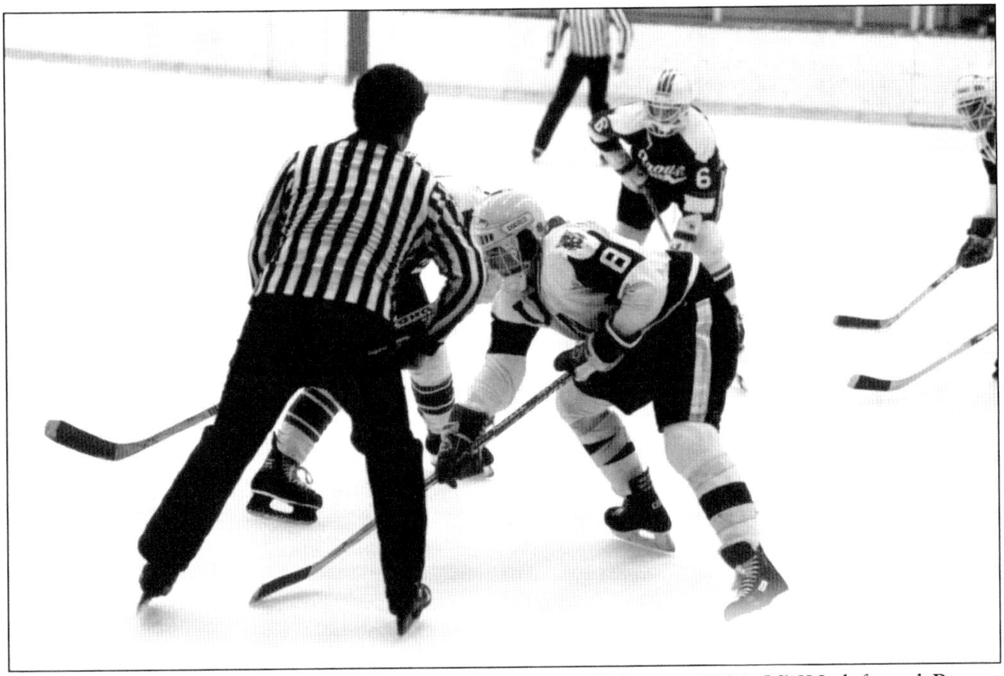

Beth Barnhill squares off against Brown University in February 1984. UNH defeated Brown 8-1. (UNH Archives.)

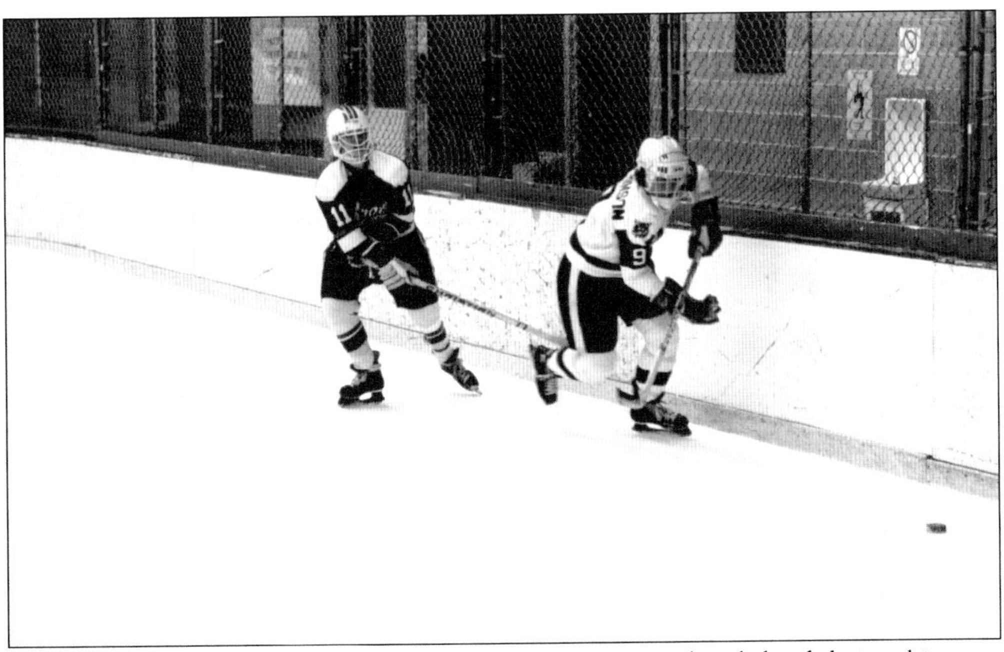

Lorie Hutchinson skates along the boards with her opponent close behind during this game against Brown in February 1984. (John Bardwell photograph. UNH Archives.)

Four

To the Whitt and Beyond

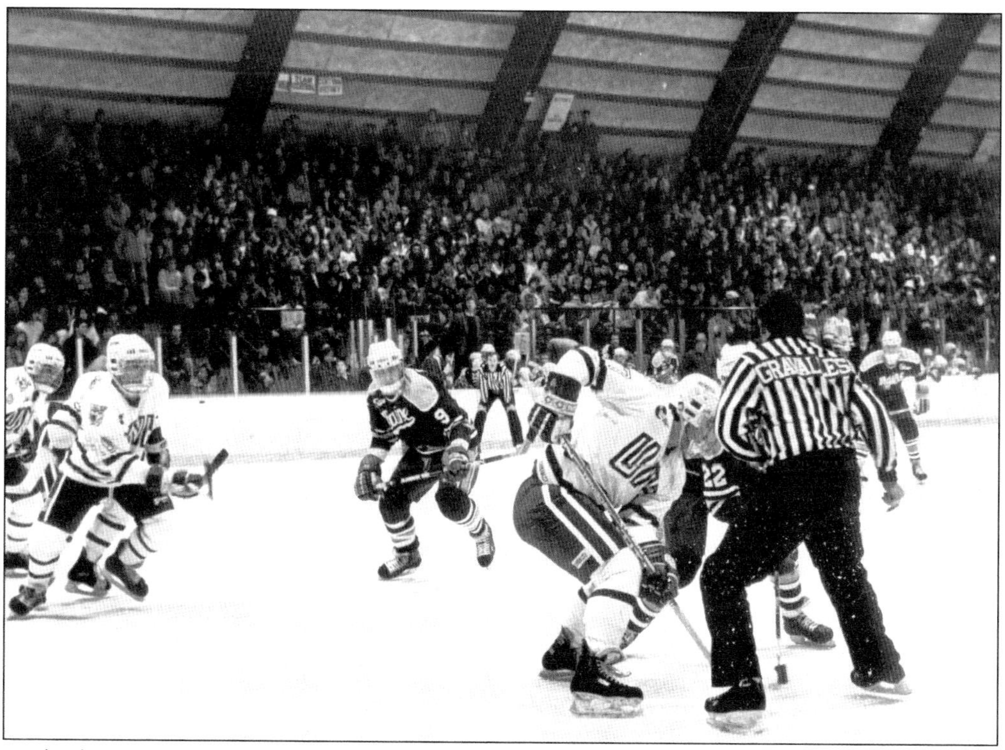

In the late 1980s, the Wildcats suffered through a succession of losing seasons. In particular, archrival Maine seemed to have the Wildcat's number. In the final game of the 1987–1988 season, UNH fell to the Black Bears 6-2. (UNH Archives.)

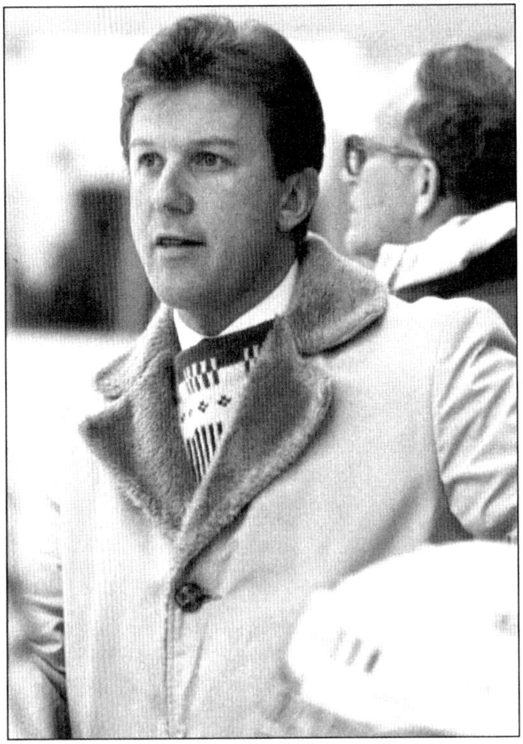

After serving as assistant coach under Charlie Holt, Bob Kullen became head coach of the Wildcats in the summer of 1986. However, Kullen suffered from a heart condition and underwent a heart transplant in 1987. He coached hockey for two more seasons and resigned in 1990 because of poor health. He died shortly thereafter. His record was 37-66-3. The Unsung Hero Award was renamed the Robert A. Kullen Award in his honor. (Hank Ellsmore photograph. UNH Archives.)

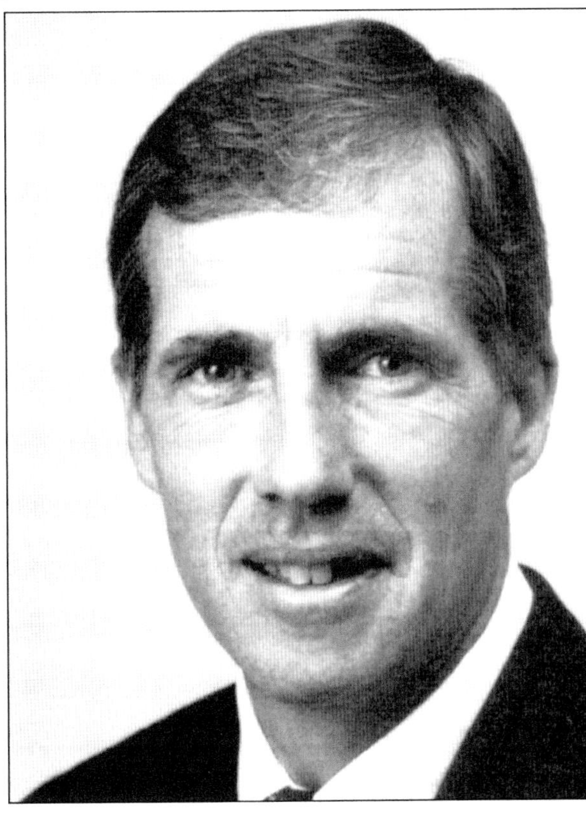

David O'Connor was an assistant coach under Charlie Holt from 1976 to 1987, a recruiter for hockey and football, and a football coach from 1972 through to 1976. He is currently senior associate director of athletics at UNH. He took over as head coach for hockey in the 1987–1988 season, when Kullen stepped down for health reasons. (UNH Archives.)

Dom Amodeo played at UNH from 1988 to 1992. He was named to the All-American second team in 1992 and awarded the Guy Smith Award in 1992. Amodeo is currently number 15 in the Wildcat Century Club, with 168 points and number 7 for points in a single season (68 in 1991–1992). (Ron Bergeron photograph. UNH Photographic Services.)

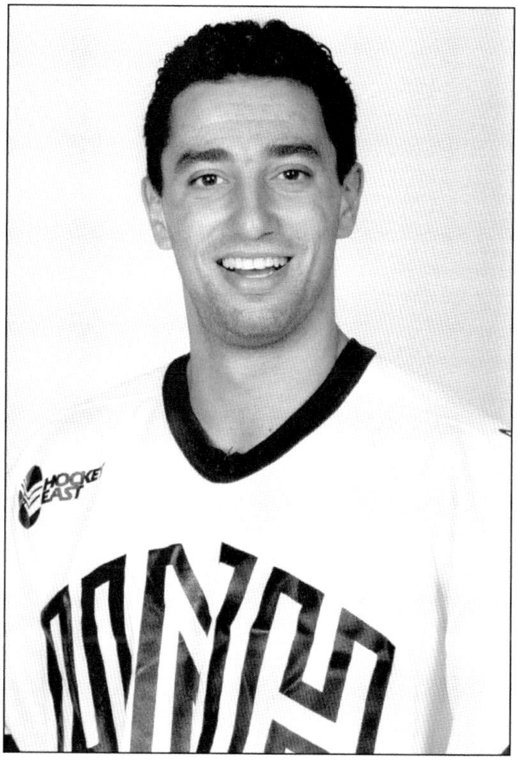

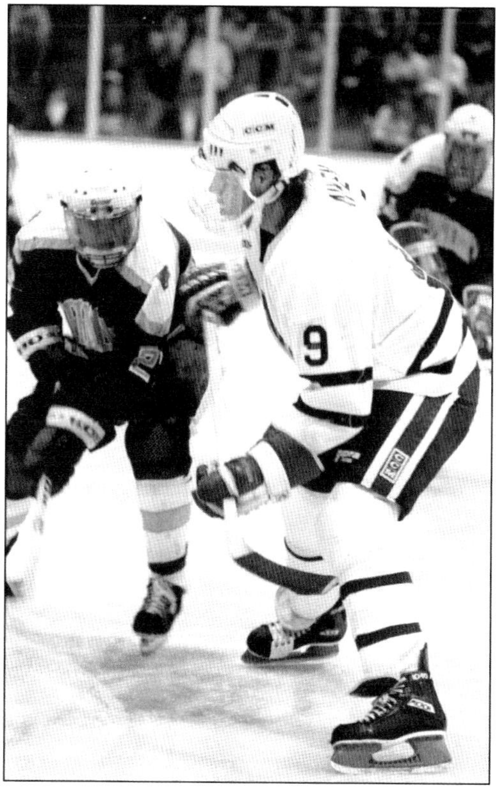

Forward David Aitken of St. Andrews, New Brunswick, provided the Wildcats with much needed firepower in the late 1980s. Aitken finished his career with 112 career points. (UNH Archives.)

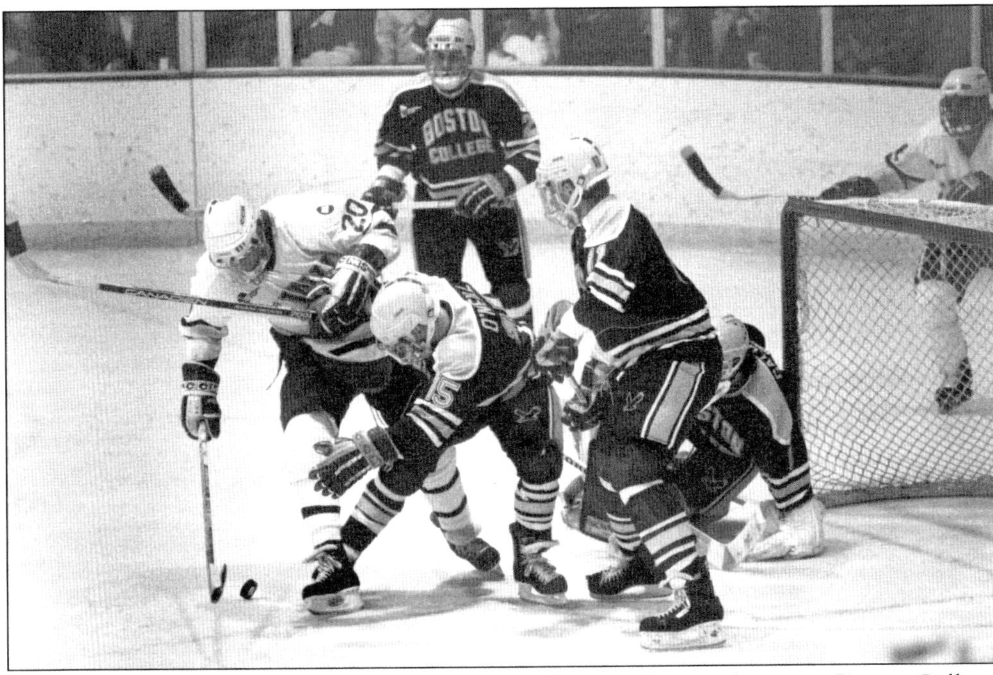

Scott Morrow (No. 28) and Savo Mitrovic (No. 26) are on the attack against Boston College. Morrow and Mitrovic contributed greatly to UNH men's hockey from 1988 through 1992. Both were awarded the Charles E. Holt Coaches Award; Morrow in 1991, Mitrovic in 1992. This award is given to the player who made large contributions to the team, whether on the ice or off, as voted by the coaching staff. (UNH Archives.)

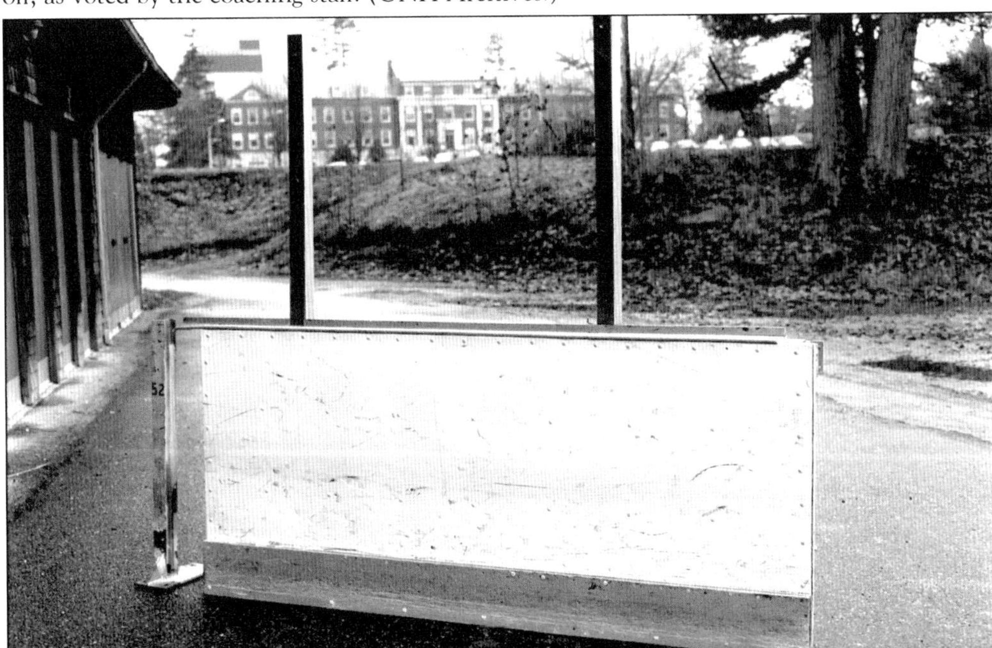

This old board was removed from Snively Arena during renovation of the rink in November 1989. (Ron Bergeron photograph. UNH Photographic Services.)

Shown is the program from the 25th anniversary year of Snively Arena. The anniversary game was played on February 16, 1990. UNH lost to Maine 3-2. (UNH Archives.)

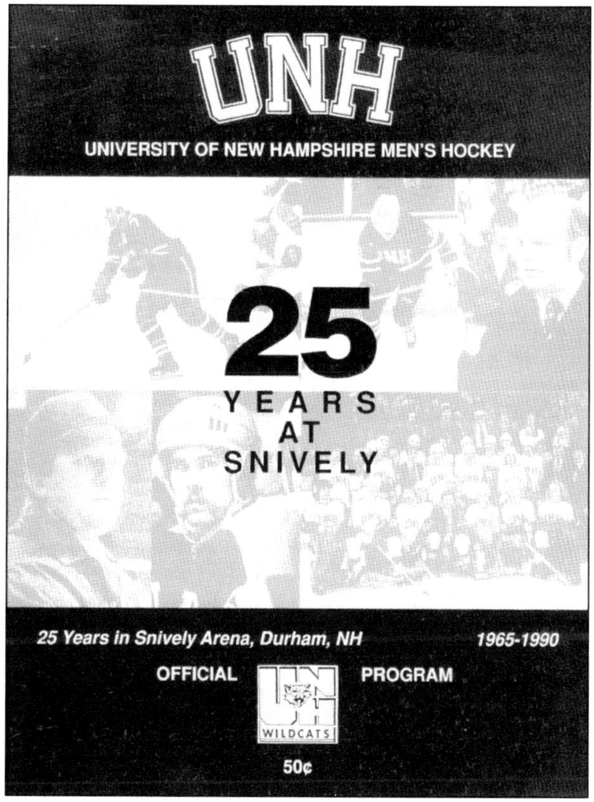

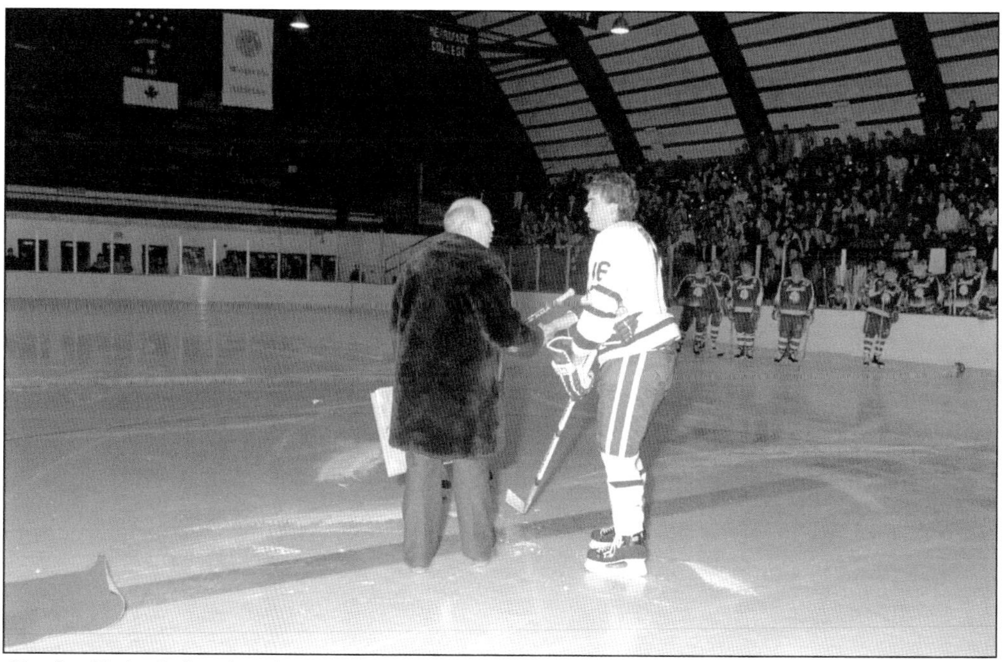

Charlie Holt shakes hands with defenseman Chris Grassie, captain of the 1989–1990 team, after the honorary puck drop in January 1990. Grassie was later awarded the Charles E. Holt Coaches Award. (Ron Bergeron photograph. UNH Photographic Services.)

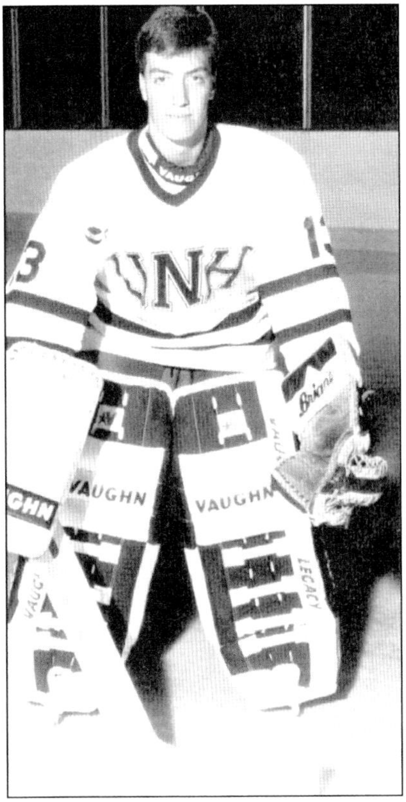

Goaltender Jeff Levy was an impact player in his freshman year. He won the Hockey East Rookie of the week award five times and posted the best save percentage in the nation (.905). He was named All-American, second team, in 1991. He is the fifth goalie in career goals against average, with an average of 3.26, and eleventh in career saves, with 1,746. (UNH Archives.)

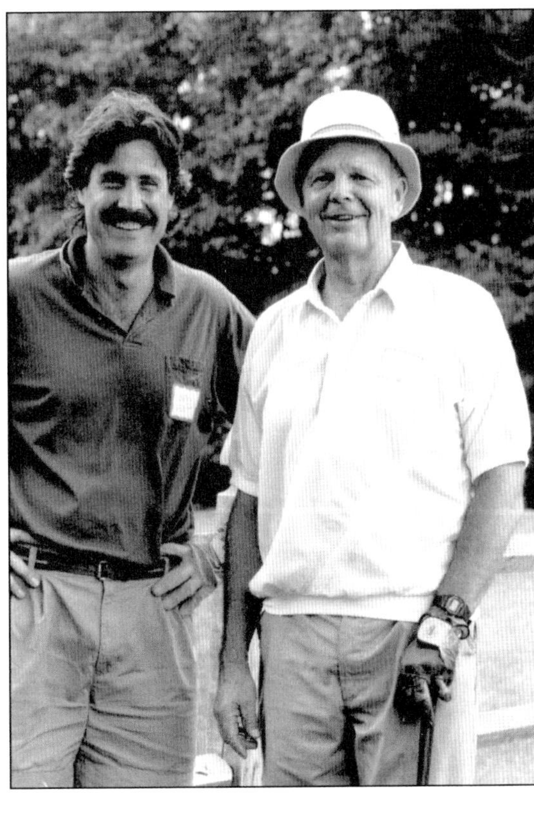

Charlie and Brad Holt gather at the UNH Friends of Hockey annual golf outing. Brad Holt (left) played for the Wildcats from 1976 to 1979. The Friends of Hockey was established in the fall of 1972 and has supported UNH hockey through the years. It is now the largest group of its kind on the East Coast. The group sponsors such activities as the annual golf outing and the annual alumni game. Incidentally, Charlie Holt coached the UNH golf team for several years. (UNH Archives.)

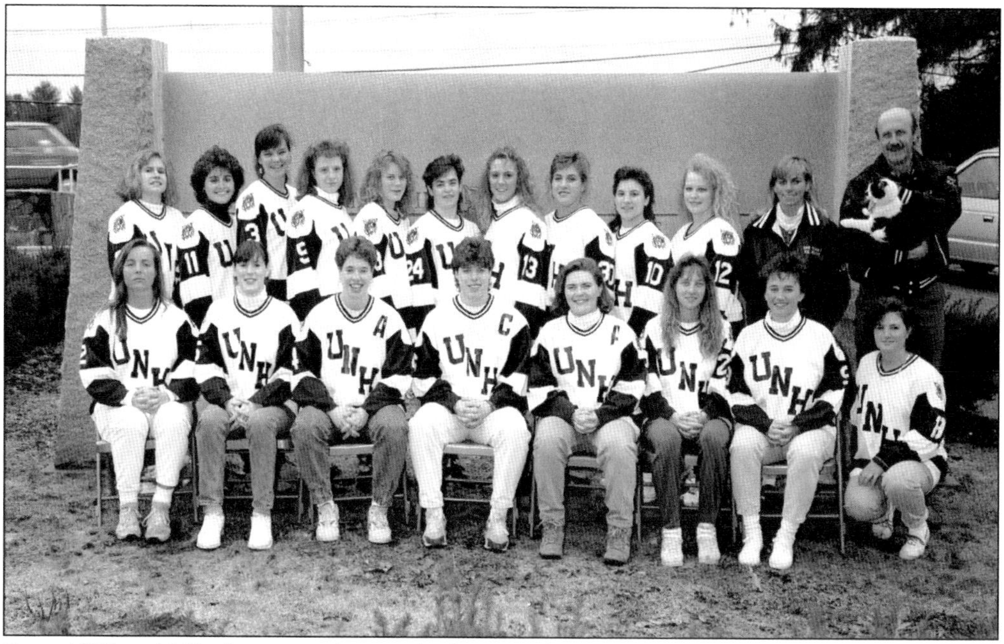

From 1991 to 1992, the women's team had a record of 15-6-2 and broke many records besides. This team featured players such as Karen Bye, Colleen Coyne, and Sue Merz, all of whom were on the gold-winning U.S. Olympic team in the 1998 Olympics. Bye earned a career point total of 164. Annie Camins set records for most goals (three), most assists (four), and most points (five) in a single period. Wendy Tatarouns had 149 career points, putting her in the UNH top 10. Goalie Erin Whitten finished with 51 career wins, which ranks fourth in UNH records books. (UNH Photographic Services.)

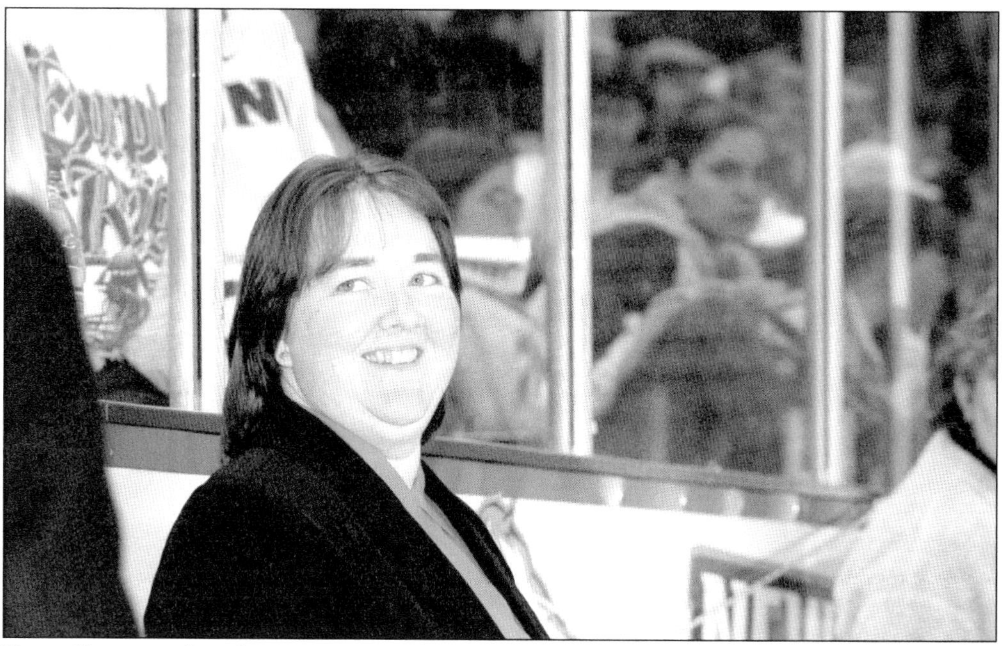

Karen Kay served as the women's coach from 1992 through 2001. She amassed a 215-90-25 record. (Lisa Nugent photograph. UNH Photographic Services.)

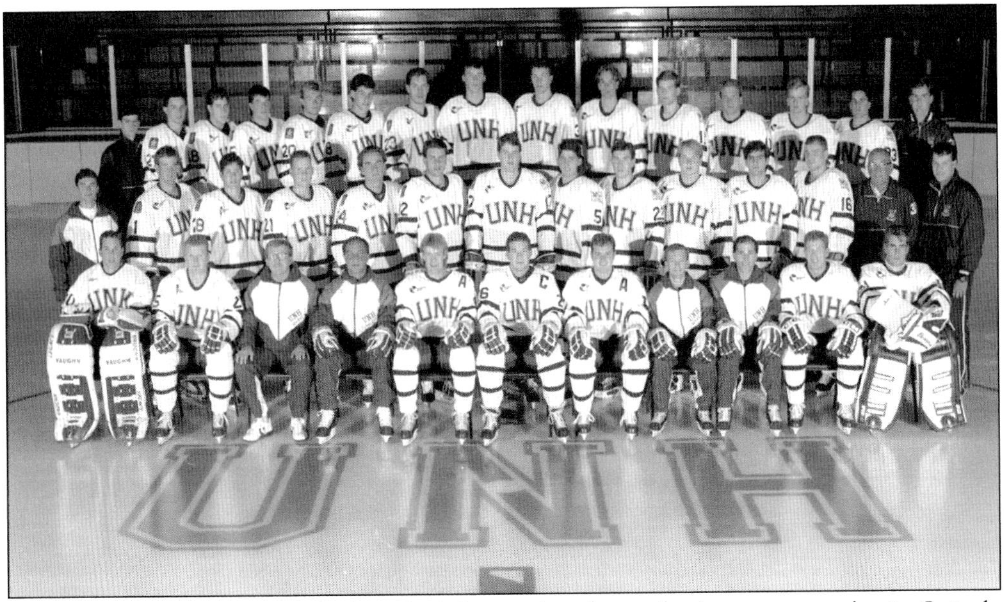

The men's 1993–1994 team had a 25-12-3 record and was the last team to play in Snively Arena. Tim Murray, a member of the team, was named to the All-American second team in 1997 and was awarded the Leclerc Trophy in 1997. Other members of this team—Mike Sullivan, Glenn Stewart, Nick Poole, Tom Nolan, Eric Boguniecki, and Eric Flinton—became Wildcat Century Club members during their careers at UNH. (UNH Photographic Services.)

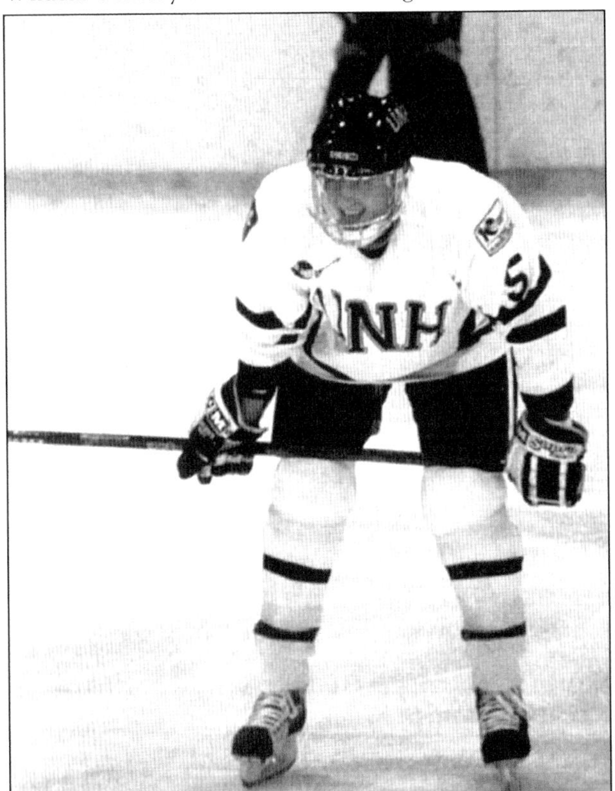

Eric Royal was a star player and three-time most valuable player for Spaulding High School in Rochester, New Hampshire, and then played for UNH from 1991 to 1995. He was chosen by his team to receive the Guy Smith Award for Best Offensive Player in 1995. (UNH Archives.)

Tricia Dunn played for the Wildcats from 1992 to 1996 and finished her career with 117 points. A five-time member of the U.S. National team, she played on both the 1998 and 2002 U.S. Olympic teams, earning gold in Nagano and silver in Salt Lake City. (UNH Photographic Services.)

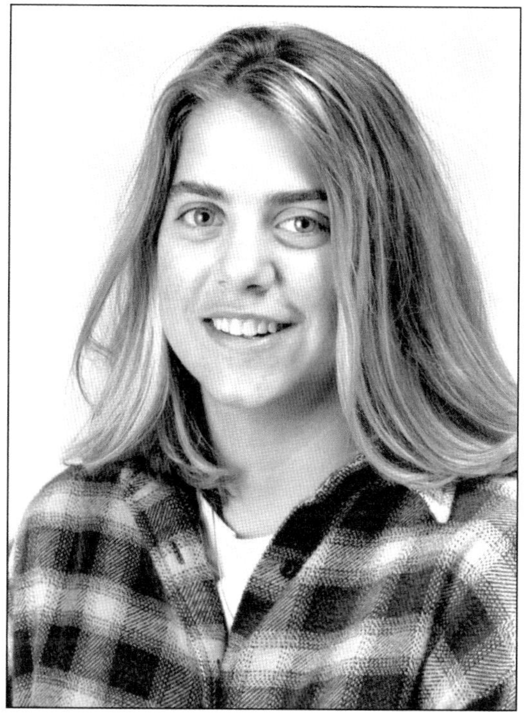

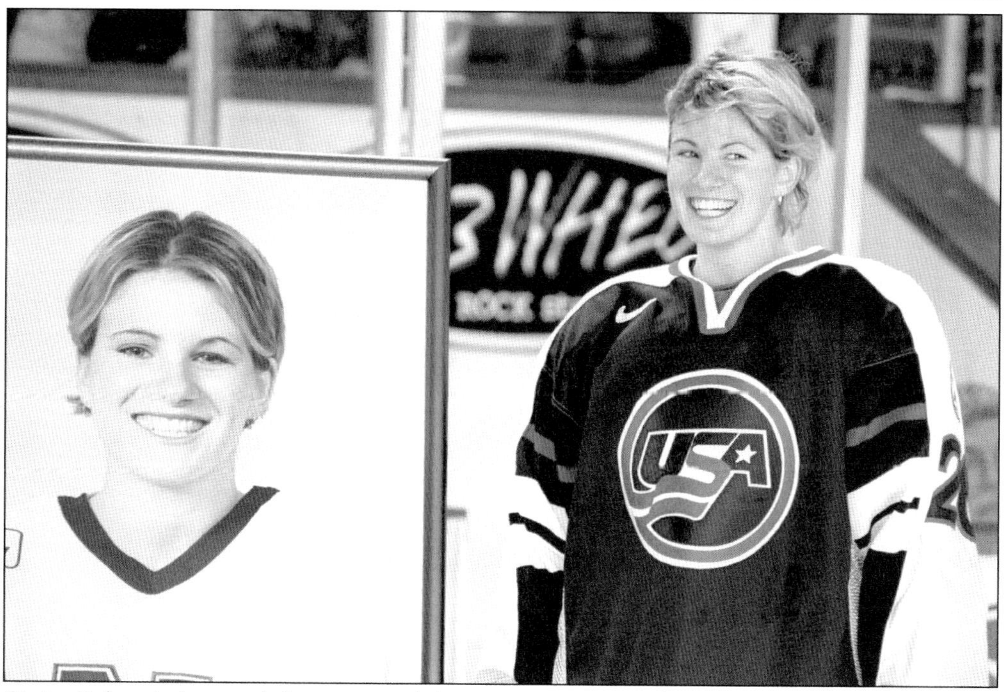

Carisa Zaban is honored during an exhibition game in March 2001 between UNH and the United States National team. Zaban passed Kathy Bryant's scoring record in 2000 and is now the top career scorer with 263 points (118 goals) and is tied with Bryant for most career assists (145). She was named All-American in 2000 and a Patty Kazmaier Memorial Award finalist. (Lisa Nugent photograph. UNH Photographic Services.)

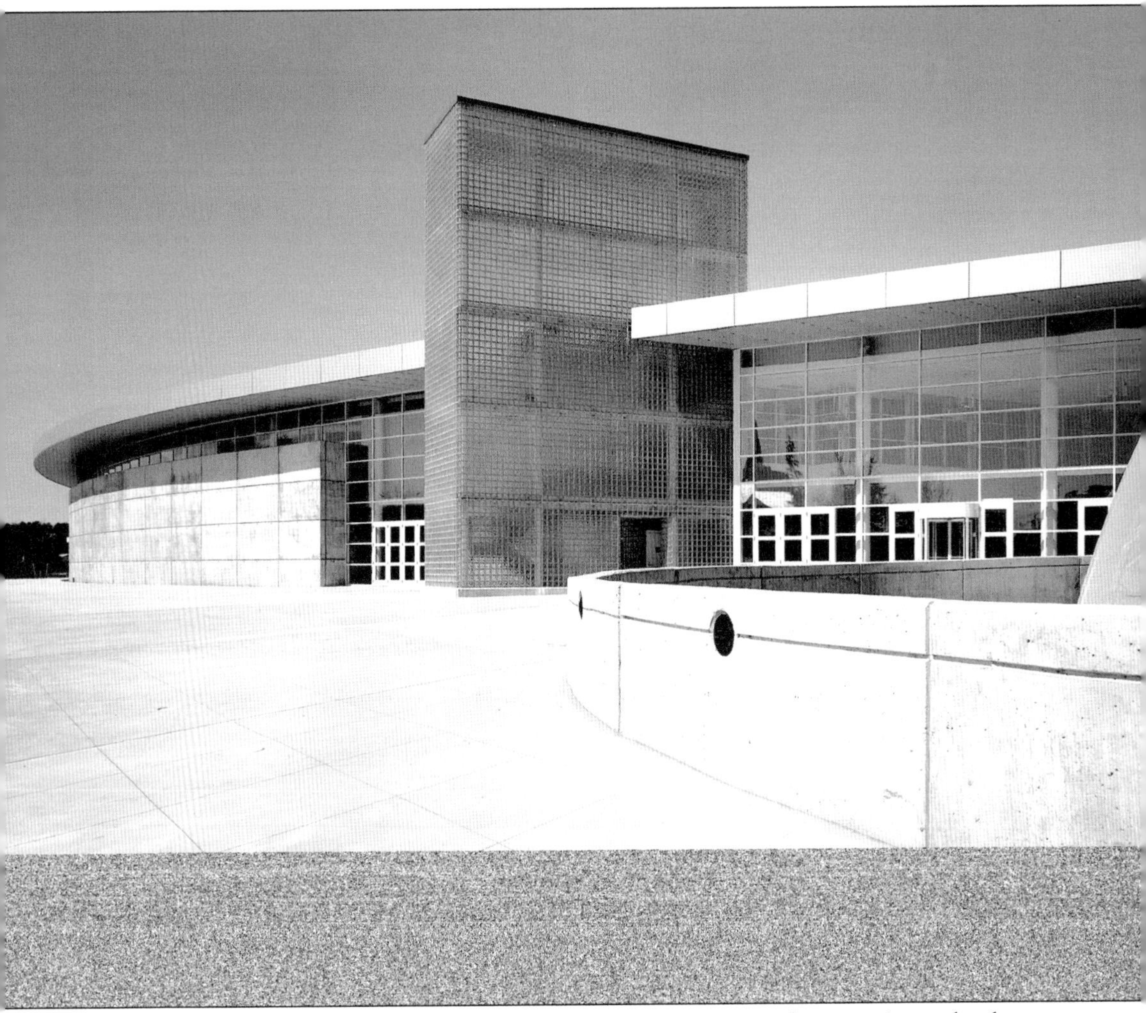

Snively Arena closed at the end of the 1993–1994 season with a men's ice hockey team double-overtime win over Boston College, the longest game ever played in Snively. The new home for UNH hockey would be the Whittemore Center. The new arena would seat 6,000 for hockey, nearly double the capacity of Snively. (UNH Photographic Services.)

This is a program from the inaugural season at the Whittemore Center. (UNH Archives.)

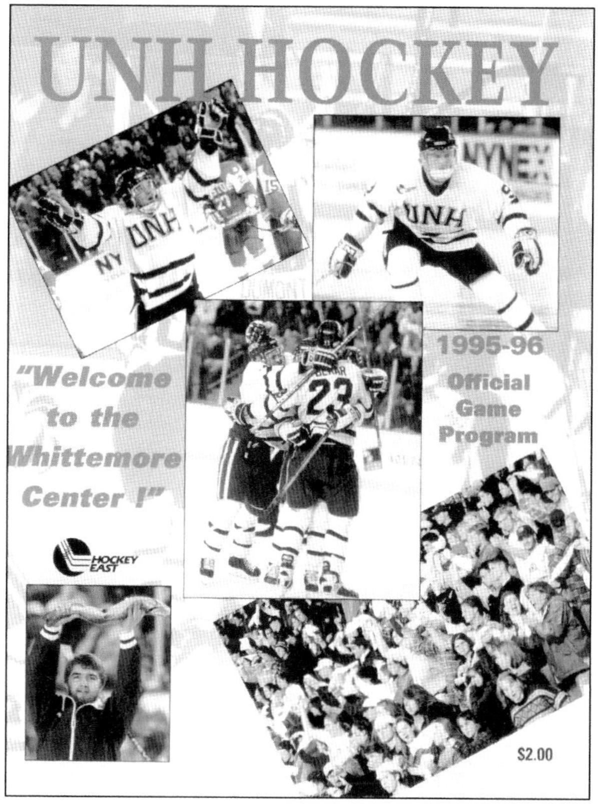

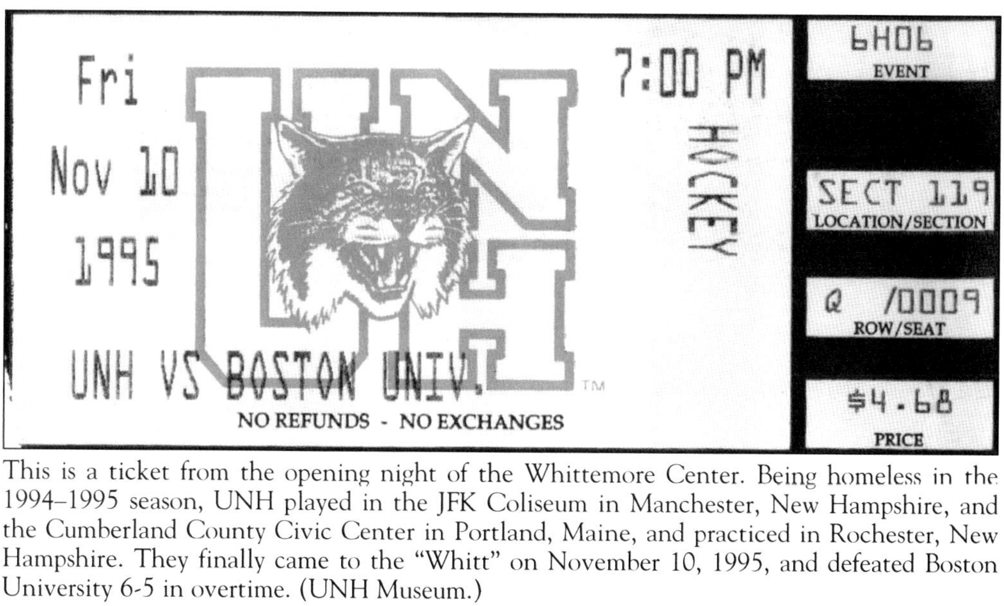

This is a ticket from the opening night of the Whittemore Center. Being homeless in the 1994–1995 season, UNH played in the JFK Coliseum in Manchester, New Hampshire, and the Cumberland County Civic Center in Portland, Maine, and practiced in Rochester, New Hampshire. They finally came to the "Whitt" on November 10, 1995, and defeated Boston University 6-5 in overtime. (UNH Museum.)

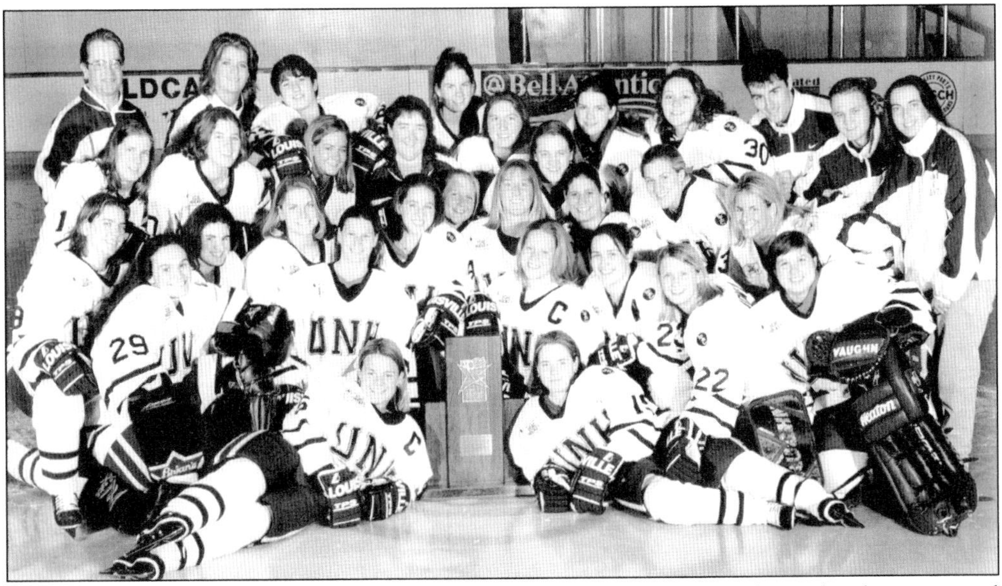

Members of the women's 1997–1998 team pose with their trophy from the first national championship held in 1998 by the American Women's College Hockey Alliance (AWCHA). They defeated Brown University 4-1. Their record for the regular season was 31-5-3. (UNH Photographic Services.)

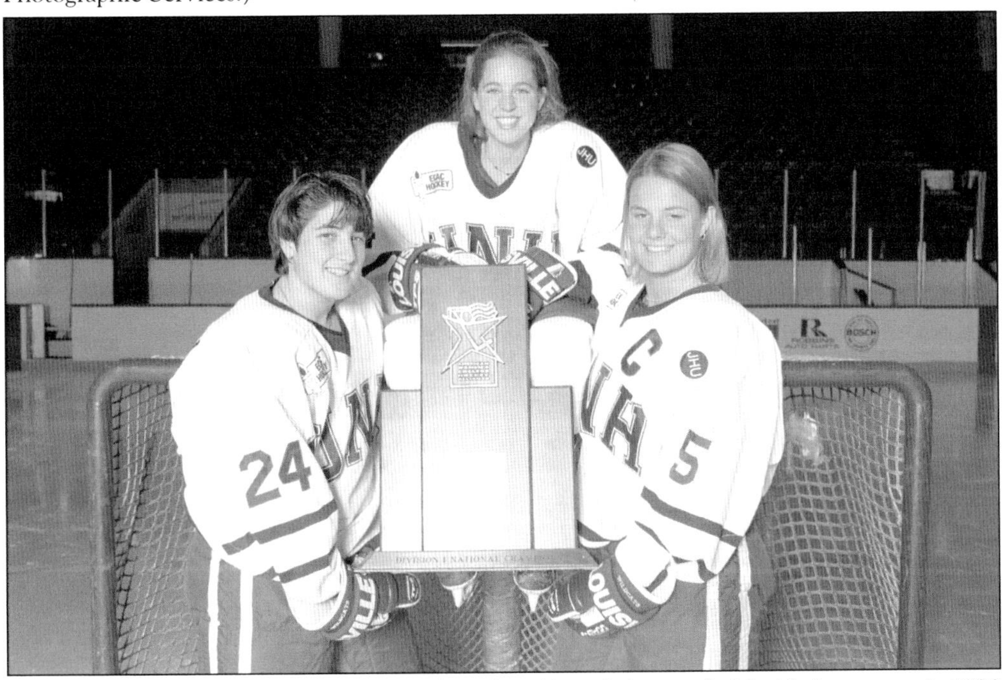

Nicki Luongo, Winnie Brodt, and Brandy Fisher (from left to right) hold the women's 1998 first national championship trophy. Fisher won the Patty Kazmaier Memorial Award in 1998, the first year it was awarded, and is the third top career scorer with 240 points. Luongo was a Patty Kazmaier Memorial Award finalist in 1999 and is sixth all-time defensive scorer, with 84 points. She holds the record for most assists in a single game (seven). In addition, she was named All-American in 1998 and 1999. (UNH Photographic Services.)

Jason Krog was co-captain of the 1998–1999 team. Krog is UNH's only Hobey Baker Memorial Award winner and was Hockey East Player of the Year. He is the second all-time point scorer with 238 points and holds the record for most assists, 144. He was named a Hobey Baker finalist in 1998, All-American twice in 1997 and in 1999, three-time winner of the Guy Smith Award for best offensive player, Most Exciting Player in 1999, and Leclerc Trophy winner in 1999. (Ron Bergeron photograph. UNH Photographic Services.)

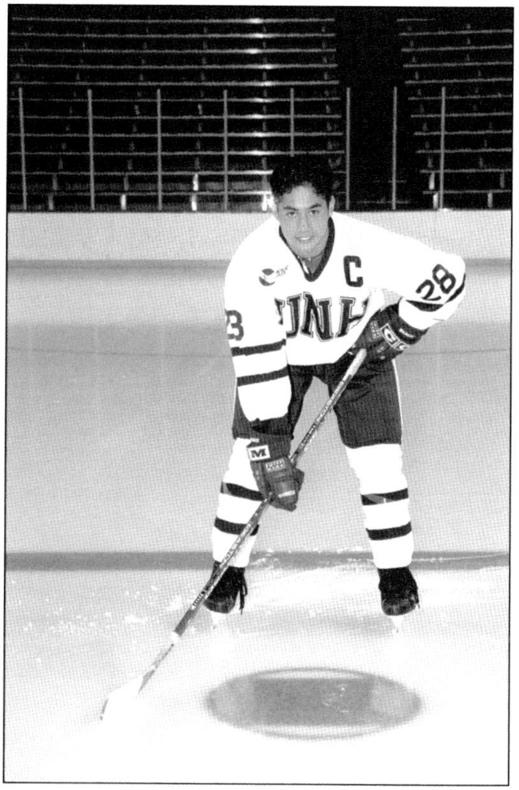

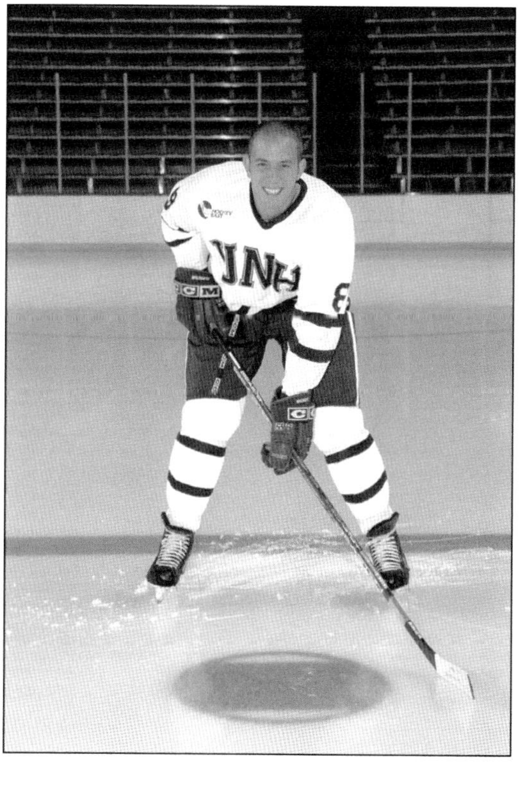

Jayme Filipowicz was awarded the Best Defenseman Award in both 1998 and 1999. He and goalie Ty Conklin were named All-American, second team, in 1999. (Ron Bergeron photograph. UNH Photographic Services.)

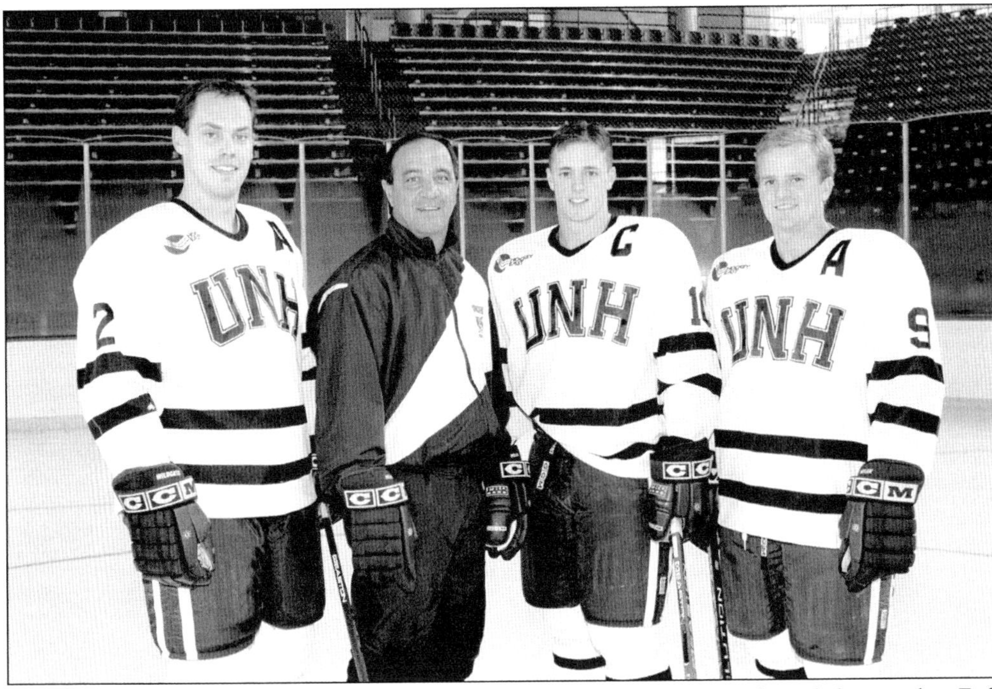

The captain and assistant captains from the 1997–1998 team were, from left to right, Erik Johnson, Dick Umile, Mark Mowers, and Tom Nolan. Mowers twice received the Leclerc Trophy as most valuable player and was named All-American in 1998. Johnson was named the Most Improved Player in 1995, and Nolan received the Charles E. Holt Coaches Award in 1998. (Ron Bergeron photograph. UNH Photographic Services.)

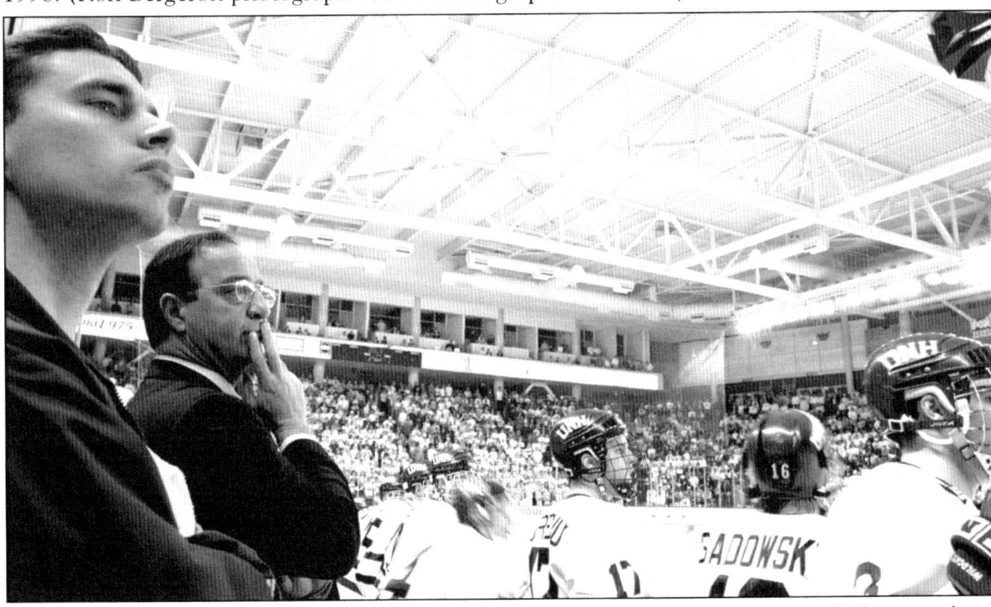

Dick Umile (second from left) watches the action during a 1999 game. Umile became head coach of the Wildcats in 1990 and has amassed a 279-138-37 record. He has won 20 or more games in 10 of his 12 seasons and has been named Coach of the Year by Hockey East four times. (Lisa Nugent photograph. UNH Photographic Services.)

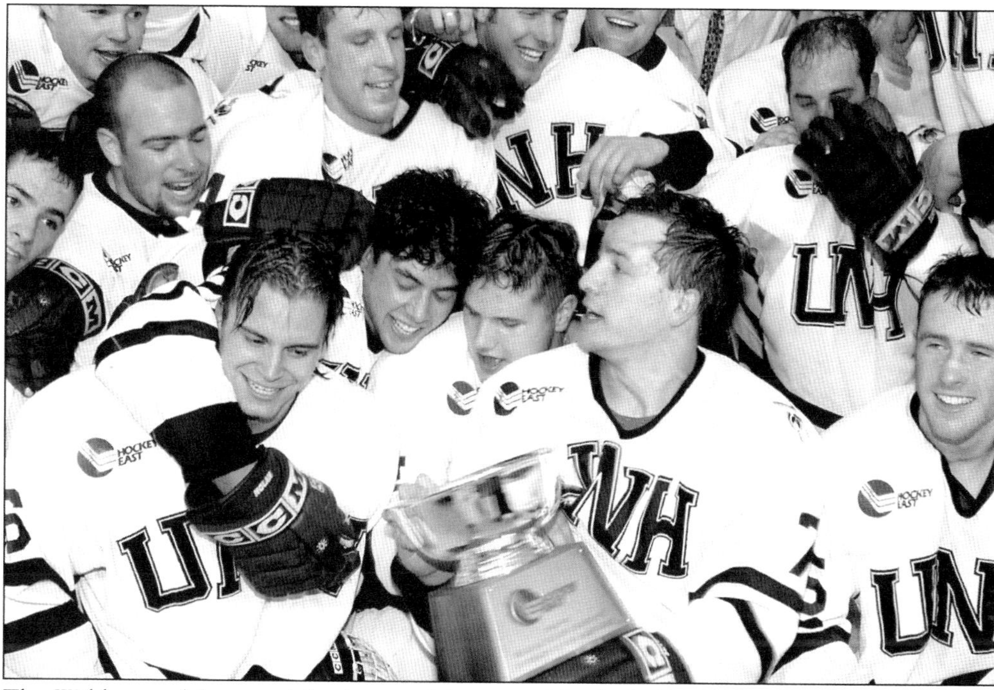

The Wildcats celebrate a 4-1 win over Maine on March 3, 1999. The win earned them the Hockey East regular season championship. It also marked Dick Umile's 200th career win. (Lisa Nugent photograph. UNH Photographic Services.)

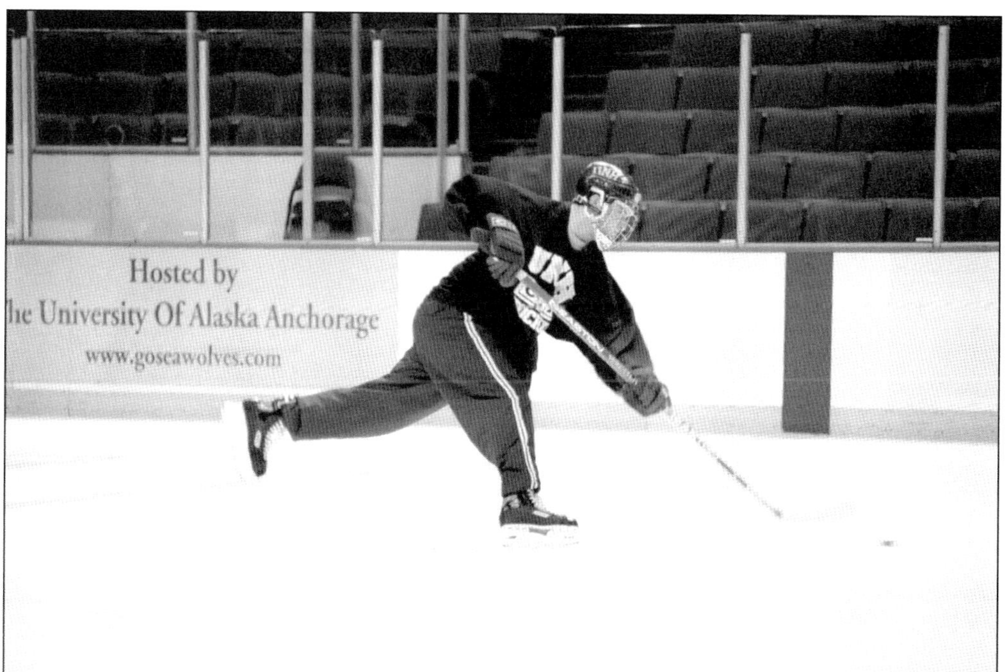

The Wildcats warm up on the Anahiem Pond in Anahiem, California, site of the 1999 Frozen Four. (Lisa Nugent photograph. UNH Photographic Services.)

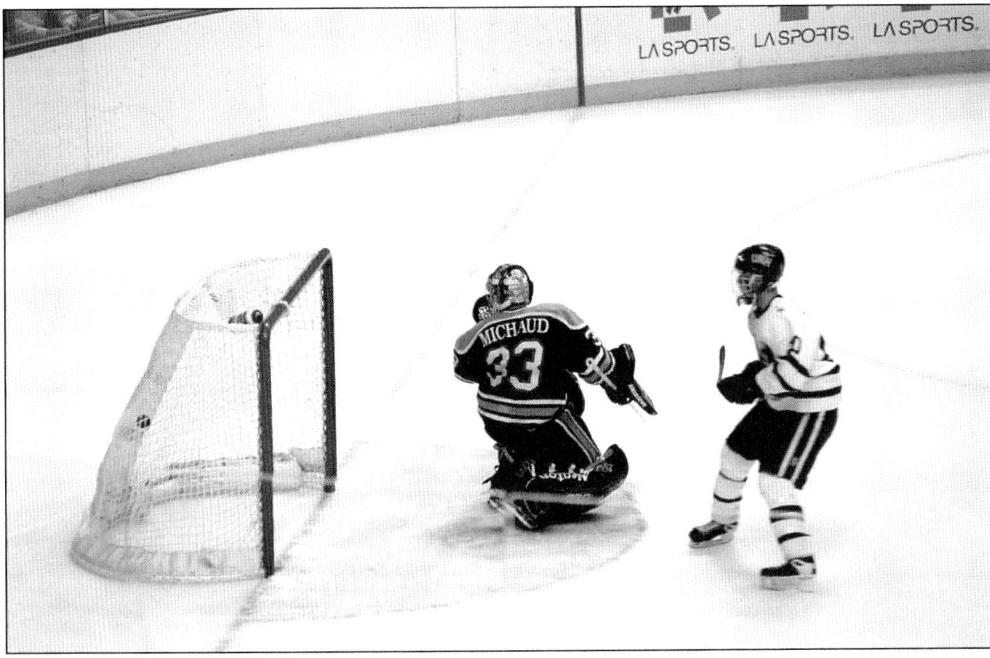

Mike Souza scores against Maine in the NCAA 1999 final on April 3, 1999. He held UNH's records for most career and most consecutive games played (156) until surpassed by Darren Haydar in 2002. Souza graduated with a career point total of 156. (Lisa Nugent photograph. UNH Photographic Services.)

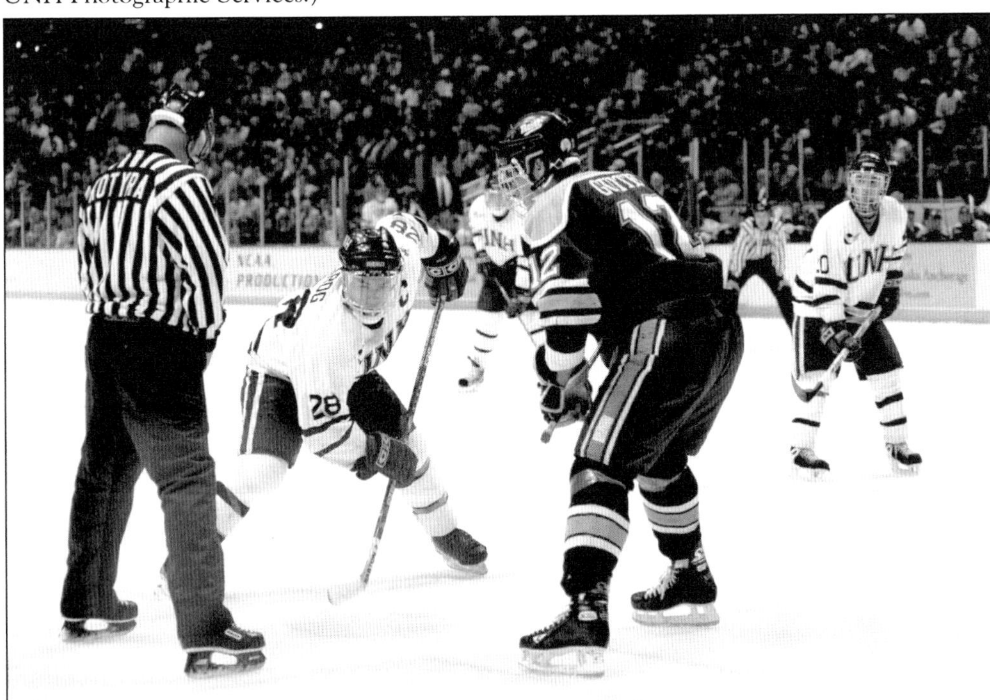

Jason Krog faces off against Maine in the NCAA finals. Maine won 3-2 in overtime to earn the national championship. (Lisa Nugent photograph. UNH Photographic Services.)

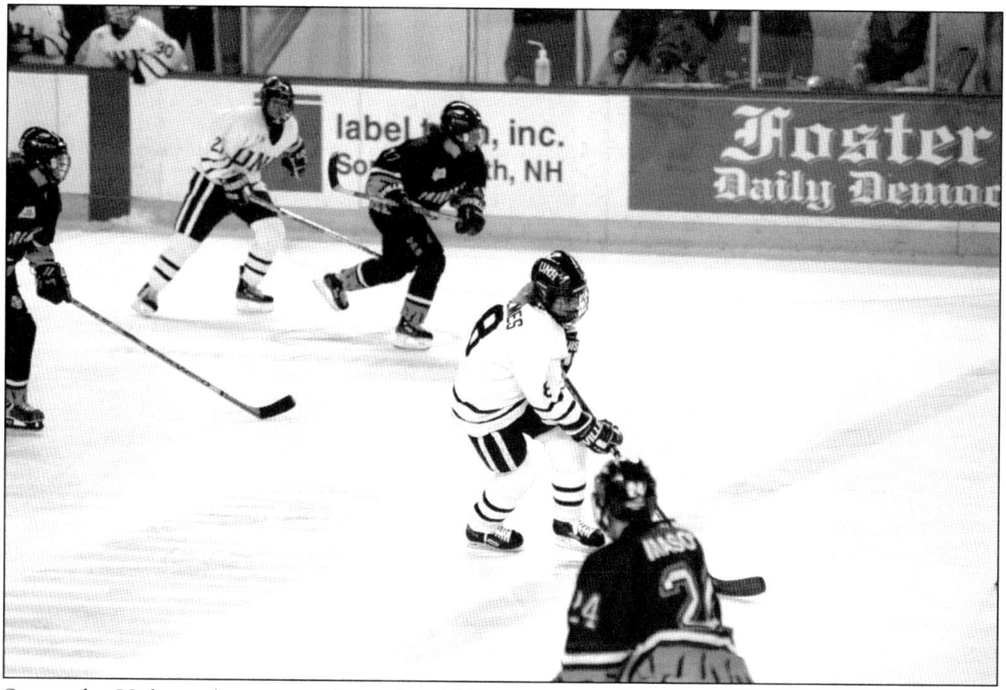

Samantha Holmes skates in a November 1999 game against Princeton. Holmes is the fifth top career scorer, with 185 points. (Lisa Nugent photograph. UNH Photographic Services.)

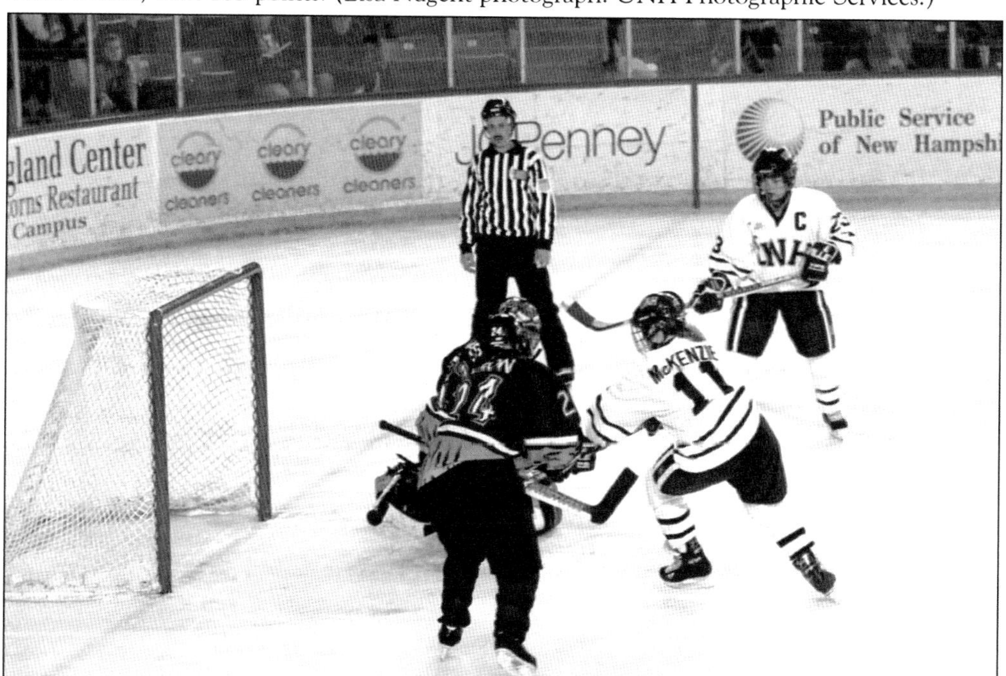

Melissa McKenzie tries to score a goal against Princeton in March 1999 while Kim Knox looks on. McKenzie holds the nineteenth spot in the Women's Century Club with her 120 career points Carisa Zaban stands at the top spot in the club with 263 points. (Lisa Nugent photograph. UNH Photographic Services.)

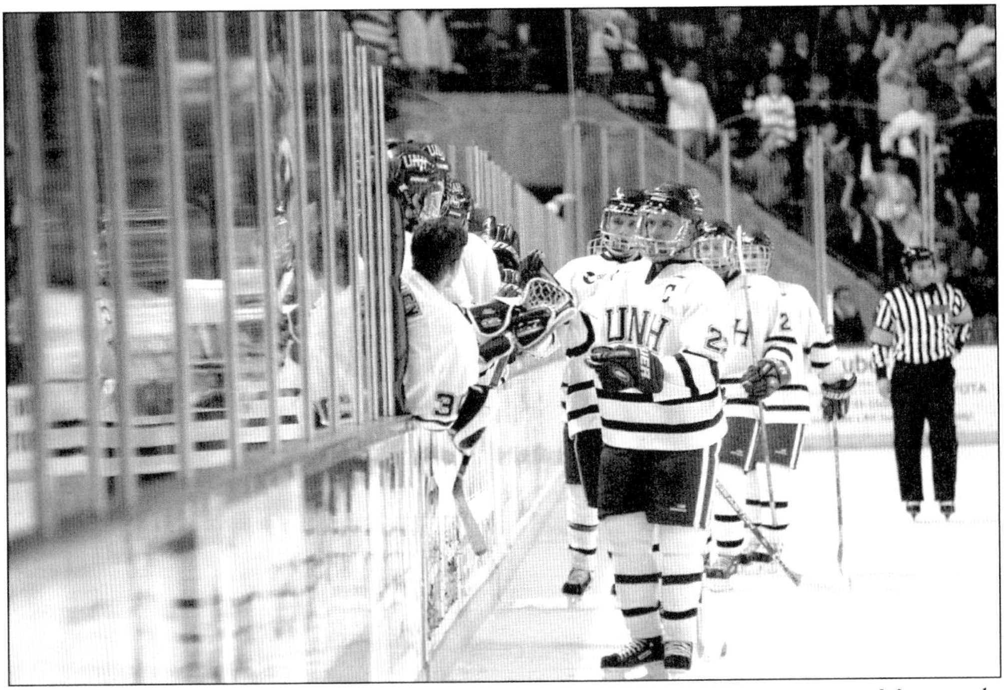

The men's ice hockey team takes a breather during a January 2000 game versus Merrimack. (Lisa Nugent photograph. UNH Photographic Services.)

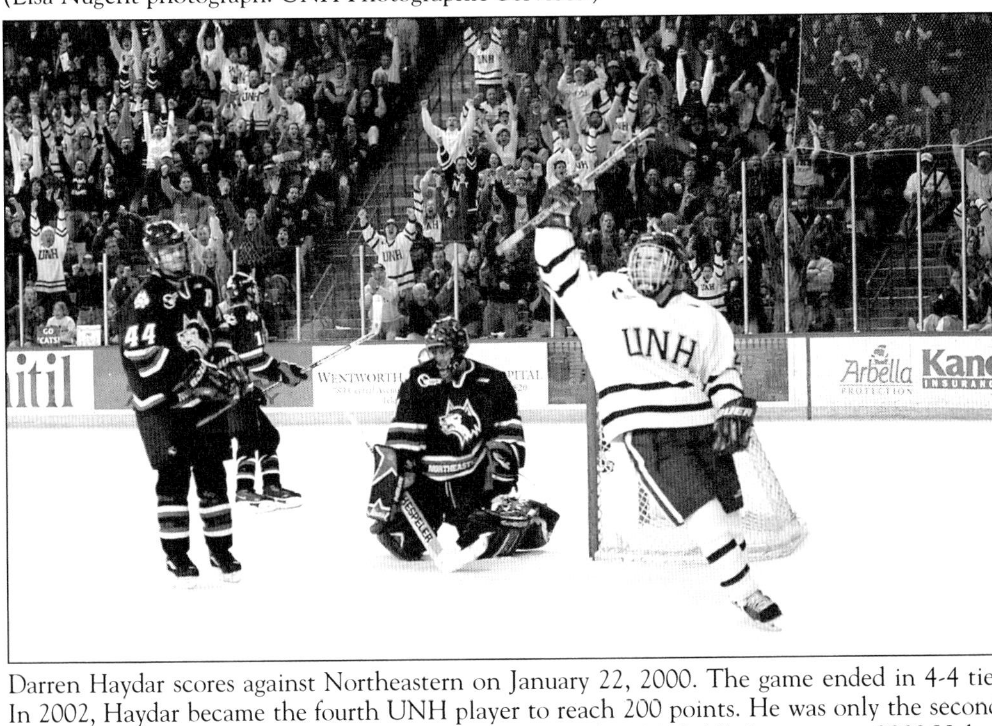

Darren Haydar scores against Northeastern on January 22, 2000. The game ended in 4-4 tie. In 2002, Haydar became the fourth UNH player to reach 200 points. He was only the second UNH player to score 100 career goals. Haydar was named an 2002 All-American, a 2002 Hobey Baker finalist, and 2002 Hockey East Player of the Year. (Lisa Nugent photograph. UNH Photographic Services.)

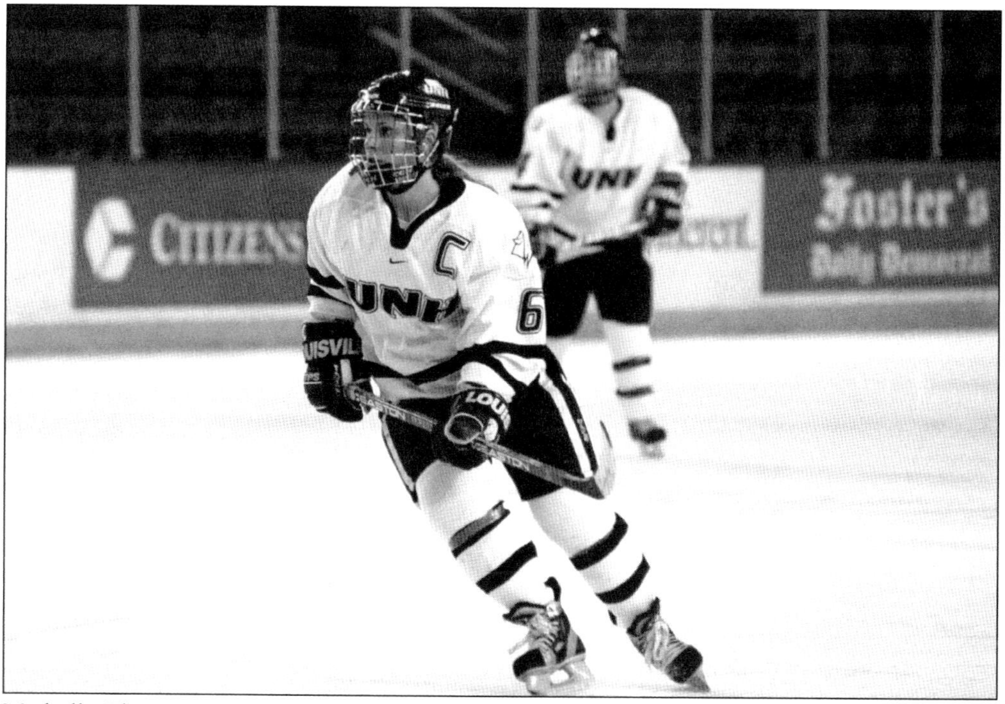

Michelle Thornton, captain of the women's 2000–2001 team, finished her career at UNH as the ninth top career scorer, with 157 points. In the 2000–2001 season, she had a six-game scoring streak and was a Patty Kazmaier Memorial Award candidate. She also played soccer at UNH and was a three-time letter winner in that sport. (Lisa Nugent photograph. UNH Photographic Services.)

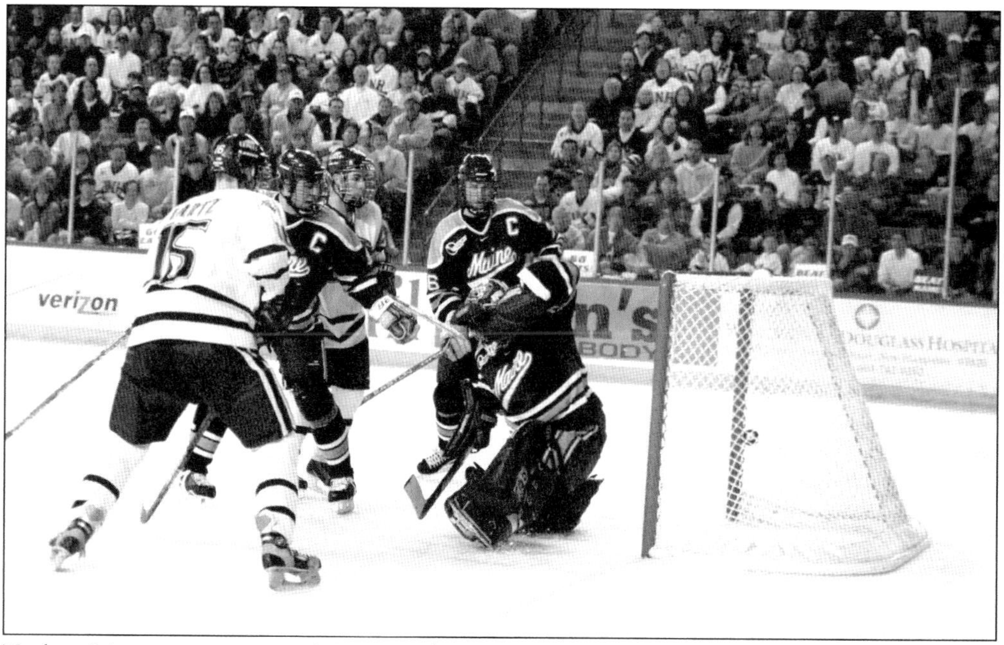

Nathan Martz scores against Maine in the January 6, 2001 game. UNH went on to win 4-0. (Lisa Nugent photograph. UNH Photographic Services.)

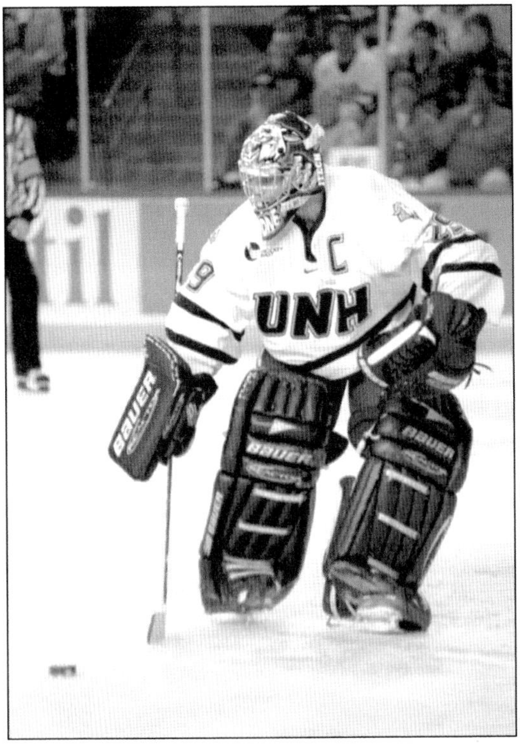

Ty Conklin is shown in action against Maine in January 2001. In his career at UNH, Conklin set records for career goals against average (2.18), career save percent (.915 over 93 games), career games (93 played), and career wins (57). Conklin was named to the All-American second team in 1999 and the All-American first team in 2000. He was a 2000 and 2001 Hobey Baker Award finalist, winner of the Walter Brown Award in 2001, and winner of the Leclerc Trophy in 2000 and 2001. (Lisa Nugent photograph. UNH Photographic Services.)

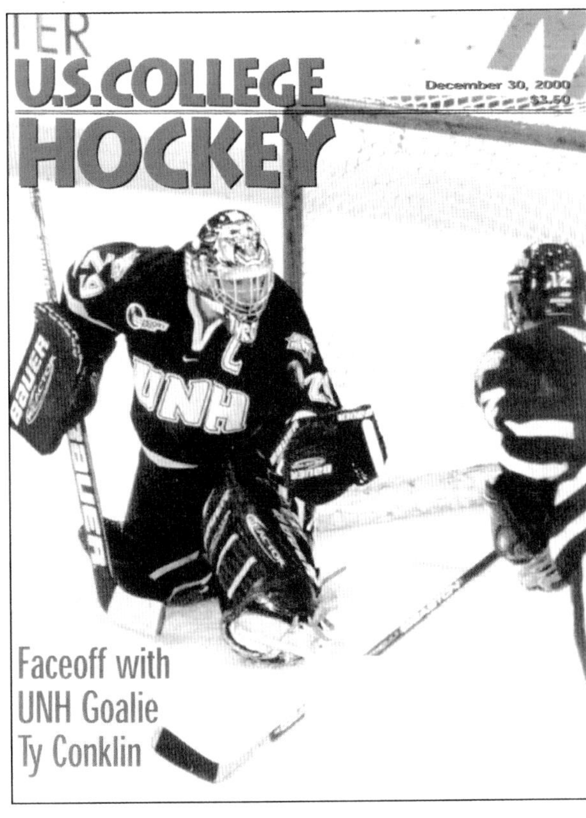

Ty Conklin is featured on the cover of the December 30, 2000 *U.S. College Hockey* magazine. (UNH Archives.)

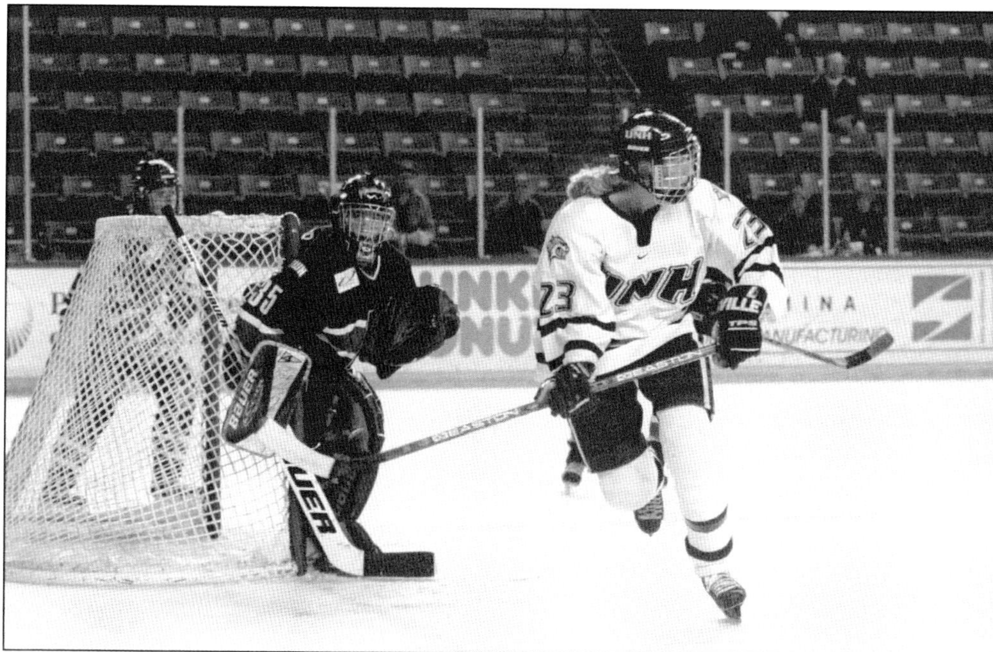

Kira Misikowetz performs in a March 2001 game against Harvard. After transferring from the University of Maine, she played two years at UNH, with a record of 67 points, 28 goals, and 39 assists. In 2002, she was a Patty Kazmaier Memorial Award candidate and was named to the New England All-Star Team. (Lisa Nugent photograph. UNH Photographic Services.)

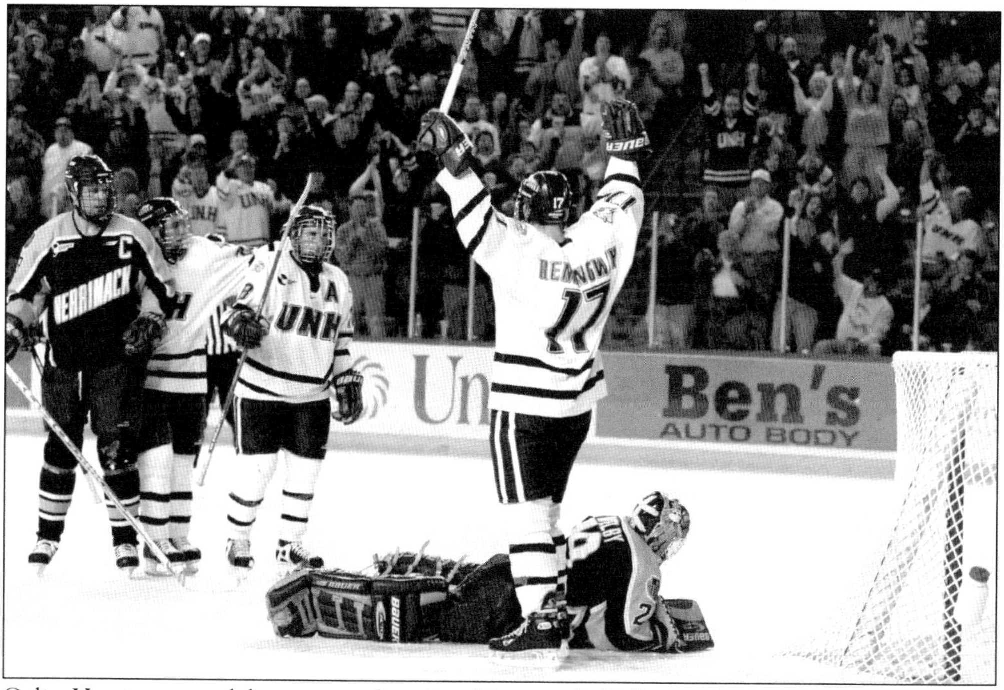

Colin Hemingway celebrates a goal against Merrimack College in January 2001. As a junior in 2001–2002, Hemingway cracked the top-10 all-time assists list and was named to the All-American team. (Lisa Nugent photograph. UNH Photographic Services.)

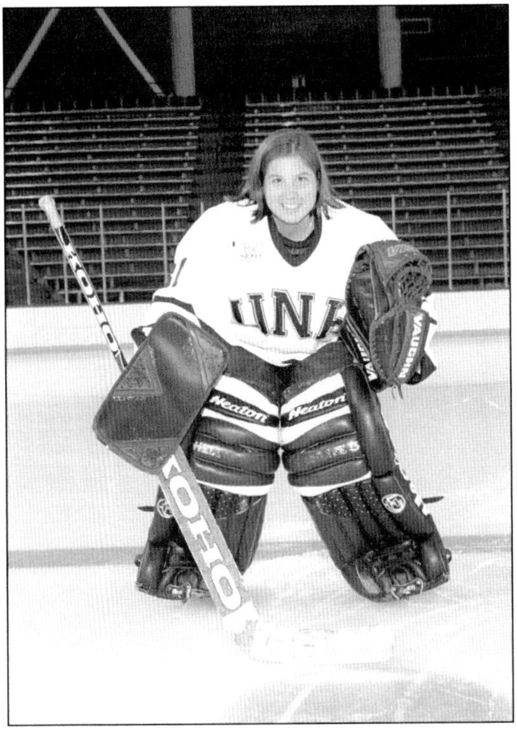

A member of the 1997–1998 team, Alicia Roberts collected several goaltending records during her years at UNH. She tops the record books with 76 wins, 2,090 career saves, and the most saves in a single game (48), a game against Harvard in 1999. (UNH Photographic Services.)

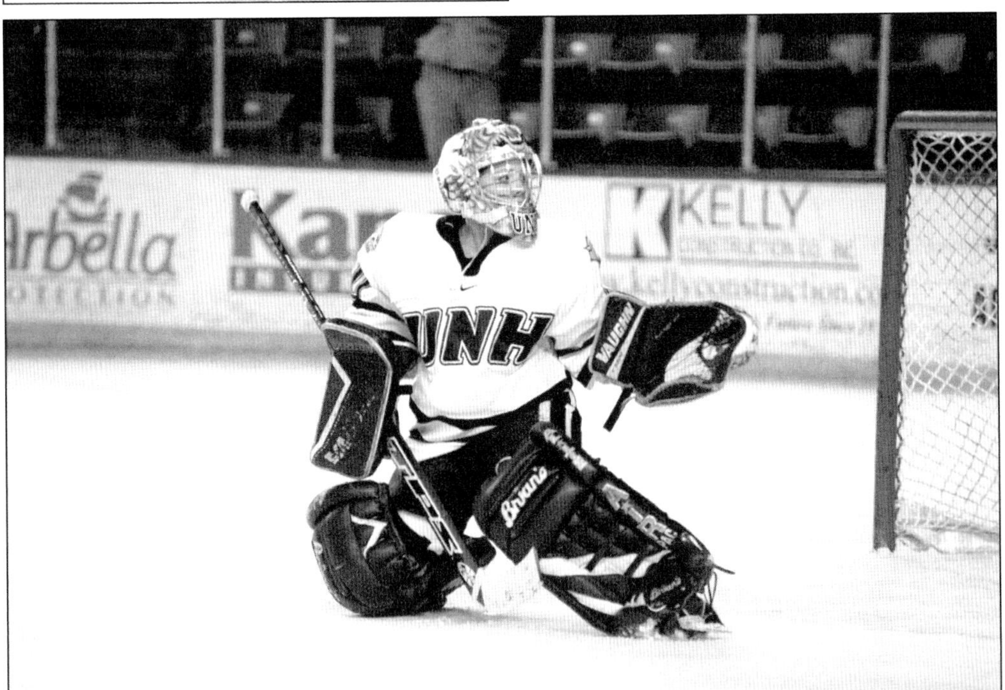

Jen Huggon defends the goal in a game against Harvard in March 2001. In the middle of her career at UNH, Huggon already held the record for most saves in a single season (841) and most saves in a single period (22), and she appeared as the fifth goalie in career saves (1,337). (Lisa Nugent photograph. UNH Photographic Services.)

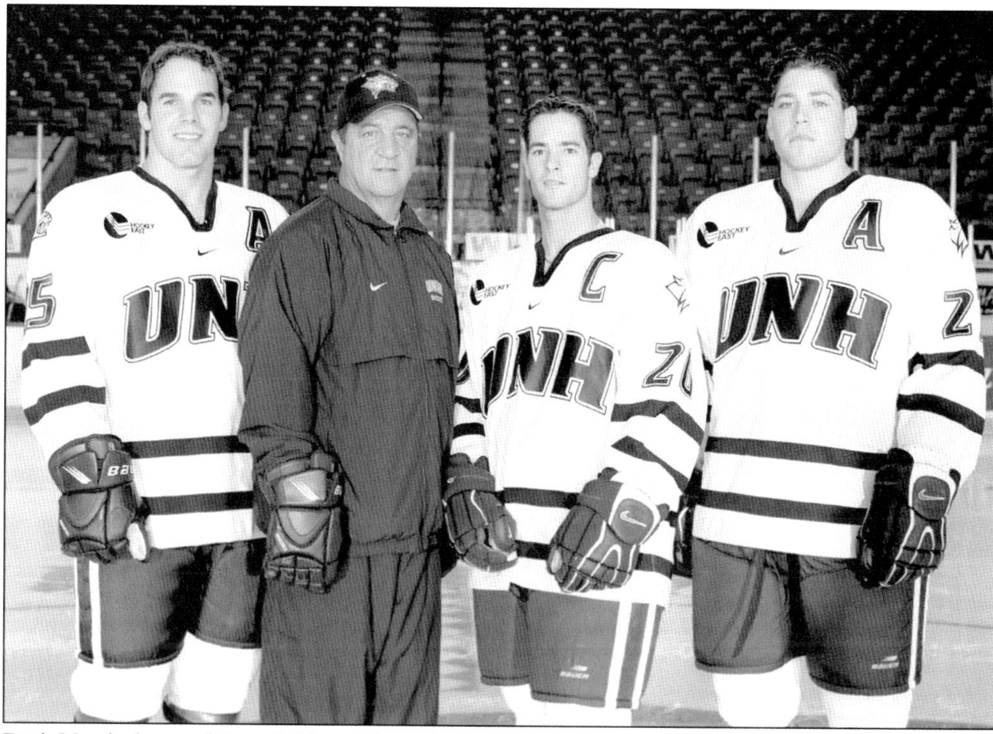

Dick Umile (second from left) stands with the captains and assistant captains of the 2001–2002 team. They are, from left to right, forward Patrick Foley, forward Darren Haydar, and defenseman Garrett Stafford. (UNH Photographic Services.)

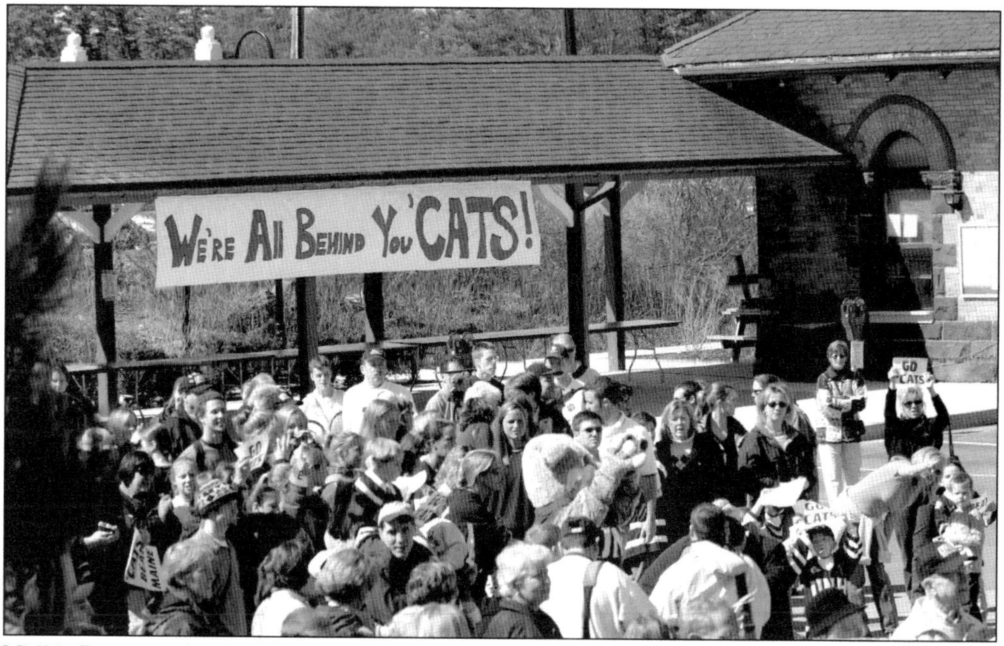

UNH Fans at the UNH Dairy Bar rally to support the men's ice hockey team as it departs for the 2002 Frozen Four in St. Paul, Minnesota. (Lisa Nugent photograph. UNH Photographic Services.)

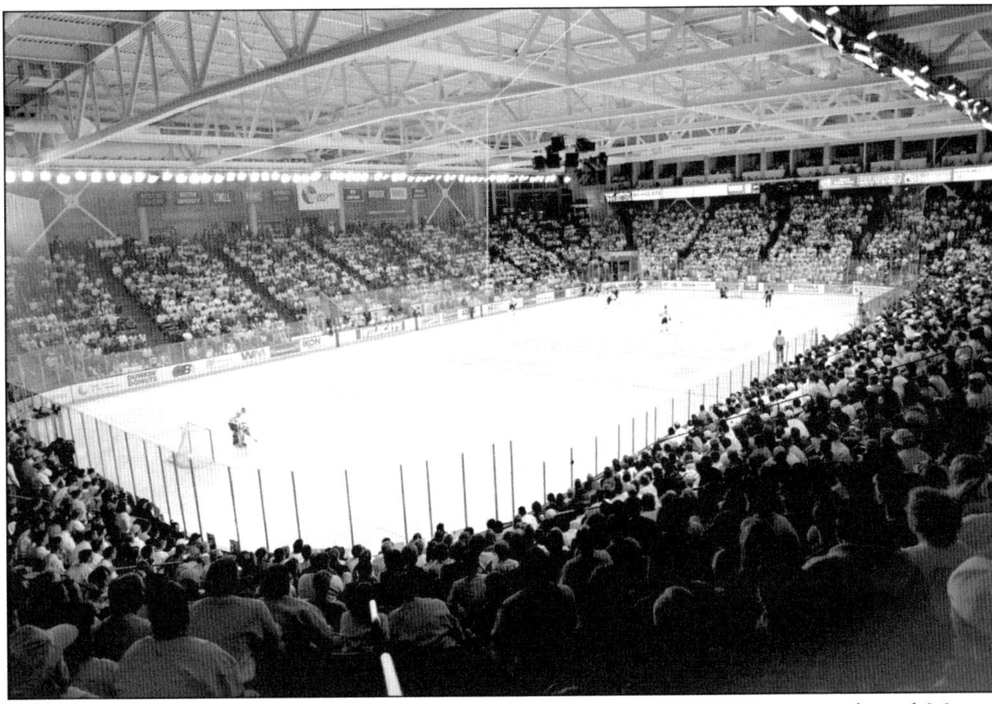

This is a packed Whittemore Center during a March 5, 1999 game against archrival Maine. (Lisa Nugent photograph. UNH Photographic Services.)

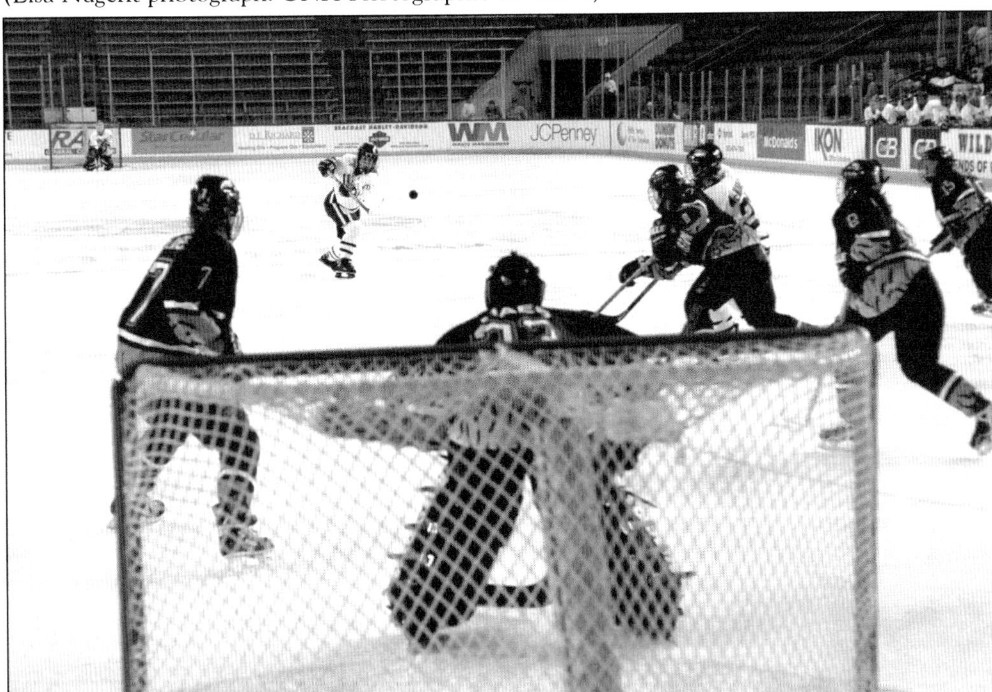

In this view of Towse Rink from behind the net, the UNH women's team launches one in a game against Princeton in November 1999. (Lisa Nugent photograph. UNH Photographic Services.)

The halftime blimp soars around the women's championship banners in Towse Rink in December 1999. (Lisa Nugent photograph. UNH Photographic Services.)

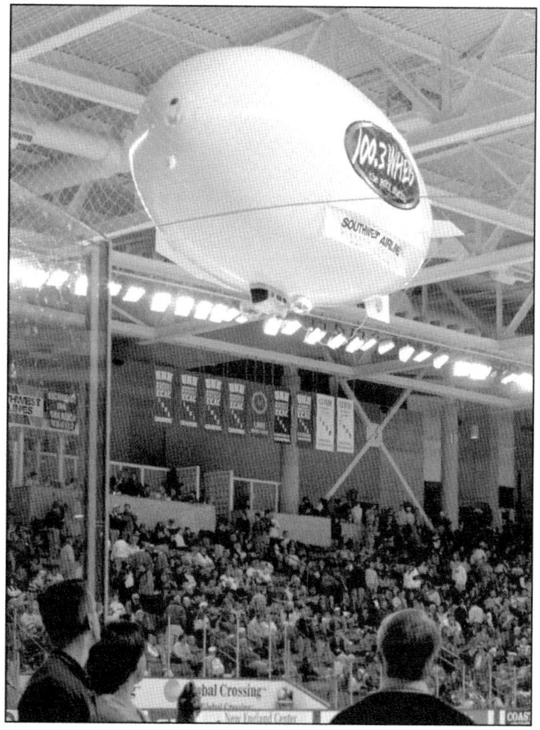

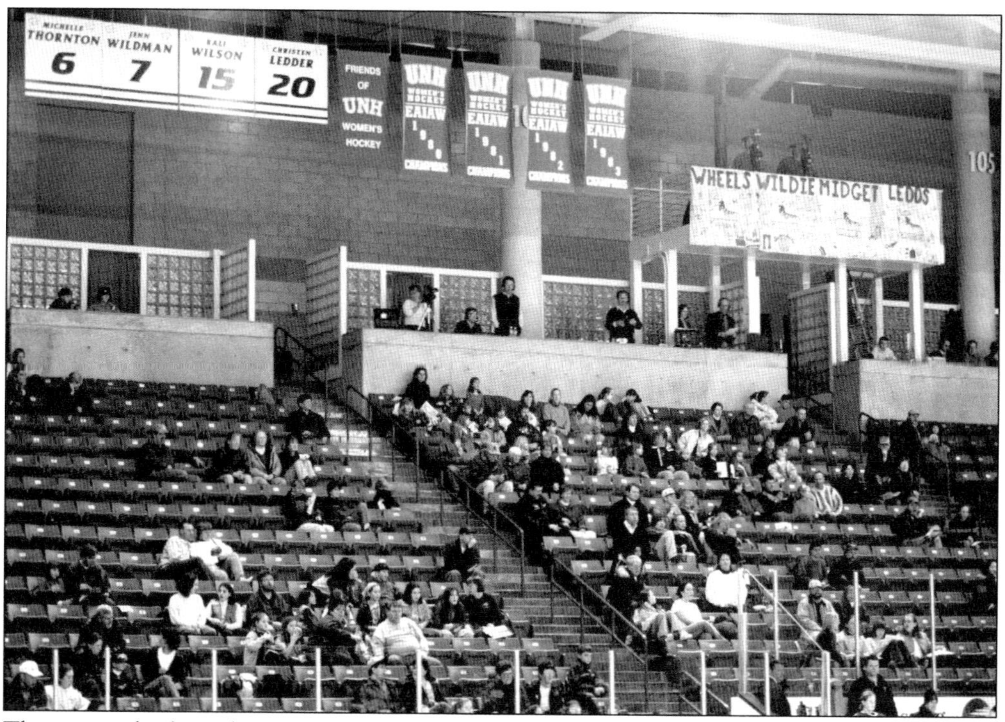

This view displays the women's championship banners, retired numbers, and a view of the press box around Towse Rink in December 1999. (Lisa Nugent photograph. UNH Photographic Services.)

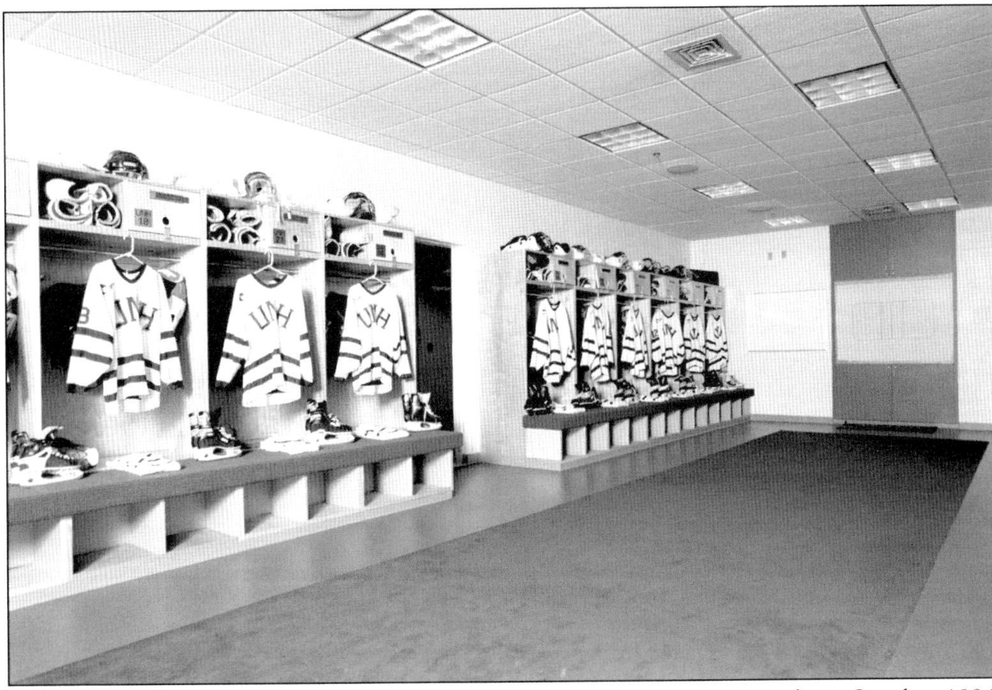

The locker room in the Whittemore Center appears quiet in this image from October 1996. (UNH Photographic Services.)

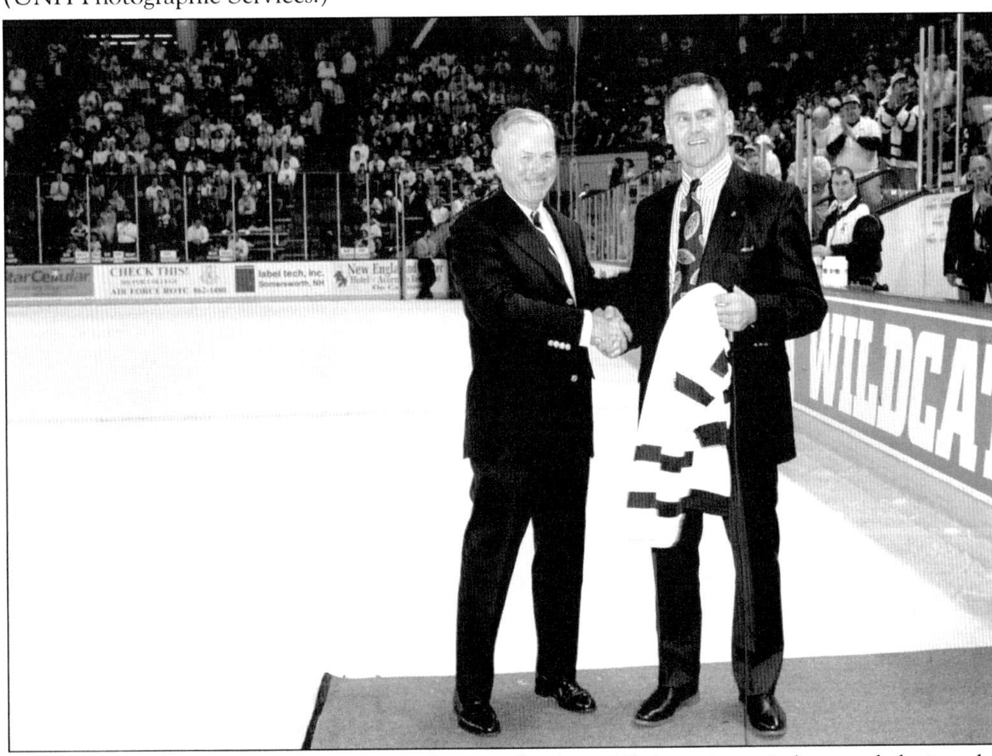

Goalie Rod Blackburn (right), UNH's first ice hockey All-American, is honored during the March 5, 1999 game. (Lisa Nugent photograph. UNH Photographic Services.)

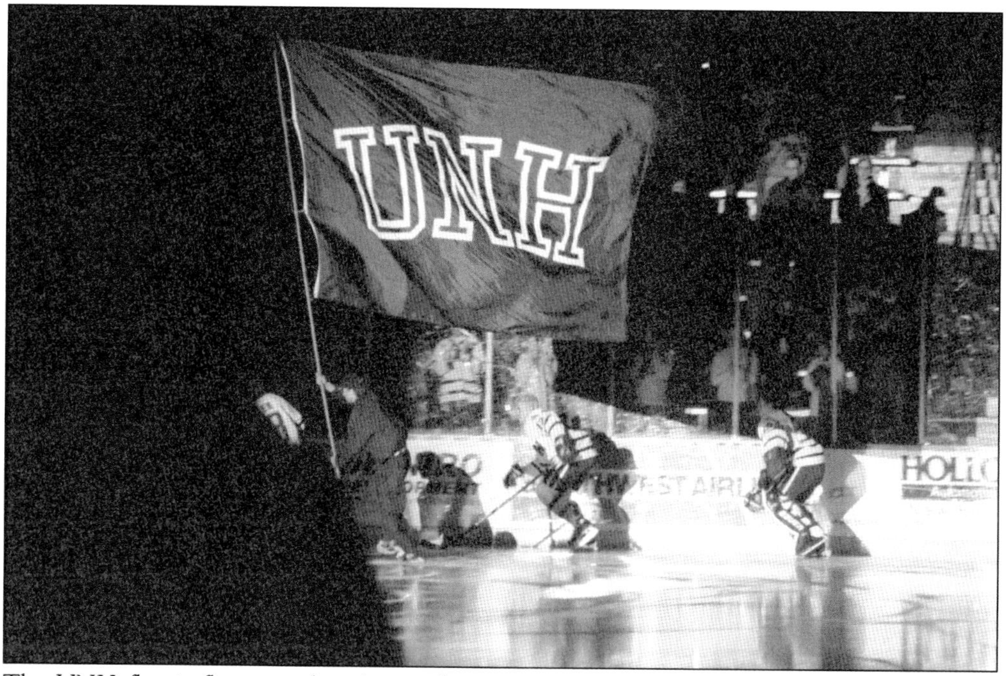

The UNH flag is flown as the players skate onto the ice. (Lisa Nugent photograph. UNH Photographic Services.)

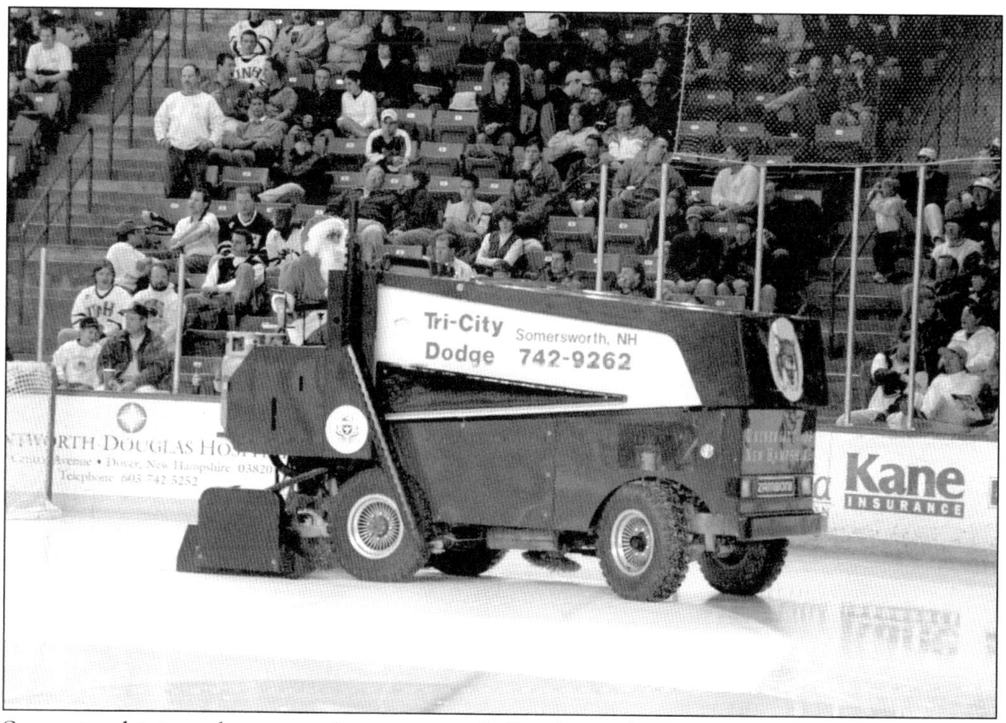

Santa is driving the natural-gas powered Zamboni during a December 1999 game. UNH recently added an electric Zamboni to the fleet. (Lisa Nugent photograph. UNH Photographic Services.)

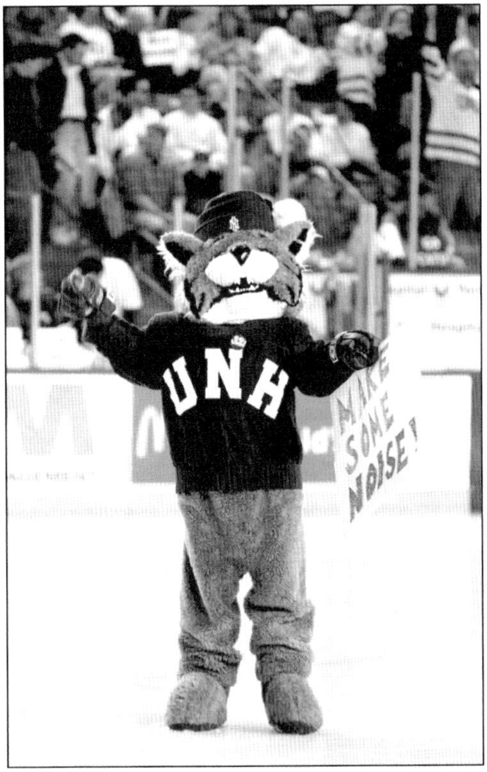

Wild E. Cat, the university mascot, encourages fans during a March 5, 1999 game against Maine—not that UNH fans need much encouragement when Maine is in town. (Lisa Nugent photograph. UNH Photographic Services.)

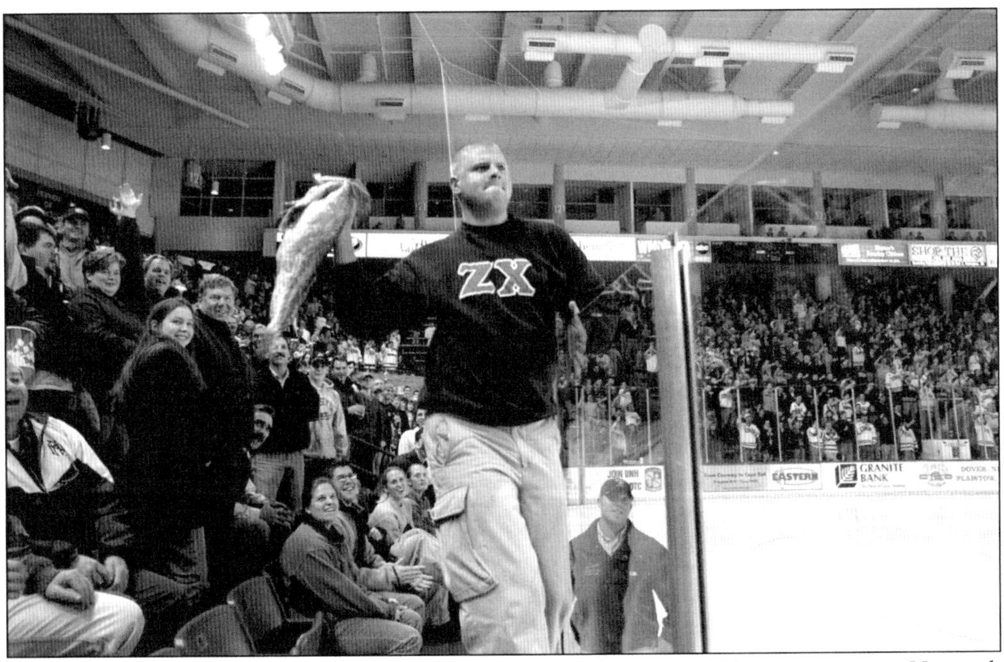

A Zeta Chi brother throws out the fish in a December 12, 2000 game against Harvard. Members of the Zeta Chi fraternity (then known as Theta Chi) became responsible for throwing out the fish in the early 1980s and have done so ever since. (Lisa Nugent photograph. UNH Photographic Services.)

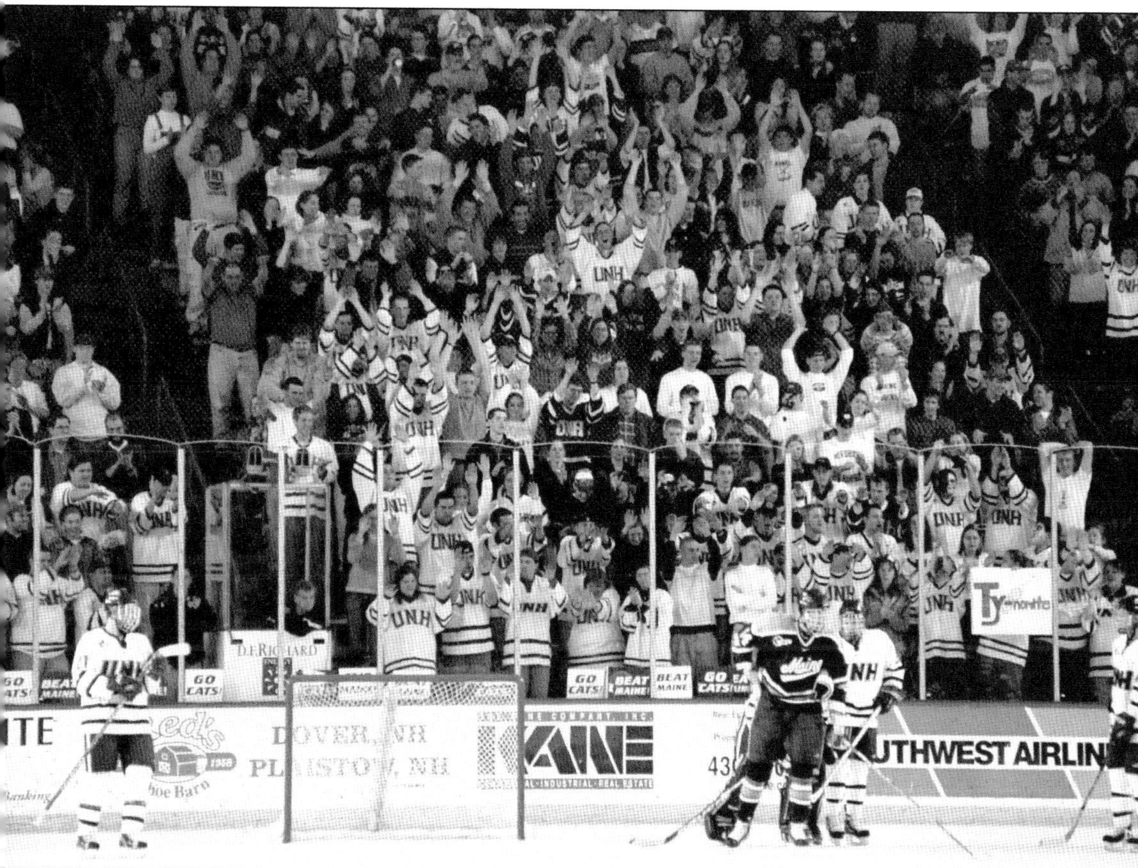

Fans show support at the Whittemore Center with their "Beat Maine" signs. The overall record for UNH versus Maine is 32-45-5, which includes the loss to Maine in the 2002 NCAA Semifinals. (Lisa Nugent photograph. UNH Photographic Services.)

UNH hockey players contribute much to local community groups, from appearances in community events to donating signed hockey equipment for charity auctions. These trading cards were produced for local DARE programs and were signed by the players. (UNH Museum.)

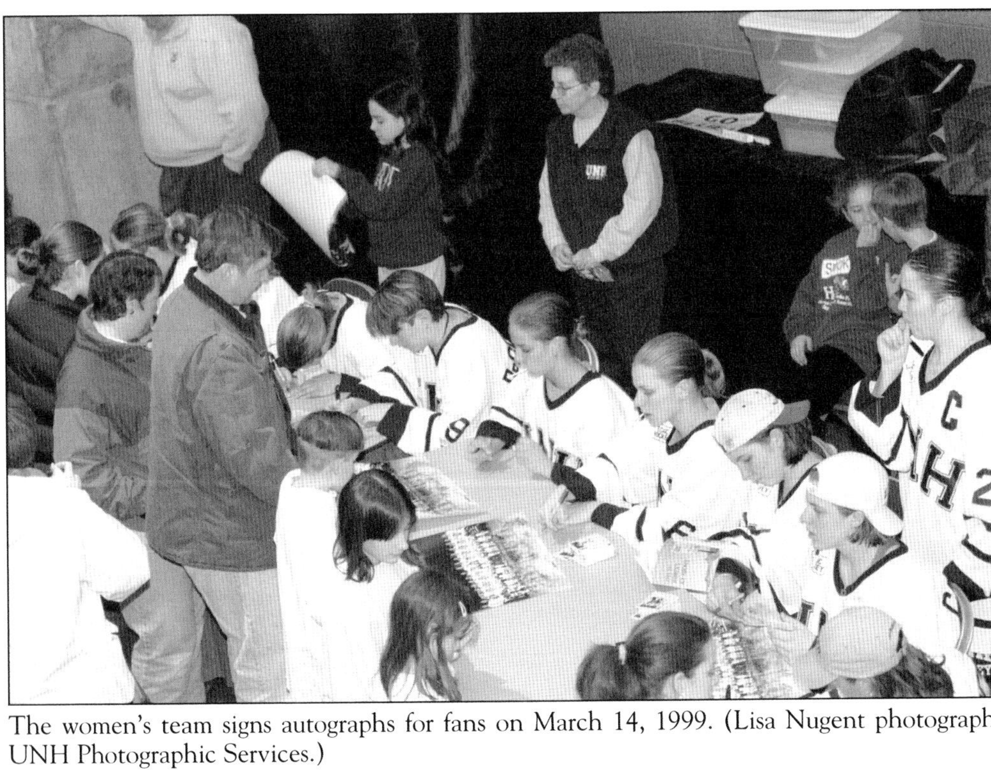

The women's team signs autographs for fans on March 14, 1999. (Lisa Nugent photograph. UNH Photographic Services.)

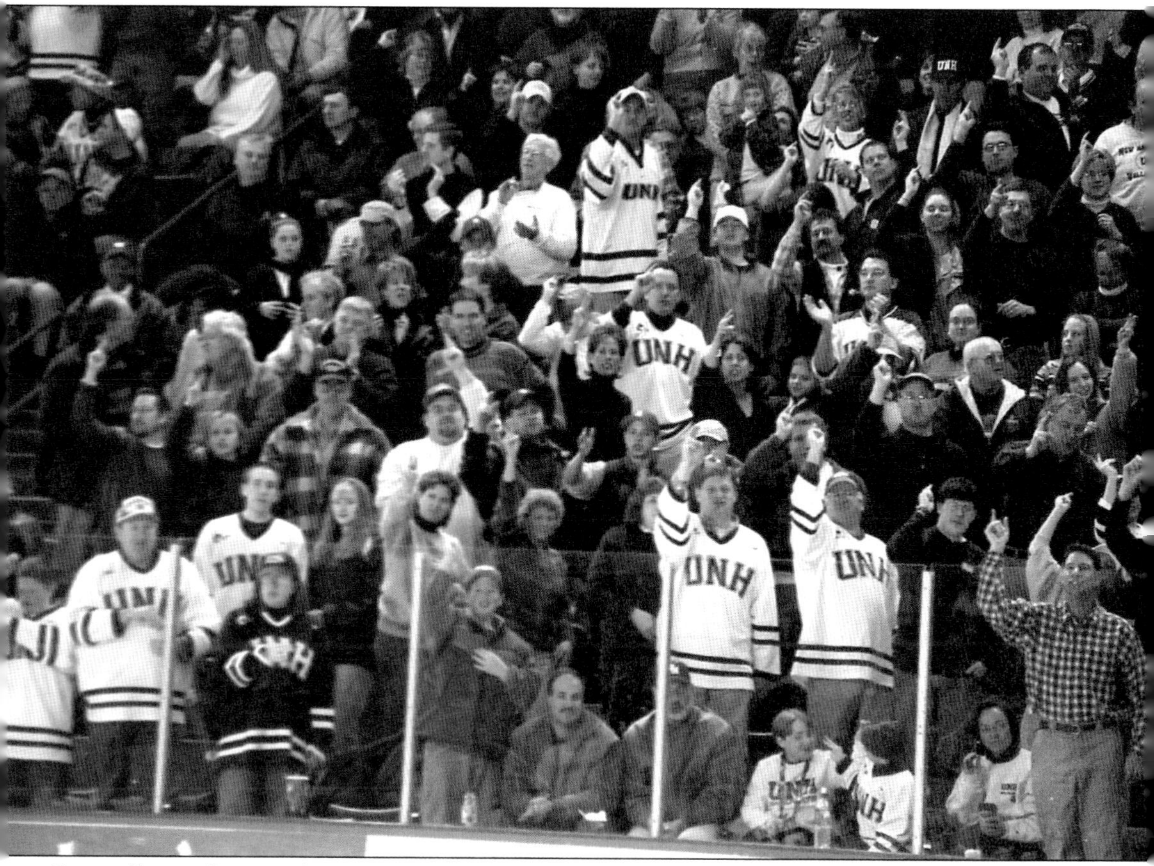

Fans rally at a January 2001 game against Merrimack. When the Whittemore Center opened, there was concern that the special fan atmosphere of Snively Arena would disappear. However, the fans got even louder in the Whitt and started new traditions. During the March 6, 1999 game against Maine, fans began "White Out the Whitt," in which fans wear white UNH jerseys and chant "UNH, UNH" over and over again. (Lisa Nugent photograph. UNH Photographic Services.)

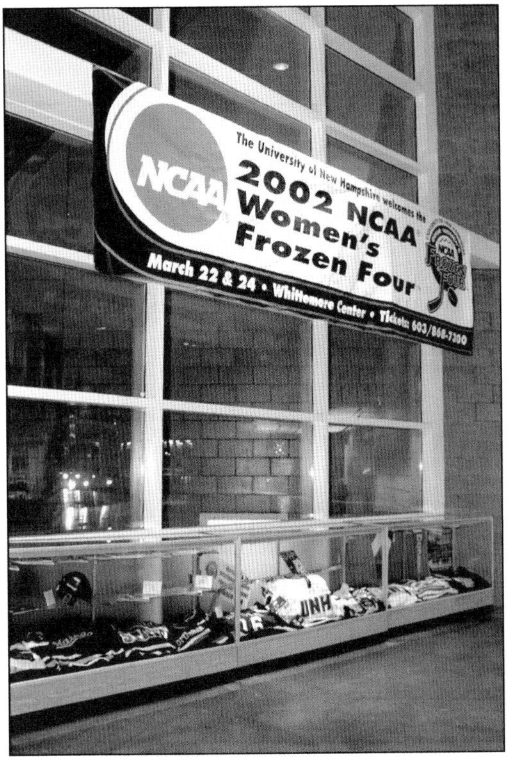

The lobby of the Whittemore Center is decorated for the first Women's Frozen Four in March 2002. UNH was chosen to host the first NCAA tournament for women's hockey in recognition of the strength of the women's program at UNH. The women also celebrated their 25th anniversary in the 2001–2002 season. The program has an overall record through the 2001–2002 season of 479-126-35, with a winning percentage of .776. In addition, the women join the newly-formed Hockey East Women's League in the 2002–2003 season. (Lisa Nugent photograph. UNH Photographic Services.)

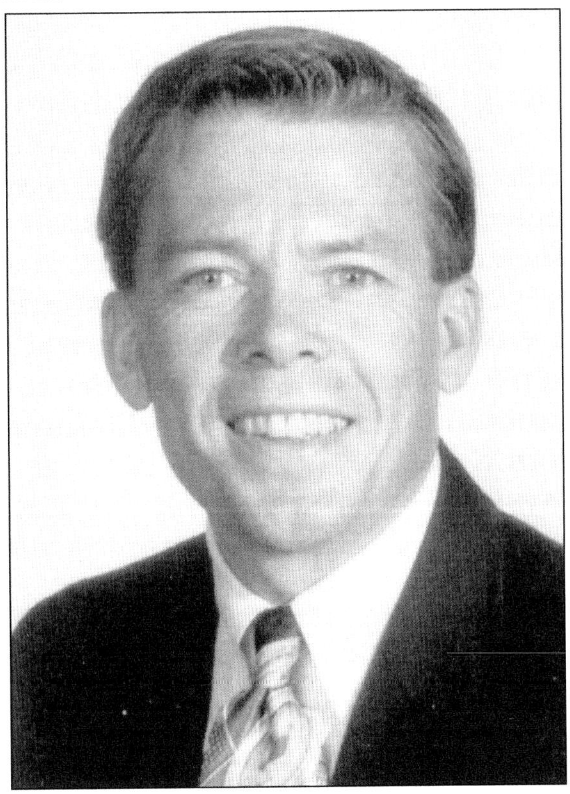

Brian McCloskey was appointed the new women's hockey coach in May 2002. McCloskey was associate head coach of the men's team from 1992 to 1997 and from 1998 to 2002 was director of UNH's national recruiting program. (UNH Archives.)